Wednesday 12 -20.?
Solina ?

M000247357

THE CHOICE

OF

HAPPINESS

May Every Reader of This Volume
Have Ever-Increasing Joy,
Delectable Delights,
Miraculous Unfoldings,
And
Easefulness,
Forever Embrace Their Lives.

THE CHOICE OF HAPPINESS

Glimpses From An Extraordinary Ordinary Scientific Mystical Life

Sundari Dembe

Inner SunLight
Productions
Lafayette, CA

Copyright © 2012 by Sundari Dembe

All rights reserved. No part of this book may be reproduced, distributed, or transmitted in any form or by any means, including photocopying, recording, or other electronic or mechanical methods or in the form of an audio recording, nor may it be stored in a retrieval system, transmitted, or otherwise be copied for public or private use - other than for "fair use" as brief quotations embodied in articles and reviews - without the prior written permission of the publisher. For permission requests, write to the publisher at the address below.

Inner SunLight Productions
3912 Quail Ridge Rd
Lafayette, CA 94549
www.InnerSunLight.com
cdembe1@comcast.net

Printed in the United States of America
First Printing, 2016

Publisher's Cataloging-in-Publication data
Dembe, Sundari
The Choice of Happiness: Glimpses From An Extraordinary Ordinary Scientific Mystical Life / Sundari Dembe.
ISBN-13 978-0-9982991-9-8
ISBN-10 0998299197
1. Personal Awareness and Self Improvement. Stress Management and Coping. Self Esteem and Values Clarification. Personal Decision Making Skills. 2. Chemistry, Other   3. Leisure and Recreational Activities. Travel and Exploration. 4. Religion and Religious Studies.

Library of Congress Control Number: 2016918680
Inner SunLight Productions, Lafayette, CA

First Edition
20 19 18 17 16   5 4 3 2 1

TABLE OF CONTENTS

Elan

ABDY

PADMA

ARRIVING HOME

Prologue

I was born in Cleveland, Ohio before it was a joke. That didn't happen until comedians on Saturday Night Live latched onto the fact that the ocher Cuyahoga River, which flows through the center of Cleveland, had once caught fire, melting the railroad tracks above it.

Actually Cleveland was a good place to grow up. It was far more cultural than its reputation, sporting one of the best art museums I've ever seen anywhere in the world, a fabulous symphony orchestra and a better than decent opera company.

For me there was one very uncomfortable aspect of the area that, more than any other, gave birth to a desire to escape that bastion of Mid-western attitudes. Somehow, the inhabitants of the city were locked into a provincial mode of thought where social interactions, who you knew, where you ate and where you prayed mattered above all else. Conversations centered on trivia and to this day I can recognize, nearly immediately, from the details of an exchange, whether I am sitting next to a native of Cleveland. I always knew that the one thing I did not want to end up being was a housewife in Cleveland.

My Grandma had inherited a six-suite apartment building from her grandmother in a changing area of East Cleveland. Mom, Dad and I lived in one suite, Grandma and Grandpa in another, my uncle, aunt and two cousins in another. The other three were rented out. As a kid I loved crawling

xi

around under the table at all the large family dinners.

When I was six, Mom found out she was pregnant on the same day that Grandpa died of a heart attack. I remember watching the rain fall that day as I looked out at the empty covered glider, that Grandma and I often had swayed on to count the seconds between the lightning and when you could hear the thunder.

Grandma moved into my bedroom for the next five years and Mom and Dad shared their bedroom with my new baby brother. Eventually we all moved into a house in the suburbs – the four of us in my immediate family, Grandma and my uncle, who was by then divorced, along with his son, my cousin. We had six phones and three different phone numbers, two each for each of the three nuclear family units sharing the space. There was one spot in the upstairs of the house where I could talk on two phones with two girlfriends at once.

My parents and most especially my mother, fit well into the small-idea mentality of suburban Cleveland life. Mom's big claim to fame was that she had once been asked to be a bobby soxer when Frank Sinatra came to town. She got to scream and pretend to faint when he arrived. She constantly flipped the radio on to hear the popular music playing.

Once in recent years, she confided to me that she had never read a book in her life. She must have had some undiagnosed learning disorder, but managed to get through high school by expanding on the book jacket descriptions of what lay under the thick covers that were never successfully traversed. She didn't go to work until I entered elementary school. Then she worked in Sears and Roebuck telephone catalogue sales and their district office for 20 years.

Dad had run for state representative when I was still a toddler. "Be a DEM, Vote for Dembe," was his slogan. The day of the election, it was announced on the radio that he'd won, but by the next day, he had slipped into a loser's slot. He had a law degree, yet ended up working for a small family-run furnace and air conditioning company, six days a week, until virtually the day he died from cancer in his 60's.

He took me to temple religiously every Sunday, and one year, he was even my Jewish history teacher there. The aspect of his life that he enjoyed and identified with most strongly was his connection to and work for the Golden Square Masonic lodge. It was likely the one aspect of his life that he wasn't compelled to share, the only corner which was his and his alone. It was a forum that surely touched the depths of his core. A number of times he was the grand poo-bah –hmmm –I guess they actually called it the Grand Master. He never had the courage to live out the life of intellectual exploration he secretly sought, perhaps as a biology teacher.

I grew up there in Cleveland, focusing on the types of activities that were acceptable. I sang in the temple choir as well as school groups from the time I was five until the end of high school. I always sang in Easter sunrise services. Once I sang as understudy for the lead of Josephine in Gilbert and Sullivan's HMS Pinafore. In the performance, I got to wear a real hoop skirt.

In high school, the four thousand-student body was tracked and I was always placed in the honor classes. Every year, for those students who received all A's, or A's and B's in the honors classes, the Cleveland Plain Dealer newspaper rewarded them with seven pairs of tickets to the Indian's games of the local baseball team over the summer. I went every year.

I never quite fit in with the kids who went to the high school I attended. I had perhaps a grand total of five dates during my whole time there. I uneasily rode the knife-edge between hanging out with a few girls who belonged to a popular Jewish girls club, which wouldn't accept me as a member, and the musical-scientific eggheads, most of whom were even weirder than I was. They were however, extraordinarily creative. We'd put physics lyrics to Bach fugues. Some of my friends wrote an operetta, which combined Moby Dick with the Scarlet Letter. I still remember some of the lyrics. Eventually a production of it was produced at Oberlin College Music School.

Strangely, when I attended my first high school reunion after a number of decades, the first person I encountered was an orthodox Jewish high school friend, who ended up teaching Sanskrit at a University in Georgia. Given the depth of my inner spiritual life, which gradually sprouted and flourished over the years, and my lifelong adult interaction with Sanskrit, led this to be a fascinating contact. Given my understanding that all we encounter matches with the reflection of what we need to understand and pursue in life at any particular time, this meeting of two high school buddies, who could speak joyfully on Sanskrit for hours, didn't surprise me.

I went off to college at The University of Michigan and then passed four years of graduate study at the University of Chicago in chemical physics doing research in superfluidity. I left abruptly less than six months before completing my doctorate when my research advisor died and I was told I'd have to start a new project with a new advisor. That event diverted my life from a highly ambitious plan to teach at some prestigious 'publish or perish' institution, which my respectable credentials supported. It led me to a more inward-directed life journey of attempting to make sense of the vagaries of life.

I embarked on a soul-searching journey out to California a short while after my advisor's death. To my surprise, I rapidly found a full-time college teaching job in less than a week's time. I envisioned working a bit before returning to the University of Chicago to finish my degree.

However, fate had another destiny in store for me. I taught three years at three colleges before settling into my teaching career as a professor of chemistry at Diablo Valley College. One chemistry department member, who had been on my hiring committee, was known as 'Cowboy'. We became good friends. I shared an office with him for two years. It was another two years before we started dating secretly, to avoid departmental gossip. After six more years of dating, we eventually married, I for the first time, he for the third. Two kids came along soon after.

For decades the strength of both my secular and spiritual lives led me to use two different first names and two different last names in every possible combination. As time unfolded, the depths of my being, like a spring, started to bubble ever-increasing nurturing waters, which were scented with a different kind of perspective. These currents brought me a deeper spiritual perspective of the ebbs and flows of an individual's existence. I started to live my "ordinary" life during the year and my secret ashram-connected spiritual life over the summers.

My fascination with the Truth of the nature of reality slowly became the burning passion of my life. What I at first thought science would provide, that is the ultimate Truth, became over time a search for a spiritual window offering a clearer view of the way things truly were. My Jewish background gave way to an exploration of Buddhist practices for a number of years, a Sufi mystery school of sorts, a settling into the Hindu practices of my guru, Baba, and eventually profound Christian mystical experiences. At the opening of this book I am in the Hindu ashram after many, many years of one-pointed dedication to this spiritual path.

Believing in the potential of existing as Super-Mom, I attempted to live out the myth, through working, being mom, engaging in semi-professional singing, all the while keeping up a rigorous and disciplined meditation practice. I was the Chemistry Department Chair for three two-year terms. For a while I assumed an interim position as Division Chair of Physical Science and Engineering and in that capacity was in charge of 100 faculty. During that period, I was the head of a team, which selected architects for a 12 million dollar physical science building and also joined the faculty contingent, who for the first time in the school's history, were allowed to design every aspect of the facility over a three-year period.

After my two children arrived, year-by-year these parallel yet disparate existences slowly and with difficulty began to merge. Gradually my 'Cheryl' Cleveland origins came to blend and then dissolve totally into the flowering of my 'Sundari' beingness.

This book is the first place I have dared to pull up all the segmental divides of my existence and present myself fully as who and what I am. I suspect that each of us has that extraordinary underlying experience of universality bubbling up from the cracks of our mundane lives.

A colleague once shocked me with her pronouncement that I was the most superficial person she'd ever encountered. Each of us I believe is a well of richness, offering our own amazing and unique perspective of what we often tend to assume to be a shared mutual reality. I think that if you really look below the surface of any person, there is not one of us who doesn't actually live out an extraordinary, ordinary life.

Introduction

There was an appealing little group of writers that met once a week at the ashram I attended. They read their compositions to each other and offered technical and editing feedback. Although I have decades of journals and other material I've written, which occupy an entire shelf in my library and extend back to the day I turned sweet sixteen, I had never shared them or read them aloud. Not even the poems or songs I'd written had been heard before, other than by one or two close friends.

So it was with considerable trepidation that I dared to join these gatherings. Gradually, after reading a few items to the group, I came to realize that their ears were connected to their hearts. The manner in which feedback was given was kind, probing in such a way as to inspire self-inquiry and catalytic in sending one ever deeper into the subtleties of one's own material.

Over time, I read to them ever more exposed writings I had produced, yet I never thought that I'd dare to read them 'The Poem'. Finally however, after one particularly inspiring session of feedback, I knew I would do it – share with them that piece that more than any other revealed the soft underside of my essential beingness and alluded to those experiences that had led to the initial blossoming of my inner ecstasy.

However, I became worried that rather than just listening to the poem, they might ask me where it came from or what experiences had elicited it. I felt the true stories would forever need to remain hidden, as they were so strange and outside of the accepted dogma of usualness, that I couldn't allow them to reach the light of day. So I started making up in my mind two or three sentence semi-truthful yet incomplete responses to various questions about the piece that I thought might surface.

At the next session, I decided to seek advise from them on a few paragraphs I had been revamping, which were among my contributions to a book being compiled in England. I was utterly amazed at the depth and clarity of their responses and the delicate probing, leading me to an ever more profound level of interaction with my short selection. One of the members even suggested that I write an entire book expanding upon the short piece I had just offered.

That suggestion shook my core and produced a totally unexpected result. As I was driving home that day, I knew that the true stories underlying my poem 'Union' were demanding to see the light of day. I saw a funnel opening over the crown of my head and the contents of three books I had been imagining swirled into one book. All the words were written there, simply waiting to be recorded. It took me about six weeks to type the first two thirds of this book. Yet I knew even then that some material was not ready to be downloaded, because I had more to learn before it became fully assessable.

Until that happened five years later in 2010, I really didn't know what the theme of this book was to be. Eventually the pattern unfolded to show me that these experiences were my journey to standing in my own wisdom and power. They were the steps that life offered to me in my transition from the gift and energetic catalysis of following a true or satguru, through lessons I learned in a nine-year journey, of three three-year segments with three different spiritual mentors. Finally I came to stand in the grace and gentleness of understanding that I am, when aligned with Divine intention, the source of anything I might ever need. This is the tale of my coming to identify with the power, knowledge and peace within that is accessible to each of us, if we dare to consciously ask for that and choose it consistently.

I have at times changed the names of those who preferred not to be identified, but this is in fact a glimpse of the true unfolding of my journey through life.

And it is thus that this retelling of my journey down the rabbit's hole into the mythical realms of True Reality came to be told.

I am eternally grateful to my guru, his successor, these three mentors who have so enriched my existence, my daughter who gave me such great editing advise, my son, and my husband who never stopped loving me or seeing my beauty. And I especially thank you dear ONE who have chosen to join minds with me through this medium and share the joy and love that we are.

Elan

Chapter One: Catalytic Encounter

The juice of my journey peeks out
from the layers of this poem titled,

UNION

I drank deeply of the nectar from the chalice that is you,
Expecting some exotic brew,
But in shock discovered that the flavor I partook of
Was none other than that of my very own Self.

How could it be?
The molecules of your energy field entered me,
Mingling - merging - diffusing through my being,
Producing the most exquisite spiritual Union imaginable.

No barrier existed in this,
Since what I was sampling only tasted of me,
The highest me,
The me I have sought through all lives - through all times.

No more perfect intimacy could be imagined.
The ultimate intimacy of all lifetimes,
The sampling of one's highest flavor as the other,
In the other.
But what other?
There is only my Self here,
But no longer alone,
Seen and appreciated fully.

The innocence of Eden envelops the Union.
I stand in the Garden,
All fear is gone.
How can I fear being naked and exposed
before my own Self?

It matters not to me that you see my personal idiocies,
The fragile foibles of a struggling soul,
The ponderous proddings of a ballooned ego.
My Being lies before you exposed.
Unfearful, I allow myself the fullness of my Totality.

Where is there to hide when that which is you
sits there within me.
Surprisingly, as my weakness lies exposed,
So is it also true
That the fear of stepping into my Strength and Wisdom
Also evaporates.

I expand into the fullness.
With our essential mingling
All is possible.
I taste my Godhood.
The Union does not subside
Nor will it ever.

We walk together now.
Such exquisite joy exists in showing you the vistas of my life.
Certainly half of me has become you.
A subtle shift, visual shading occurs,
And it is you in here that is me.
I feel the still well of appreciation,
The calm tranquility of your energy as mine.

My thoughts cease.
I settle into your body.
I walk in it showing you
My lake and reservoir.
You run surprisingly well
Not yet used to sharing my vehicle in this way.
More natural to you
is the expansive vista of Mt. Diablo from my new office,
And the placid 11 acres overlooking Happy Valley,
The view from my backyard.

I am drowning in you.
The process is not complete, but now I know to my surprise,
That it is not Freedom that I will blend into,
But rather the perfect Bliss of the Eternal,
The ultimate Stillness of all that is,
Which will eventually become
The ocean of my penultimate expansion.

The cup of you was truly the Holy Grail,
Bringing comfort and joy,
Bliss and love,
Beyond any conceptual measure
Throughout all time.

THE ORIGIN of 'UNION'

It had happened about four times previously in a 27 year period, where I had been able to chant all 182 verses of the Sanskrit *Sri Guru Gita* text with one thought, one emotion – one continuous one-pointedness of devotion, love and focus. Not one stray idea or wandering of attention. I'd probably done it once contemplating Uma-Guru, maybe twice for Baba, my guru who was no longer living, and once with just the emotional laser of the chant's essential feeling. But I'd never before tried doing it for Babe Baba, my Guru's Guru. This was the perfect day, Babe Baba's lunar Punyatithi, the anniversary of his death.

I had been spending a month, along with my teenage daughter, at the ashram of Swami Chandra-Prakashananda, also known affectionately as Uma-Guru, in the Catskill Mountains near South Fallsburg, New York. We took Amtrak trains across the country, looking at possible colleges for my daughter, and then culminated our summer vacation with a month-long sojourn at the ashram. I knew this time together would likely be our last before she left the familial nest to embrace that destiny that awaited her in her collegial years and beyond.

I was on staff for the month, and although I'd done this much seva, or service, many times before, this was the first instance in which I had offered my labor since the designation of 'staff' had become a distinct category there. At the official staff orientation, we had been told that "this month will change your life", and I remembered

Thinking, "Sure, as if this month was going to drastically revise a path I'd been treading for so many years." Little did I know how radically the last week of this period would alter every aspect of my vision and understanding of the world.

The first three weeks of the month had been as trying as any of my sadhana, or spiritual path, and profound levels of surrender had been growing in my heart. The day before the altering event, I had stood before Babe Baba's statue. From the depth of my being, I made a vow to him from a well of deep gratitude. I pledged to protect, honor and serve God's energy and intention completely, not only in this life, but throughout all my lives. Not only in this time, but throughout the past, present and future of the past, present and future, if only I might merge with God – even if that meant the end of my life, my identity and even my existence.

So on this day I went for it. Riding the fullness of love and devotion for Babe Baba, one pure thought was successfully maintained throughout the entirety of the chant. Bathing in the extraordinary bubble of bliss and self-satisfaction that ensued, and relishing the formidable accomplishment I had just achieved, I left the hall.

The validity and worth of what I had just created was rapidly reflected back to me, as the newly appointed seva head of Babe Baba's Temple in South Fallsburg approached me. She asked if I would like to dress Babe Baba's murti or statue in a few days time for Krishna's birthday. I was also invited to pass out prasad, or blessed treats, after a midday chant in the temple. I gratefully accepted both these gifts of acknowledgement from the Universe.

After my morning seva, chopping vegetables in the kitchen, I barely had time to bathe and wrap myself in a scintillating blue sari, which I had purchased when I was last visiting the mother ashram in Ganeshpuri, India. I arrived at the Temple and was asked to seat people for the midday chant. Afterwards, two of us were given large trays of wondrous treats to distribute. I did so sparkling internally with a ripple of "Blessings from Babe Baba" that spontaneously emanated from my heart as each morsel was placed in an outstretched hand.

After a deliciously lovely period of time, my tray emptied. I went into the Temple, pranamed or bowed, and started to leave. As I did so the young man who had also been serving the delectable morsels presented one to me. As I reached up to receive the offering, he placed it in my hand, not removing his. Startled, I looked up. Our eyes locked. His gaze fixed me, paralyzing me in place, with his most extraordinary eyes and time stood still. I most certainly knew him – VERY WELL. My heart leapt. We didn't speak.

For the next few days my mind raced. "Who is he?" my mind constantly demanded to know. At first I thought that it might be Sanjay, the younger of Uma-Guru's two brothers. I had been his chemistry tutor one summer in Ganeshpuri, when he was only 12 years old. I had gone everyday to her parent's house for three months and designed chemical experiments for Sanjay and me to investigate. But I did some calculations and realized that this young man could not possibly be the right age to be my former student. I asked the Temple supervisor the young man's identity, but she said that he simply showed up to help occasionally and that she had no idea who he was.

Eventually I saw him again. Our seva stations were close. We came to talk. There was nothing casual or superficial in these exchanges. The depth of human communication potential happened effortlessly and instantly, sometimes without words. Often, he would only speak one sentence.

One day he told me to contemplate "I am liberated by my Guru's Grace." I did so continuously for the next three hours. Strangely, his every word became a command that completely consumed my attention and being.

He appeared again and I told him that what had arisen for me was that the word 'my' implied duality for me. I perceive Guru's Grace as simultaneously being my own Grace as well. The phrase 'my Guru's Grace ' seems to separate me from the Essential Guru, or teacher that each of us is for ourselves. At the heart of the matter there is no difference for me between the core energy of the Guru and my Self. So, I didn't resonate with saying 'my'.

He said, "OK, do that then." And I did. I went back to my seva and repeated, "I am liberated by Guru's Grace", knowing that that was also my own Grace.

One time he asked me "How was Baba with you?" It was a strange question, as if he were a father checking up on him. Another time he inquired how much I was meditating each day. I told him that it was about a half-hour. He 'tsked' that it wasn't long enough. The next day without effort, I began to meditate 1-1½ hours a day. That practice continued fairly effortlessly, for the next number of years.

Interestingly, in my early years with Baba, who was both Swami Chandra-Prakashananda's and my Guru, I had not realized what was happening when I had first been given shaktipat, or spiritual awakening. I thought that the Guru had to touch one to activate this inner energy. I went up to Baba on three separate occasions and asked him what I could do to receive his Grace. Each time he looked at me sternly and said, "Meditate more." It felt as if it were a command.

At the time, I thought that perhaps I was not pure enough to receive such a gift. One day, I realized that in fact, I had already experienced this sought after awakening during the opening talk Baba gave at a retreat at Cottontail Ranch in Calabasas, California.

At that time, I had felt a great aching and pain at the base of my spine and saw a fire burning all around me. The experience had continued for three days. I thought I was ill. However, spontaneously the idea of saying Baba's mantra "Om Namah Shivaya" from the area around the base of my spine arose in me. As soon as I repeated it in this way, all the pain left me and I felt totally refreshed.

This experience later recapitulated for me in meditation, and I finally saw that in fact, I had already been given shaktipat. The realization that the fire burning around me had been my spiritual awakening became clear. I had already received that for which I was so earnestly striving.

I laughed soundly. A few minutes later, participants were invited to approach Baba for darshan, or going up to greet him. He took one look at me, took the hat off his head and soundly patted it onto mine, giving me the very touch which I had been seeking for so long.

Baba only granted me what I wanted after I came to the realization through my meditative process, that I already had it. My continuing self-inquiry into the nature of shaktipat led me to this epiphany. My young friend's command to "meditate more" perfectly reflected the very command Baba had set before me so long ago.

I quickly came to believe that my new friend, Elan, was a great and powerful being in a young, unassuming body. Much later he told me that I was the first one in his life to recognize him for who he really was.

At one point he had told me that he could transmit shaktipat with one finger and one day I experienced it. There was a birthday party being given for him and he invited me both to a lunch at the ashram's snack area and to a dinner outing with his friends that evening. "Let no one be left out," he said, and I was shocked that I could be someone who was not to be left out in his worldview.

I didn't want to go out with the young people that evening. The food sounded fattening and I had just lost a lovely amount of weight with Weight Watchers. It was also my last few days in the sacred environment of the Guru's house and I wanted to relish every moment of it.

I felt very fortunate later to have stayed to hear a tape of Uma-Guru thanking those of us leaving after spending the month on staff. I recall her saying that it doesn't matter what mistakes you make or how many times you fall but rather only your devotion matters. This thought has buoyed my spirit innumerable times since.

I decided to go to the ashram snack area gathering and wanted to find a perfect gift for Elan. I had told him that I thought I had known him from some other time around, some other life in the Himalayas or the Hindu Kush mountains, but definitely in the highest, etheric mountain regions.

" In the Himalayas", he said, and I knew it was so. I felt he had been my dearest buddy, my best friend. I have had access internally for a long time to what I imagine to be my 'past lives'. In this particular 'past life', I saw us as being two young men living out life's great adventures together. We were on a spiritual quest through dangerous mountain regions, living in the ecstatic joy of nature and of our youthful exuberance, engaging in profound spiritual sharing.

I found him the perfect gift at the neighborhood store – a perfect quartz crystal. It reminded me of our joyous mountain existence together. I had it wrapped and bought a little card with a beautiful peacock feather for him.

That day I went into the snack area at noon. It was fairly empty, as food service had not yet begun. My daughter was there, taking pictures of some of her friends. I looked around and finally spotted him. He was sitting alone, eating something on a tray with his back to me. I went over, into the warm bubble of energy that transported us to another realm. No one else existed. He had told me to be there for the party at noon, yet no one else arrived for the next 40 minutes.

I gave him the gift. With incredible one-pointedness of attention and care, he opened the card. After reading it aloud with a heart-felt depth of appreciation, he placed it deliberately in his wallet. Then he opened the crystal and the fullness of our Himalayan peaks and the life we lived there seemed to surround us.

With his left hand he placed one finger on the back of my right hand. The casual contact was electric and plunged me instantly into a state of unity, spiritual and physical, leaving the totality of my body buzzing. I experienced a perfect fullness and a perfect energy match. All distinctions vanished, as did 'the World'.

This moment gave me a reality to associate with the idea that an individual's separateness can vanish, like a drop of water merging into the ocean. It was as if I had fallen into the most exquisite and complete form of MY OWN energy that I ever could experience. Even after the momentary contact ceased, the depth of that energetic encounter left my body and soul trembling for the next few days. While chopping vegetables at my seva all the next day, I was still literally shaking.

It was amazing that between the time he touched my hand and when I left a few days later, every single time I wanted to see him, he appeared – randomly- right there and then – maybe 15 or 20 times! He was totally there for me.

It had once happened like that for me with Baba as well. It was during one of the eight three-month summers I had spent with Baba – this one also in South Fallsburg. Baba had a habit that year of hiding behind a curtain after the evening chant of the Sanskrit Shiva Mahimnah Stotram in the area of the building where he resided. He would peek out every once in a while to check on devotees as they climbed the stairs up to their dormitory rooms.

I was part way up the stairs one evening, when Baba peeked out. His glance was like an arrow that pierced my heart so palpably, that I reached up and grabbed it. I saw his name write itself on my heart in golden light and I can still find it there to this day. Tears of love flowed from my eyes.

I went up to my room with the eight girls in the four bunk beds. I sat in my lower bunk, sitting up against the wall in the dark. The purest longing for God welled up within me and consumed the totality of my consciousness. I had never before experienced such yearning. It had the intensity of the craving for air, which one would experience if one were trapped underwater. It was an immediate feeling that I would cease to exist if I couldn't have God that very moment. There was no aspect of me that was not crying out for God's immediate presence.

The intensity of the longing continued for much more than an hour, until all aspects of the ashram life had faded into the quiet oblivion of the sleeping hours. All of a sudden, from the depths of my being I heard the words, "Go to Him." To me in that moment, it meant 'Go to God, Go to Baba.' Not in some abstract sense, but in physical reality. Somehow, completely trusting the voice of the inner Guru, the voice of my Soul within, I got up, still dressed and left the room.

I started down the staircase that I had ascended hours before. There, standing entirely alone was Baba, waiting for me. Without any thoughts, without any intention, I walked up to him and like a magnet, my head was drawn down to his feet, where it remained.

It is a considered a breach of etiquette in India to point one's feet at another person. It is believed that this is the part of the body from which the most energy of an individual is released. Therefore, with great beings, it is considered to be a privilege and a blessing to place one's head on their feet. Even footwear, which they have worn, is considered to have picked up their sacred energy. So a guru's sandals and feet are considered to be holy. Knowing this and having contemplated it, must certainly have led my head to it's resting place on his feet.

Tears, welling up from the depths of gratitude and fulfillment, sprang from my eyes. Somehow I realized in that moment, that if one truly calls upon God with all of one's being, God cannot refuse to manifest.

After what was for me an immeasurable period, outside of time, Baba drew me up. Then he, who I thought only spoke Hindi, surprised me by saying in perfect flawless unaccented English, "What is your name? What work do you do?" even though he was well aware of the more mundane answers to these questions. My new young friend Elan was as much there for me in that moment in the snack area, as Baba had been there for me that night so long ago.

Two days before I left, on the day before Krishna's birthday, I was looking for Elan. I could not find him anywhere, so I gave up. At just that moment, I turned, and there he was walking right up to me.

He told me to follow him. He headed out into the woods. I lingered, holding back. I wanted to leave my bag and go to a rest room. But somehow I knew it was a test. I breathed deeply releasing all the mind trips holding me back. I followed ten paces behind and walked into that forest, following the path that God was illuminating for me.

Eventually we came to a magical grove of trees. It will forever be with me as one of those penultimate places – etched forever in beauty beyond belief. It was a place that surely could never really exist, but it does. Mysteriously, sitting there, were two comfortable wooden lawn chairs awaiting us.

I knew what was about to ensue. He had told me that he had never before met anyone who was able to tolerate looking into his eyes. Without a word we sat. Our eyes locked instantaneously. I gazed into the infinity of his eyes meeting mine. Time and thought stopped. Perfect contentment, satisfaction and fullness were present, but no thought-process to even acknowledge them. This was the most precious and perfect of moments imaginable.

I had practiced this 'traspaso' or transmission before. In Sufi groups I'd been a part of, certain sacred ceremonies involved this steady unblinking looking. Most often the other person's face would flash for me with what I imagined to be the undulating images of faces they had had over many lifetimes, with the multitudinous flavors of energies with which their Soul's had clothed themselves. I knew this process and had previously told him that I would be able to look into his eyes.

It was different with him. His face was stiller than anyone I had known. There were no undulating images to mark the passage of time, just the one unchanging energy that he was, meeting and merging with me in a pure spiritual Unity. We might have been there a half-hour with eyes locked or perhaps two hours. I have no idea.

Finally one other-life face flashed from his countenance into the awareness of my being. It was a different, foreign, maybe Arab-looking face, with sharper features and more ego in it. I thought perhaps it might be my visage reflected to me from him, from that past-life which we had shared.

Instantly a story of a past life with him emerged. We were two young men traveling together through dangerous and remote areas of the high Himalayas. Our journey was a spiritual pilgrimage. We had spent many a quiet night around a fire, beneath the stars in the clarified air of those high mountains sharing Soul Essence. We lived through many adventures.

One day the trail we were following narrowed to a slim ledge on a high precipice. He started across first. We heard a cracking sound and I realized that the very rock we were standing on was giving way. I shoved him forward to safety, just as the ledge collapsed, plunging me to my death.

On the way down, I felt jolted by the force of Love, Grace and Blessing, which had exploded from his core, enveloping me in the most ecstatic Bliss imaginable. I think it was the first time in that life, in which he realized that he could exude Grace. It was the sweetest of deaths and I embraced the light and joy of it, even as I plunged to my doom. So he, as Babe Baba, and I had met before.

Sitting there, gazing at each other there in the forest, Elan reached over and placed one finger again on the back of my right hand and again transmitted his energy to me. To receive it more effectively, my hand flipped clasping his. He stayed engaged. It was only much later, that I realized that I had matched his energy in that moment, equalizing what was happening in some way. I felt that I became a Siddha, a perfected being, in that instant. We detached.

In a strange voice, which I could scarcely recognize as my own, from a deep viscous well of pure loving energy within me, I shared with him one experience of 'traspaso' which had transpired with my Guru, Baba. Baba had been unable to attend the beginning of a month long retreat, which was held on the campus of Humboldt State University in Arcata, California, during the summer of 1975. He had suffered a heart attack and was recuperating in a hospital in San Francisco. On my way up to the retreat, the driver said we could visit Baba at the hospital.

On our arrival we had been directed to a small family waiting room with a few other people. Within a short time Baba had walked in wearing a robe and his dark glasses. He sat in a chair. I went over to him and pranamed, that is bowed. Baba leaned forward and embraced me. He then lowered his glasses and looked directly and deeply into my eyes. I fell down a tunnel that for me led to infinity through the vehicle of his gaze.

So, in the woods that day, many years later, as my new friend listened to this story, his energy field expanded. He looked at me and said, in a commanding tone, "Say it! You know who I am. Say it!"

Until that moment, I had never considered who exactly he might be. I froze, paralyzed in shock. I didn't dare let myself come to any decision. For a long moment, my gaze rested on his feet in their running shoes. I longed to lay my head on them, as I had on Baba's, but I was afraid of how he might react or that we might be seen.

I don't remember quite how I arrived back at my room that day or how I finished that, my last official day as a staff member at the ashram.

The next day, which was my departure day from the ashram, was also Krishna's birthday. I awoke at 1:30 AM for my seva of dressing Babe Baba's murti, or statue, in the Temple, which was in a different building from my dormitory. The usual bus shuttles were not running at that hour and we were not allowed to walk the road at that time of night, so I was fortunate indeed that someone had offered me the use of their car.

I entered the ashram at 2:30 AM and pulled an angel card, which said 'Moksha' meaning 'Liberation'. Interestingly, this alone, liberation, had been my only goal for the month that I had served as staff. It was what I had stated as my intention, which prospective staff members had been asked to formulate in writing, on their application materials. It had been the deepest longing of my heart for a very long time, far exceeding any other concern of ANY kind.

I see liberation or freedom as a different state than enlightenment. I believe enlightenment to be an ongoing experience of some aspect of the inner light, while I see liberation as the ability to choose one's inner state at any moment so that inner bliss becomes a possible choice at any time regardless of external circumstances.

That last morning was an exquisitely perfect jewel, leaving me bathed in the powerful energy of the intimate contact spent within the heart of the Temple. I shared the ritualized seva of dressing the statue with someone named Ganesh. In Indian mythology Ganesh is the elephant-headed God, the son of Shiva, who is the remover of all obstacles and difficulties. This pairing with Ganesh felt auspicious to me.

As I participated in these early morning practices in the Temple, I recalled that Uma-Guru had once given me a command to 'Go to the Temple'. Her directive had occurred many years before, when my son was just a toddler. I had ended up at a private moment, when others were forbidden entrance, enclosed in the breezeway of the Temple at the Oakland ashram with Swami Chandra-Prakashananda, my son and just a few of her staff. I had looked at her and seen her lips move. Yet, I heard no external sound. Instead her voice resonated inside me, exactly with the same vibrational quality as when I talk, except it was her voice that I heard inside myself. It thundered within me, "Go to the Temple."

I knew in that moment that I had been given a Command from the Guru. Temple meant many things to me. It meant Babe Baba's Temple in the Oakland ashram. It meant Baba's Mahasamadhi Shrine (honoring his death) in Ganeshpuri, India, where his body was interred. It also meant the body, the Self, my very physical vehicle with which I exist in this corporeal realm. The meanings, experiences and unfoldings her command created for me, evolved in innumerable ways over the years.

I spent the dawn of that final morning at the South Fallsburg ashram that summer, in perfect attunement with that order which she had uttered within my heart so many years before. I had a hunch that Uma-Guru would be in the Temple during the middle of the morning seva session and I felt an appointment with destiny to meet her at that place of Babe Baba's murti, which I had just helped to dress. Therefore, I planned to spend my last free morning aligned with both Baba and her indications to me, meditating in the Temple. I had also been asked to assist with seating people for a noon chant there, so everything seemed perfectly aligned to see her before my early afternoon departure.

So, at this time, as in all my spare moments of the summer, I again started off to the Temple. But on the way, I passed Elan, lounging on the lawn resting and I couldn't resist visiting him for a while. We talked. After some time, in a deliberate manner, he said, "You know, she's in the Temple right now. You had better go."

I was furious with myself, knowing somehow that I had blown it by being distracted on the way to my date with destiny. I had fallen asleep to my intention.

I arrived at the Temple, but because Uma-Guru was already inside, entrance was denied. I sat down on a bench in the adjoining cloakroom where shoes were stored during programs, as is the Indian custom.

Immediately, I felt myself embraced between the tremendous ecstasy of interaction, which I imagined must have been occurring between Swami Chandra-Prakashanada and the statue of Babe Baba. It was as if I were inside the room with them. Waves of shakti, energy, washed over me leaving me weak-kneed and literally unable to stand. For that reason, when one of the Guru's staff asked me to stand by a door and open it for her if she passed that way, I declined. Moments later, she exited, going through that very same door that I would have been holding had I acquiesced to the offer.

I kicked myself internally, feeling Hell's doors open and the realm of Liberation's close. I fully realized how I'd not only missed being with her in the Temple, ignoring the key command she had placed in my heart those many years past, but I had even turned down a seva opportunity to serve her directly. "Three strikes and you're out," I thought.

 1. You weren't in the Temple when you should have been because my new friend's presence distracted me.

2. You didn't meditate and hence didn't follow Baba's prime directive that morning.

3. You refused a seva opportunity to directly serve the Guru.

The Gates of Heaven had flung open for me and I was asleep.

THE GATES of PARADISE

I had previously been, for many years, a participant and group leader in a Sufi group of Claudio Naranjo's called SAT. SAT stands for 'Seekers After Truth'. We often read Sufi stories as a spiritual practice. Kathy Speeth, who helped lead Claudio's groups, had introduced Baba to the Nasruddhin stories of which he became so fond. One of those Sufi Tales came to mind at this moment. It is called "The Gates of Paradise". One version of this story can be found in Idries Shah's *Tales of the Dervishes*.

There was once a good man. He had spent his whole life in cultivating the qualities enjoined upon those who would reach Paradise. He gave freely to the poor, he loved his fellow creatures and he served them. Remembering the need to have patience, he endured great and unexpected hardships, often for the sake of others. He made journeys in search of knowledge. His humility and exemplary behavior were such that his repute as a wise and good citizen resounded from the East to the West, and from the North to the South.

All these qualities he did indeed exercise – whenever he remembered to do so. But he had one shortcoming, and that was heedlessness. This tendency was not strong in him, and he considered that, balanced against the other things that he did practice, it could only be regarded as a small fault. There were some poor people who he did not help, because from time to time he was insensitive to their needs. Love and service, too, were sometimes forgotten when what he thought to be personal needs, or at least desires, welled up in him.

He was fond of sleep; and sometimes when he was asleep, opportunities to seek knowledge, or to understand it, or to practice real humility, or to add to the sum total of good behavior – such opportunities passed by, and they did not return.

Just as the good qualities left their impression upon his essential self, so did the characteristic of heedlessness.

And then he died. Finding himself beyond this life, and making his way towards the doors of the Walled Garden, the man paused, to examine his conscience. And he felt that his opportunity of entering the High Portals was enough.

The gates, he saw, were shut; and then a voice addressed him, saying: 'Be watchful; for the gates will open only once in every hundred years.' He settled down to wait, excited at the prospect. But, deprived of chances to exercise virtues towards humankind, he found that his capacity of attention was not enough for him. After watching for what seemed like an age, his head nodded in sleep. For an instant his eyelids closed. And in that infinitesimal moment, the gates yawned open. Before his eyes were fully open again, they closed, with a roar loud enough to wake the dead.

As Uma-Guru walked through that door, this story jumped into my consciousness and I could almost hear those Gates of Paradise slamming closed right before me. Excruciatingly, I felt the depth of my own heedlessness.

I watched Swami Chandra-Prakashananda as she went through that very door which I had been asked to hold. She walked half way down the hall and then exited out a side panel I hadn't noticed before, which led outside. No one was around any longer after she passed through, so I walked to the still open portal she had traversed and stood there watching, as she approached a crowd of mothers, children and other devotees who were congregated at the front door of the ashram. She was almost up to the group, when I became aware that she felt me looking at her. She stopped, turned and locked eyes with me for a long time.

Deliberately, she reversed her direction, slowly walking back to me, until she was directly before me. She stopped a minute saying nothing, but intently gazing into me. I had no thoughts or emotions. I was simply there. Then, she continued across the narrow corridor to a door on the opposite wall, and exited toward the private, rear area of the main meditation hall, which adjoined the Temple.

Traspaso, eye transmission, again.

I went on with my activities of the day. I encountered Elan a short time later and bemoaned missing what I felt was my destined mystical appointment with Uma-Guru by 'falling asleep'.

He stopped me in disgust and said, "What's wrong with you? You're not grateful for what you've been given? She's given you so much." And I knew immediately that he was totally right. But what was truly amazing was that his comment instantly gave birth to a cornucopic abundance of gratitude within my being. It sprang from my heart like a stream washing and bathing every fiber of my being.

Somehow, with incredible will power, I knew that Grace would come in its own time and way and that my ultimate job was to savor with the deepest gratitude what was, as it was exactly, and that that was perfect and enough.

I walked to the front of the ashram and picked another angel card. Synchronistically, it said "Gratitude'. I dove into its message deciding consciously to settle into gratitude for what I had been given this magical month, culminating in these precious moments, rather than feeling self-condemnation for what I felt I could have received. Besides the usual choices we are given of half empty or half full, it is always possible to realize that the glass has been totally full all along.

At the morning's *Sri Guru Gita* chant, my last of the visit, that very morning of my departure, once again I was able to chant all 182 verses of the Sanskrit with perfect focus. Every instant was chanted in the emotional and mental fullness of gratitude to Uma-Guru for the gifts she had given me during the visit.

Much later, after arriving home,
I wrote her this letter-poem.

GRATITUDE

I give you my heart,

Its tiny rivulets tenderly touching all other hearts,
Reveling in the delicious delicacy of their more than
Baskin Robbins number of flavors,
An infinite number of munchable morsels of love,
Vanilla, chocolate, coconut, pistachio and mango hearts,
All for the sweet tasting
All flowing in the mutual, but as yet undiscovered
unity of their love,

I give you my heart.

I give you my devotion,

Steady, serene, sure,
The joyous realization that the nectarian sweetness of
Guru's feet has pervaded
every nook and cranny of my reality,
Every corner of my mind,
No longer a place searched for in order to be nurtured,
It is soothingly, comfortably, supportively everywhere,
Lifting me constantly through to the realm of
contentment and satisfaction.

I give you my devotion.

I give you my Grace,

That all permeating force, supporting all that is there
and all that is not.
The material, corporeal, existence and
the subtle, etheric continuum.
That which rests in what seems to be
the tiny space existent between thoughts,
But is finally seen as the infinite matrix of beneficence
punctuated by concreteness,
Much as the planets
(having the nature of discreet thoughts)
rest in space,
Grace's expression of unlimited expansiveness
is much like that space between the thoughts,
My Grace
(originating from Guru's intention streamed to me,
God's newly tuned instrument),
I boomerang to you,
In support, protection and service for your great work.

I give you my Grace.

I give my soul to you,

For - not now, not always-
But beyond time itself.
Through the past, present and future
of the past, present and future,
I am yours.

I give my soul to you.

I give my Gratitude to you,

For every millisecond spent in service in your house,
For every rug pulled out from under my feet,
For each shattered expectation,
For the brutal pulling of attachments,
For the excruciating loss of ego bolstering identification,
As a musician,
As a scholar,
As a scientist,
As a mother,
As a wife,
As a teacher,
As a friend,
As a knower,
As a member of this Yogic community,

For the amazing connections and associations
you allowed me to experience,

For the gift of intentions,
For the existence of the ashrams,
For the Temple,
For the support of
the sangham (the community),
For the nurturing eye-opening
parent satsangs (gatherings),

For every course, intensive and program
Delivering in fullness exactly what it promises,
For the lifeline of sweet sevites and service
That pulls one through the eye of the needle,
For He whom you have allowed me to meet,
know, and learn from in ways unimaginable,

I give you my constant and eternal Gratitude.

I give you my love,

For all you do,
For all you create,
For Him, having become my source of everything,
For being Baba,
And so as well for being Babe Baba,
For your great seva,

I give you my love.

THE FLIGHT HOME

After that powerful, fully focused *Sri Guru Gita* chant on my final morning at the ashram that summer, my daughter and I were ready to leave. I headed over to registration to pick up my room deposit. Walking through the dining hall I came up behind my unsuspecting friend, Elan, and patted him soundly on the back as I quickly sped by him, quite late for the taxi to the airport. He let out a surprised yelp, not realizing that anyone else was in the room. We didn't speak, but as I stood in line moments later waiting for my deposit, and although he was no longer present, I felt his energy, blessings and goodbye descend upon me. I picked the angel card of 'Self-Inquiry' and we left.

The taxi sped my daughter and me quickly away from the ashram and after a time we arrived at the Newark airport. We took a United flight, which was to make a stopover in Denver on the way back to our home in the San Francisco Bay Area.

I settled into my seat and the plane took off. I fell into a very deep state far inside myself. The moment of traspaso with my friend reestablished itself within my consciousness. It felt as if his eyes were inside my face still looking at me, but separate from me. After a while, a strange shift occurred where he became my Self, looking out. A still, eternal calmness and contentment arose inside me as he took up residency throughout the inner landscape of my being. It was as if my body had two occupants. I could feel and share the flavor of his state.

As the plane circled for its arrival at the Denver airport, all that my mind could say over and over and over was "I am so happy, I am so happy, I am so happy."

It was a level of bliss that was incomprehensible to me before that moment and it was so all-encompassing that I was not sure if I would be able to walk off the plane.

Even in that moment I was immediately reminded of one of my favorite Sufi stories, called "The Land of Truth", retold in *Thinkers of the East* by Idries Shah.

THE LAND of TRUTH

A certain man believed that the ordinary waking life, as people know it, could not possibly be complete.

He sought the real Teacher of the Age. He read many books and joined many circles, and he heard the words and witnessed the deeds of one master after another. He carried out the commands and spiritual exercises which seemed to him to be most attractive.

He became elated with some of his experiences. At other times he was confused; and he had no idea at all of what his stage was, or where and when his search might end.

This man was reviewing his behavior one day when he suddenly found himself near the house of a certain sage of high repute. In the garden of that house he encountered Khidr, the secret guide who shows the way to Truth.

Khidr took him to a place where he saw people in great distress and woe, and he asked who they were. "We are those who did not follow real teachings, who were not true to our undertakings, who revered self-appointed teachers,' they said.

Then the man was taken by Khidr to a place where everyone was attractive and full of joy. He asked who they were. 'We are those who did not follow the real Signs of the Way,' they said.

'But if you ignored the Signs, how can you be happy?' asked the traveler.

'Because we chose happiness instead of Truth,' said the people, 'just as those who chose the self-appointed chose also misery.'

'But is happiness not the ideal of man?' asked the man.

'The goal of man is Truth. Truth is more than happiness. The man who has Truth can have whatever mood he wishes, or none,' they told him. 'We have pretended that Truth is happiness and happiness Truth, and people have believed us, therefore you, too, have until now imagined that happiness must be the same as Truth. But happiness makes you its prisoner, as does woe.'

Then the man found himself back in the garden, with Khidr beside him.

'I will grant you one desire,' said Khidr.

I wish to know why I have failed in my search and how I can succeed in it,' said the man.

'You have all but wasted your life,' said Khidr, 'because you have been a liar. Your lie has been in seeking personal gratification when you could have been seeking Truth.'

'And yet I came to the point where I found you,' said the man, 'and that is something that happens to hardly anyone at all.'

'And you met me,' said Khidr, 'because you had sufficient desire to find Truth for its own sake, just for an instant. It was that sincerity, in that single instant, which made me answer your call.'

Now the man felt an overwhelming desire to find Truth, even if he lost himself.

Khidr, however, was starting to walk away, and the man began to run after him.

'You may not follow me,' said Khidr, 'because I am returning to the ordinary world, the world of lies, for that is where I have to be, if I am to do my work.'

And when the man looked around him again, he realized that he was no longer in the garden of the sage, but standing in the Land of Truth.

This story came strongly to mind, as we were landing in Denver. In that moment, I truly felt that I had entered the Garden of Truth.

DENVER

We had a long layover until the next flight and I was so grateful when my daughter suggested that she peruse the shops on her own. I had to find a place to meditate and adjust to this state, so that I could at least maintain the pretext of functioning. Little did I then realize that it would be four or five months until I could accept this fresh inner realm as a vague approximation of a new normalcy.

I needed to sit down. There was a phone booth empty. It was the only quiet and appealing space I could find. At first I pretended that I was on the phone, but in minutes that became far too difficult a ploy to maintain. So, I gave up all pretexts, folded up into a lotus posture and sank into the state.

He had said that no one could look into his eyes, and I had thought to myself, "I can look into anyone's eyes." I was wrong. That moment changed, forever I hope, who and what I am. That eternal moment of traspaso embedded his being in mine.

I later wrote a poem about this moment, feeling the compassion of looking out through my friend's eyes. I felt that this was much as it would be staring out through the eyes of the 'living' statue (murti) of Baba's guru, Bhagawan, meaning Lord. I had dressed this statue once a week in Oakland at 4AM for many years. This was also the spot ashram residents would gather once a month for a full moon bathing of the statue, called an abhishek, in the early morning.

I titled the poem of looking through
the eyes of the Divine:

THROUGH BHAGAWAN'S EYES

I looked to my depths for that vision of God within,
But instead, see God's self same vision "peering " out as me.

Looking out, I merge with Him,
Sweet abhishek (ritual bath) water flows over my skin,
I feel the devoted hands washing my form,
Such love, such blessing.

I glance out from Oakland's Temple,
Warmly welcoming the tender hearts
Filled with longing, wishes, hopes, and desires.
Their darshan perfect in the ebb and flow
Of mutual Blessings and Grace.

I warmly welcome those in South Fallsburg.
Dear hearts brimming with such fullness and devotion.

The Corporeal one, having taken life within my being,
Peers both inwardly and without,
Constantly present,
Etched into the core of my Self,
In the fire of the glance,
Unifying us forever.

Having taken the hand,
That pulled me through the needle's eye,
Has given birth to the constancy of this facet
Of God's vision,
Looking outward from within.

Uma-Guru's sweet gaze lives in me as well,
Knowingly conveying,
The moon's ecstatic beauty,
The ocean's serene taste of Infinity.

We are all here,
God's nearly merged vision within,
Sealed in the abundant blessings
Of the present moment,
Now.

After a while, sitting in the phone booth at the Denver airport, I felt another consciousness. I opened my eyes and my daughter was outside the booth. "Mom, are you alright?" she asked. I told her I was fine. Years later she confided in me that she had watched me from the time I was pretending to be on the phone and had found me to be acting in quite a peculiar fashion.

Chapter Two:
Reality Ripples of Bliss

THE ENTROPY of SEPTEMBER 11, 2001

Much later I came to think that it was no coincidence that I was able to attain my less chaotic state on this particular air route. In fact, I came to realize that these two events, 9/11 and my personal peak spiritual leap, existing in such close spatial and time proximity, were profoundly, energetically interconnected through the Second Law of Thermodynamics, which describes the nature of disorder, or entropy, in the universe.

There are at least 15 very different sounding formulations of this highly accepted law. I am selecting just one version to discuss, which is that statement of the law, which I perceive to be most readily extended from the classical scientific realm to the metaphysical. This law has caught the attention of poets and philosophers over the years and has been called by some the greatest scientific achievement of the nineteenth century. Engels disliked it, while Pope Pius XII regarded it as proving the existence of a higher being (Bazarow, 1964, Sect. 20). It is often projected into other than normal scientific realms, but not in the manner in which I will extend it here.

One statement of this immutable, acknowledged, yet incredibly subtle scientific law is that for any spontaneous process, the disorder, or entropy of a system must increase. So, one's house spontaneously gets dirty, which is more chaotic, and cleaning it up, which creates more order or less randomness, surely is not spontaneous. It takes a lot of work! The process that occurs naturally is always the one where the messiness, chaos and disorder increase.

Let me offer some classically simple examples of the Second Law. A somewhat trivial manifestation of this principle is that socks get mixed up naturally because that increases their disorder in the drawer or wash. On the other hand, papers take work to keep them organized and this process involves a lowering of the entropy, that is, their messiness decreases when they are arranged. Children are natural dynamos generating randomness, chaos and disorder, hence displaying an increase in entropy and teachers are paid for the non-spontaneous, entropy lowering function of educating them.

I propose that this law can successfully describe many natural phenomena in the metaphysical realm. The Second Law of Thermodynamics is why thoughts arise in meditation. The thought free state is one, which would most often arise after an extended period perhaps years of a regular meditation practice. This involves discipline and effort and hence an increase in order.

That is, one's entropy has decreased when the thought free state is entered. If one achieves this state, even for a short time, somewhere in the cosmic connectedness of realities, chaos must have increased to more than compensate for that newly generated order. When a thought free meditation or one-pointed chanting of the *Sri Guru Gita* occurs, it must be joined with a new randomness somewhere, so that when added together, the disorder of the system will still have overall increased.

I always enjoyed the thermodynamic implications of one of Baba Jivananda's, comments about chanting. He had been Uma-Guru's predecessor and teacher. He said that one could achieve Liberation in the Kaliyuga simply by chanting the name of God for 24 hours.

The Kaliyuga, our present age, is the most chaotic and disordered of the yuga's, or Vedic cosmological time cycles. It is a dark age with a lack of righteousness and hence a naturally more rapidly increasing entropy than in other ages. Therefore, all the societal disorganization during the Kaliyuga, more than at other nobler, ordered periods of human history, naturally increases the entropy. Because of this, it is an easier time for an individual to be in a state of lowered disorder, which attaining the Liberated state represents.

Therefore Baba's comment is really saying that in a time of great agitation as the Kaliyuga is, the ordered state of realization can require as little as one day of effort, since the second law mandate of increased disorder is already being met.

Some more serious examples of Second Law processes present themselves in this modern era. Our present society is expanding into ever increasing states of disorder. War, the spread of HIV/AIDS, deaths, molestation scandals within the church, sexual predators on the internet and the suicide bombers in Afghanistan, Iraq, Israel, London, Bali and elsewhere all effectively add to the system's entropy. It is these very events, which allow the development of more ordered processes, such as genetic engineering, vaccine production and an expansion of human consciousness because they are already producing so much chaos, that the huge entropic increase that these incidents represent opens the way for new order in the world.

Looking at the events of the terrorist attacks of 9/11, it is obvious that the entropy of the entire world increased enormously that day, not only with the huge loss of life and its ripple effect on all those connected to these victims, but also from the agitation, fear, worry and other such highly chaotic emotions that were generated around the globe and continue to be so. These very happenings have opened a window for the expansion of individual, local, national and global unity.

The cold, uncaring reputation of New Yorkers has been replaced by a rejuvenated sense of community, a process representing lowered entropy.

Similarly, the profound devastation of the Indonesian tsunami of December 2004, Hurricane Katrina flooding New Orleans and the huge earthquake in Pakistan and Kashmirian India in 2005 has again created a shift in the total world entropy, where leaps in a unified global consciousness are possible. The extraordinary outpouring of philanthropic efforts to assist those impacted by these events is again an example of the lowering of disorder that the alignment of hearts represents.

When I realized that the air corridor that I had been on, as I entered my new more aligned and certainly lower entropy state, had been at the focal point of such chaotic death and destruction, I was horrified. For a while I felt some universal culpability for what had later ensued, based on my knowledge of the Second Law of Thermodynamics. Were those on board that aircraft that lost their lives on 9/11 somehow generating tremendous disorder in that same airspace and hence paying the entropic price for the more ordered state which had been generated within me on that plane?

THE NONLINEARITY of TIME

Later, I realized we were a system, that event and I. We assume that time is linear, but that is actually an illusion. I believe that there is really only NOW sending its ripples out into what we perceive as the past, the future and even the present. So what we see, feel, do and experience NOW is all we are and all we ever will be. Therefore, not only does the future come to unfold, but the past as well is mutable through the events of the present. So, there is a past, present and future of the past, present and future. And, it is possible to alter the past.

There was a time in my life, my sophomore year of college, when I was on the edge of madness and despair. I had worked for an obstetrician and gynecologist that summer and had casually been provided some amphetamine medication for weight loss. It was only years later that I came to realize that on returning to school, I began to experience withdrawal symptoms. I locked myself in my dorm room for three days "looking for the vector" to push my mind back. As a Chemistry major, I spoke to myself with such analogies. I remember the feeling that an energetic hand came to me and somehow provided me with the love and support I needed to be pulled out of the pit into which I had sunk.

At a time of some clarity many years later, I consciously did visualization work, where I became that hand that rescued me. The future me greatly assisted the past me, by consciously helping myself to make it through hard times.

In the same way, as I contemplated the time distortion aspects of that amazing flight I took to Denver, I came to believe that the chaos emanating from Flight 93 on 9/11, was entropically bound to my own consciousness leap, but not in a linear time continuum. The future disorder that would eventually ensue there was already incipient in the descending electromagnetic fields at the time of my flight. I believe that we enter life with a certain predetermined electromagnetic twist or spiraling. This field results in arranging all events, meetings, marriages, affairs and encounters of our entire life. We call this Karma.

From this perspective every aspect of our existence is already decided. What you do, who you're with, the details of each day are already established. Your reaction to all that is happening is your only freedom. So it is IMPOSSIBLE to be wrong. Everything is always unfolding perfectly. You may therefore relax totally into the divine spiral of your very own life, knowing that it and you are God's intention, manifesting perfectly.

So I came to accept my connection to these events of September 11, 2001 knowing that we were part of the same unfolding of Divine manifestation in the world. I also came to believe that both the chaos and the order, the starving child and the societal excess, the murderers and the saints, cannot exist the one without the other. That is, until the time that we choose to forgive all that we see and step into existing as the Divine Matrix of all that is, consciously experiencing the Bliss of Itself. That is living as God is. All this is outside the artificial designations of time and space.

THE HEART'S FLAME

I had played with time distortion previously. There have been numerous dramatic highs and lows in my life. Many years ago, as I came to realize that the past could be impacted, I chose three memory images from among the worst moments of my life – a childhood molestation, a rape from my mid-20's, and the crazy me in the dorm room lying on my bed looking for the vector to push back my mind. I brought those three images of me into my core. I saw Baba Jivananda on a golden throne in my heart, and I allowed those three of me to sit there, like small children, and be totally comforted.

I had undergone therapeutic counseling, which had soothed, but not dissipated the pain of these past events. However this time, as they sat there, bathed in Grace and Love, these three of me became ever more increasingly filled with Light. Their individual features melted away gradually over time. They held hands in a circle as their luminosity increased. Eventually, all distinctions melted into one form of pure golden-white light.

Shortly thereafter, when Uma-Guru was visiting the Oakland ashram, I was at my seva, chopping vegetables in the kitchen, looking at a picture of Bade Baba seated on a bench. To my shock, in what I might call a vision but what was actually more of a reality for me, his right toe leapt into my heart and the top of it caught fire. Eventually the entirety of it was a flame. It became a perpetual light within my heart that still burns to this day.

I believe that the permanent experience of the inner Light is in fact enlightenment and that this is actually not so advanced a place along the journey as is often assumed. However it is a well-defined place. Liberation seems to me a more advanced state beyond the ongoing consciousness of one's light, involving the knowledge and experience of one's unity with all others. The inner shift is from having been the seeker to being the finder.

An ashram friend of mine who also distinguishes these two states believes enlightenment to be a constant connected awareness of the Self or actually being at one with one's Self. He views liberation to be the inner contact with the divinity of all or the union with God. Certainly, even after these seemingly 'end' states, there must be multitudinous and continuing levels of unfoldment.

As I explored this newfound light within me that day and later, an internal awareness arose that, in fact, the flame within me was actually made of my deepest pains having been transmuted into the Light of my Heart. It seemed that reclaiming the energy I had left in painful events long past and transporting that to the present was the fuel that was needed to ignite my own flame.

I discovered after this experience, that whenever I internally went to those ancient memory aches of old, that I was no longer there. The scenes still remained, but I no longer see myself present in them. The 'charge' of these events no longer lingers within me and it is possible to forgive everyone and everything in them-even my Self.

From the perspective of NOW, the only place where in fact reality ever exists, there is no difference between the memory of an event from a past life and a memory of an event already passed in this life. They equally exist in the unreal world of Not Now-ness and eventually they can assume an equal level of insignificance.

At the lunch break that day, right after the seva session in which my Heart's flame was kindled, I went to the Temple at the Oakland ashram and sat in a full lotus for meditation. I experienced Babe Baba materialize before me not as flesh and blood, not so someone else could see or feel him, but stronger than just imagining.

My head fell over towards his feet, but just before it reached them, a blue bolt of lightening erupted outward from those feet into the region of my ajna, or sixth chakra, the region of the third eye between the eyebrows.

From that day, he appeared to me at least weekly, sometimes daily, for the next year. He often put his hand in my mouth extending his fingers internally into the area of my third eye from inside my head. Once he shocked me by blowing his prana, or breath, into my mouth and lungs. I felt I was being healed from the nine years of smoking in my youth.

One day when I was feeling particularly skeptical of these ongoing experiences, I demanded to know if I were just imagining them. He once again appeared before me, reached into my mouth and again vigorously probed my third eye region internally.

I left the ashram that morning in a dubious frame of mind and was driving to work, contemplating my sanity in believing such visions, when my third eye region started vibrating violently in and out. I reached up to feel it and sure enough there was a highly significant physical twitching, or pulsating of that entire area. As I drove to work, I saw a flame arise in that very same internal space between the eyebrows. That flame also remains there to this day.

I asked a knowledgeable swami about it once and was told that Indian kundalini scriptures describe the kindling of the flame of the intellect in that very region. My experiences of frequent visions of Babe Baba stopped after this second flame was kindled. Interestingly, at one point of my South Fallsburg summer, Elan deeply kneaded that area of my forehead. Just as it had in my experience with Babe Baba, that region of my forehead twitched for many days.

LIGHT-
ELECTROMAGNETIC RADIATION

These internal visions comprise a level of inner experience that has a reality beyond the dramas of the mind's inner vistas. It is closer to the dream state of living out adventures where one is totally aligned with being the one in that perceptive reality. Other entities and energies from that internal realm have often appeared to me, interacted with me and given me advise or clarifying visions which have had catalytic impacts on my life.

Neither are these visions, which are emanating from someone else's stray thoughts, which I find myself to frequently intercept. Years ago, in the early seventies, I was a healer and aura and chakra reader at the Monday night healing clinic of Berkeley Psychic School. Actually, for the first year, I just watched a close friend of that era, a fellow I was enamored of, do healings. After about a year of intently 'looking', I started 'seeing' the auras and colors he was describing, as well as, at times, 'bunched up energy'. This was energy that was not flowing through a person's body freely, but got hung up somewhere in their physical field, causing problems from headaches to illness to tumors.

It is not a normal eye function that allowed these perceptions, but rather an attunement to the electromagnetic energies, the vibrational and rotational energies, of the actual molecules composing the physical body structure. It is the normal frequency differentials of wavelengths of light, which are exactly what produces different visible colors, superimposed to a different range that allows the differing colors of the aura to be seen. These 'normal' colors are thus shifted to a usually invisible range. In this way, the differing colors of the aura can be seen, using the same familiar gaps associated with the normal visible spectrum of light that we are so familiar with when we view a rainbow.

Scientists consider light to be anything that moves at the speed of light --186,000 miles per second. At this speed it takes the light from the sun 8.3 minutes to shine on the earth. The light one is seeing from the sun now, was actually emitted 8.3 minutes ago. The light from even the closest star, Alpha Centauri, was released about 4 years ago. The speed at which light travels becomes a measure of distance, so Alpha Centauri is said to be four light years away. If our sun were the size of a period on this page then the nearest star would be eight miles away. There are only 40 stars within 16 light years of earth.

Light is also known as electromagnetic radiation. It has both a wave and a particle nature, but no mass or substance. Light has a wavelength associated with it, which is the distance from the peak of one wave to the peak of the next. The shorter the wavelength, the more it needs to wiggle (this is its frequency) to get anywhere. The more it is wiggling, the more energy it has. Therefore, the shorter the wavelength, the higher is the energy and the longer the wavelength is, the less energetic is that light. High-energy light can damage human tissue.

There are many different things that are light. What distinguishes them from each other is their wavelengths. At the shortest wavelengths are the very high-energy cosmic rays from outer space. Next, having a wavelength about the size of an atom are the dangerous gamma rays emitted in many nuclear reactions. As one proceeds to longer wavelengths, the x-rays used for dental and medical diagnoses are found. Next is the ultraviolet (UV) light emitted from the sun, which can't be seen, but is responsible for giving one sunburn, due to its energy being higher than that of visible light due to its shorter wavelength.

Finally we've reached the light that one most commonly thinks about. That is the visible region of the electromagnetic spectrum, which our physical bodily senses perceive, but which is only a tiny bit of all that comprises light. The wavelength of visible light ranges from 0.00001 inches (4000 Angstroms), for the most energetic, shortest wavelength violet light, to 0.00005 inches (8000 Angstroms) for the longest wavelength, less energetic red light.

The natural rainbow formed by atmospheric water splitting white sunlight, which contains all visible wavelengths, into its spectrum always has the colors in the same order, the order of their wavelengths. The order, from the least energetic, is indicated by the acronym ROYGBIV, standing for red, orange, yellow, green, blue, indigo, and violet. Violet light is the highest visible energy color.

As one progresses to longer wavelengths, infrared (IR) light is encountered, such as that found in bathroom heating lamps. At a longer wavelength still, now between 0.01 and 10 inches, is found the microwave radiation used in microwave ovens.

These ovens are calibrated only to affect the rotational energy of the water molecule. Anything without water in it will not get hot. Food heated in this manner has only its water molecules doing rapid somersaults, that is, the rotational energy of water is increased. Higher temperature means faster molecular motion. By contrast, food heated by more conventional ovens, whether gas or electric, has ALL its molecules moving faster in lines, rather than just the water doing the somersaults or rotations that a microwave induces.

Finally one encounters the lowest energy (longest wavelength) forms of light, radio and TV waves. Radio waves, the waves carrying the sound to be captured by the radio, but not the 'noise' itself, start at about 10 inches long and TV waves are often miles long. These noise creating, yet soundless forms of light are the lowest energy of all its forms.

An extension of this classical view is that we share our space with all this radiation all the time. We are surrounded by light of every form. In every cycle of light there is the node, where the wave changes from above the line to below. It is a point of null, zero, silence. There are also places where overlapping waves cancel each other's highs and lows creating interference patterns. There are many points of cancellation, nodes, or silence at these junctions. They surround us and are available to us all the time.

Similar wavelengths exist in a different range in the aura. When disease is present, the vibration of the molecules associated with the problem area creates a field in that region of the body, which does not match the energetic flow of adjoining regions. If this deficit or excess remains for long, illness arises.

CHAKRAS and HEALING

Healers often use opposite colored energy i.e. a violet or blue for what visually looks like a hot red body area that needed cooling. This mixing of a somewhat complementary hue allows a balancing of the amplitude of the frequency associated with the disease or discomfort. When opposites are equally accepted by a system, a point of neutrality is attained. From that place all possibilities are able to manifest, so the choice for health or anything else becomes real.

I perceive that all illness or injury always involves a purification of one of the chakras associated most closely with the region of the body nearest to that site. There are seven chakras, or major energy junctions of the nadis or subtle energy channels in the body.

The first chakra, located at the lowest central positioning of the body cavity, inward from the spinal base, involves issues of survival. Jobs, finances, housing, and money concerns are all associated with this chakra. The first chakra governs survival issues of jobs, money considerations, and housing, which support one's basic survival in the physical three-dimensional realm. This chakra helps ground us to the physical realities of living on this planet.

The second chakra, or sexual chakra, is located in the belly region, below the navel and again in the center of the body cavity. It concerns one's sexual identity. Second chakra stirrings connect one to possible mates.

The third chakra existing internally in the region of the solar plexus is associated with issues of control and energy distribution throughout the body.

The focus on issues of the heart, or love, is tied to the fourth chakra in which the attention expands outward from the individual to at least some in the world 'outside'. It is the first of the 'higher' chakra's dealing with love, both in its personalized and generalized forms. Fourth chakra love can be for that one special someone or ever so much broader.

The fifth chakra, embodying the principles of communication allows one to present oneself to others and to the world. The interior region of the Adams apple of the throat is the seat of this energy junction.

The sixth chakra, or the inner region of the 'third eye', is situated just above and within the area between the eyes, at the center lower portion of the forehead. This area's functioning concerns seeing the broader perspective as life unfolds before one's eyes.

Finally, the seventh chakra located at the crown of the head is the seat of knowingness – of oneself and one's place in the universe and how things work.

Not only does the individual's body contain these seven chakra's, but I am aware of the same seven chakra's existing in the body of the planet earth as well, one on each of the seven continents at positions of the crossing of many ley lines, or subtle energy channels existing on the surface of the globe.

All disease involves some purification process associated with the chakra in closest proximity to the physical ailment or symptom. On a simplistic level, pneumonia involving the lungs will tend to be associated with issues concerning a heart or 4th chakra cleansing process. A sore throat or laryngitis would be linked with the 5th or communication chakra found in the region of the throat. I have always thought that if I am as a healer able to see these deficits or excesses in someone's body field, that what I perceive should be able to be measured.
A lifelong dream of mine was to work on instrumentation to measure subtle body fields in order to allow earlier diagnosis of problems such as cancer and AIDS, and hence

permit more effective treatments and prognoses.

SHIFTING FOCUS

On arriving home after the transformative experiences of the summer, I found that I could scarcely function. I was in such an ecstatic state. I was also so constantly aware of Elan's energy, his presence within me and to some extent his actual ongoing reality shared internally with mine that normal living was out of the question.

I had practiced what was called Guru Bhava for years, first with Baba Jivananda and then with Babe Baba. It involved feeling what one imagined was the Guru's consciousness internally as one's reality, and feeling the imagined superimposed body of the Guru as one's own.

For years I engaged in this practice off and on with Baba Jivananda as it's object. Then, after my experience with Babe Baba in the Temple, at the moment my Heart caught fire, the practice spontaneously shifted so that he internal focus of my attention became Babe Baba.

I was at first somewhat disturbed by this transition to what I thought was a different Guru. Internally I prayed to Baba, asking why this had happened. I was led to pick up one of his books and randomly opened to a page. There Jivananda stated that the greatest gift he could ever give anyone was to give them his Guru, Nityananda, also called Babe Baba, for Baba's own state had arisen from having become his guru.

I had been a previous circumstance that I perceived of as someone becoming the being of another. It was when Baba Jivananda died or as is said, he took Mahasamadhi, in 1982. He had made Uma-Guru his successor, but even though I felt her highly evolved state, I had known her as a gawky 19 year old, with normal life concerns and issues. At that time I could not conceive of ever seeing her as my Guru. So I was not around the ashram for some time during the transition period.

Eventually, there came an occasion, when Uma-Guru was visiting the Oakland ashram. I had nothing better to do that day so I decided to drop in. I ended up having a private darshan, or meeting with her, to speak about the pain and isolation I had been feeling since Baba's death.

To my surprise, as I approached her, I experienced her energy as having the identical flavor to the energy which I associated with Baba's. I knew in that moment, that in fact she had become him, that is, his energy had taken over her Being. For that reason, I could again be part of the ashram community, because for me beyond a shadow of a doubt, I knew that it was my Baba functioning through her. I could taste that energy there from that time on.

So I had gone through these internal shifts before, but nothing so radical as that which transpired this time. How could I follow this Guru Bhava practice so long, for these many years, and all of a sudden turn completely into someone else? I was in such constant Bliss that it didn't matter, but my mind could make no sense of it.

By trade, I am a Chemistry Professor at a 25,000-student community college. Even as I gave my chemistry lectures each day, I was swimming in such ecstasy that it was hard to stand. I also had the sense of seeing and living another life simultaneously, my friend Elan's life, every moment. I felt as if my body contained the reality of two distinct beings at once, fortunately with his constant joy predominating.

There was no one with whom I shared my new reality. My husband and I are both Chemistry professors and live out a richness of intellectual probing of our discipline, but my spiritual life made him a bit uncomfortable for many years. I also did not feel that the kind of allegiance shift in my energy would be accepted or understood by friends in the ashram community. Most of my closest friends were from work and wouldn't understand the adventures I had just had. I didn't understand them myself. But I sure was happy.

It wasn't that I had never experienced this degree of joy, but all instances of it in the past had been random and irreproducible. It was as if there were an internal spiral staircase to the 'Land of Paradise', but it's entrance had always been barred. I had occasionally popped up there, but invariably fell to a more normal state for my consciousness fairly soon. I often felt changed by the experience, but not able to permanently live from that new state. I neither understood the mechanism well enough to ascend the staircase, nor to prevent the eventual tumble.

What shifted for me during my reliving of the traspaso on

the plane was that the bar blocking the entrance to that internal staircase was removed. It isn't that I'm always happy now, but the moment-by-moment choice to be happy does exist for me in every instant. The bar is still there, but not locked. I have to make the continuous and conscious effort to lift it and climb the stair to be in that 'Land of Paradise'. Now however, it is always my choice. And, perhaps it always was. Yet now, I know and believe it to be so.

THE TAROT

A longing arose to describe to Elan the miracles in my life that had arisen from our meeting. I thought that he would still be at the ashram and I decided to write. Besides sharing what had transpired for me, ideas on a topic we had discussed were internally demanding to be communicated.

We had spoken on occasion about balancing the forces in one's life. I had taught the Tarot before and a story that interconnected the Tarot cards of the Wheel of Fortune, the World and the Chariot came to mind, to share with him in a letter.

The Wheel of Fortune as well as the card of the World, as depicted in the Waite deck, show four animals representing the four possible paths available to the senses by which they are able to interact with all that they encounter. These are the journeys represented by each of the four suits of the minor Arcana.

A Tarot deck has 22 Trumps or Major Arcana cards and four suits of 13 cards each, the Minor Arcana, which over the centuries, were transformed by gypsies, and have come to be our normal deck of playing cards.

The lion represents the fire path, wands, of the Minor Arcana. Unity in this path is realized in the crown of the head, M'OH, through wisdom. Each suit represents its own particular door to the very same Samadhi, or Unity, in a distinctly different way. The path of wands is a kundalini pathway. Kundalini is the coiled energy, which lies at the base of the spine and can be activated by the catalytic effect of encountering a great Being's energy field.

The entire spiritual journey is often described as the transitioning of this spiritual energy from the base of the spine to the crown of the head. From my perspective it also involves the union of earth energies from below and heavenly energies from above within the physical vehicle of the body. It clears all samskaras, or karmic impurities, from the nadis, or subtle body energy channels. It does this by cleaning and activating the spin of all the seven major energy junctions or chakras in the body, along the way. The culmination point of this energy's journey through the body is the very top of the head at the seventh or crown chakra. Reaching this place results in Yoga, the Union of all opposites, which is experienced as Samadhi, Bliss and the inner state of Liberation.

Scientifically speaking, due to the effect of an erect posture that the human being assumes, there is in fact a potential energy difference between the base of the spine and the crown of the head generated by the gravitational field of the earth. I see the transitioning of that approximately 1 meter, or three foot, difference as the 'Gateway to Heaven'.

Science traditionally describes two kinds of energy, kinetic and potential. Kinetic energy is that which originates from motion. For instance, temperature arises from the movement of the individual particles of which all substances are composed. The faster these atoms or molecules move the hotter is the object.

Potential energy is the innate energy, which has the possibility of being generated by a system. So, when a chemical bond forms, potential energy is released and it takes the same amount of energy to break that same chemical bond.

Another kind of potential energy is due to an object changing its distance from the center of the earth, that is its position. An example of this is the possible, or potential energy, stored by a boulder at the top of a cliff ready to fall. As it plunges, all its potential energy is transformed to kinetic or motion energy by the time it reaches the ground. This energy has the capacity to do work, such as cracking open a nut.

The formula for the positional energy generated by the force of gravity for differing distances from the center of the earth equals the mass (m) of the object times the acceleration due to gravity (g), times the height (h) that the object is lifted, or falls, as in:

Gravitational Potential Energy = mgh

So I perceive there to be a real force operating to create a flow, possibly of electrons, along various vertical body channels, particularly along the nerves and more subtle energy pathways of the spinal column. I believe that this is why nearly all systems of meditation recommend an erect spine. They vary as to the point of focus. Some use a mantra (sacred word), or the breath as a point of concentration. Some observe whatever thoughts arise, or concentrate on a point or some other aspect of the awareness to use as a return foci for consciousness when entropy causes its wandering. However, the straight spine is nearly always mandated. And it is this exactly, that supports the journey of the kundalini energy, the spiritual journey represented by the suit of wands in the Tarot.

The bull, or the earth route of Pentacles in the Minor Arcana, involves the "PATH" (pronounced poth), or head energy center, in which illusions are dissipated through knowledge.

The Angel, or water path, involves the suit of cups and is centered upon reaching Samadhi through finding the ecstasy of the heart center, or "OTH", through love.

Finally, the eagle represents the sword suit, which is tied to the element of air, where the search for truth involves the instinctual belly center, or "KATH". It is the activation of this deep internal region that the Taoists refer to as the dantien. The emanation of "chi" or power energy from this belly area, allows the skilled tai chi practitioner to propel an opponent with its force. Its activation results in finding oneself in the right place at the right time with the right people. It allows one to find one's way without further direction.

This wheel of fortune card also contains three other figures representing the three centers present in the human form. The Egyptian Hemananubis, the man with the head of a dog, is the emotions; the sphinx with the sword, the mind; and the golden serpent, the lower instinctual center, which has the power to be transformed by the kundalini.

This card has the potential to eat you in the jaws of karma, when the senses (the four animals and their elements) and the three creatures of the body's operative energies are given free reign. However, it can also exalt one to the highest realms of grace and synchronicity (the universal connectedness of all things). This occurs when the three body centers, along with the senses, are working in harmony with the Holy Law, the TORA (TARO). They will thereby also be in alignment with the Hebrew mantra for the never pronounced name of God (Yahweh), the four-letter tetragrammaton of Yod, He, Vov, He, depicted on the card. It is then that there is a perfect harmony in the cycles of the Wheel of Fortune, or one's destiny.

So finally I shared in my letter to Elan, this story about these particular cards:

'At the beginning of time, there was a chariot, with a master within. He gave clear commands to the chariot driver, who held his reigns so expertly, that the four animals pulling his vehicle were under perfect control. Eons passed.

Eventually the charioteer forgot even the very existence of a master within and loosened his hold on the team. They wandered here and there, losing their sense, and even their awareness of each other. Chaos ensued. Somehow after much time, the charioteer eventually heard the faint voice of the forgotten Master within. The control of the instinctual beasts was reestablished and once again a straight path was pursued through the strength of the Master's intention. The moral is: Where passion and discipline are one, 'I' lead the chariot.'

The chariot is the body, the animals are the senses and the Master is the Self. Using these principles, anything can be achieved.

And so, this is the letter I sent off to Elan. Months passed with no response. I tried to check whether he was actually at the ashram in New York or even if he ever had been. I was unable to find any information on him at all. I never doubted my very real experiences with him, but I did come to doubt whether he really existed in a 'normal' fashion.

Chapter Three:
Continuing Connections

THE PHONE RANG

I continued adjusting to my strange new state of being which took about four or five months to feel somewhat normal. My body, emotions and thoughts were wildly happy and totally foreign. I continued to raise my children, cook meals and clean house, live as a wife with my husband and teach my classes. Sometimes in lab, on the rare occasions when I showed a movie, I would sit unnoticed, in a full lotus perched on a laboratory bench at the far rear corner of the room, relishing the ecstasy of the moment and settling into the full consciousness of him, who still continued his presence in my inner realms.

Randomly, a few months later, at work during my office hour, the phone rang. Shock and joy overtook me as I heard Elan's voice on the line. A rapid shift to the realization of his flesh and blood existence reestablished itself.

Thus began a period of time where we would talk for hours, as he called me from England in which he lived. I had never before spoken internationally on the phone. As time went by, I slowly came to know of his personality self and the more mundane aspects of his life.

THE HOLY INSTANT

One day in January of 2002, the phone rang and it was again Elan. He was in the country and asked if he and a friend might drop over and spend some time visiting. I said certainly. I have a large and comfortable house and that he was most welcome. He said he was only six hours away. I frantically cleaned up a bit and in 4 ½ hours, there they were at my door.

As he and his friend walked up to the house, he walked up to me and hugged me. Instantly, the world vanished. All time, space, form, distinctions, perceptions, EVERYTHING was gone including the observer within. It was only when I returned that I could formulate the idea that I had felt complete union, peace fullness, and a sense of completeness, when I had 'been gone'. It was the very same thing that had happened in the ashram café, when he had told me he could give me shaktipat with one finger.

It wasn't until I studied *A Course in Miracles* that I could find any description that approximated what I had experienced. In Chapter 18 of the Course, called Beyond the Body (IV, 11-14), I found the following discussion, which for me seems to express what had occurred for me.

"Everyone has experienced what he would call a sense of being transported beyond himself. This feeling of liberation far exceeds the dream of freedom sometimes hoped for in special relationships. It is a sense of actual escape from limitations. If you will consider what this

"transportation" really entails, you will realize that it is a sudden unawareness of the body, and a joining of yourself and something else in which your mind enlarges to encompass it. It becomes part of you as you unite with it. And both become whole, as neither is perceived as being separate. What really happens is that you have given up the illusion of a limited awareness, and lost your fear of union. The love that instantly replaces it extends to what has freed you, and unites with it. And while this lasts, you are not uncertain of your Identity, and would not limit it. You have escaped from fear to peace, asking no questions of reality, but merely accepting it. You have accepted this instead of the body, and have let yourself be one with something beyond it, simply by not letting your mind be limited by it.

This can occur regardless of the physical distance between you and what you join; of your respective positions in space; and of your differences in size and seeming quality. Time is not relevant; It can occur with something past, present and anticipated. The "something" can be anything and anywhere; a sound, a sight, a thought, a memory and even a general idea without specific reference, Yet in every case, you join it without reservation because you love it, and would be with it. And so you rush to meet it, letting your limits melt away, suspending all the "laws" your body obeys and gently setting them aside.

There is no violence at all in this escape. The body is not attacked, but simply properly perceived. It does not limit you, merely because you would not have it so. You are not really "lifted out" of it; it cannot contain you. You go where you would be, gaining, not losing, a sense of Self. In these instants of release from physical restrictions, you experience much of what happens in the holy instant; the lifting of the barriers of time and space, the sudden experience of peace and joy, and, above all, the lack of awareness of the body, and of the questioning whether or not this is possible.

It is possible because you want it. The sudden expansion of your consciousness that takes place with your desire for it is the irresistible appeal the holy instant holds. It calls to you to be yourself, within its safe embrace. There are the laws of limit lifted for you, to welcome you to openness of mind and freedom. Come to this place of refuge, where you can be yourself in peace. Not through destruction, not through a breaking out, but merely by a quiet melting in. For peace will join you there, simply because you have been willing to let go the limits you have placed on love, and joined it where it is and where it led you, in answer to its gentle call to be at peace."

So, in what seemed to be a fraction of a second, or an entire life, I was still standing there after a momentary greeting that had dipped into eternity.

I had only that evening to visit with Elan and his friend, for the next morning my husband and I had planned a trip to Monterey. My daughter had just turned 18 years old and it was one of the first times we dared to leave her and her 15 year old brother alone. Neither one drove, and since our house is fairly isolated, we were concerned about how they might manage.

I was torn about leaving and wanted to cancel our trip. Elan wouldn't let me, but finally agreed to still stay for a few days after my husband and I returned from our excursion. So they stayed with my children for the weekend.

With some effort, I was successful at staying in the moment with my husband for this very rare weekend away. We stayed at a lovely hotel along the ocean. We walked along the rock cliffs at dusk and had lovely quiet meals. All together it was a spectacular time to be alone together.

Yet as we started driving home on Sunday, my internal focus rapidly returned to my houseguests. I was excited about having some more time with Elan and hoping that he might shed some light onto the nature of the state that had arisen within me when since meeting him the previous summer. I longed to understand who he was to me and why such profound internal shifts had occurred.

ONE WISH

I spent an enchanted afternoon with them upon my return. We did some sightseeing in San Francisco. Catching panoramic vistas of the Golden Gate Bridge, snacking at the Japanese Tea Garden and visiting Muir Beach, filled the day. Eventually he, his traveling companion and I, ended up at a beautiful, gourmet Mexican restaurant in Tiburon looking across the Bay at the skyline of San Francisco. The sun appeared to set smack dab into the center of the Golden Gate Bridge. A conversation of import ensued.

He told me to close my eyes and take back my energy. Somehow, I instantaneously retrieved my energy, but also gave him back his. All at once, I stopped feeling him living inside me. I experienced an acute and upsetting separation and a plunge from the bliss I'd been in, since that fateful arrival at the Denver airport. I felt energetically lost without the substantiality of him inside my field. I was upset as I watched him drive. "He said, "If you only spent as much time focusing on your Self as you do on me, you would be in an amazing state."

In my confusion, I took that as an external rejection. It added to what I had felt had been an internal rejection in the restaurant. A few tears fell from my eyes. I became confused and agitated, emotions that were at this point many months foreign to me.

We went to a large group session with a well-known healer. I had a very hard time being there. I had no perspective on what had just happened. There was a sense of being hollow, cleared out of that exquisite energy of his that had been residing within me the previous 4 months. The class ended. He knew I was upset.

We started driving home. I was arguing with him. Elan rightly wanted me to take responsibility for my own state and I fell into an old and familiar pattern of blaming him for my loss. Today I understand that I am powerless over all people, places and things, and that in fact my state is the sole thing that is totally under my control. It's not that I always can operate from that Truth, but at least I am ever increasingly more aware of those times that I start falling into thinking that I can control others or that anyone but me has any control over my thoughts, my feelings or my being.

On this day, I was blinder than a bat and internally angrier than a two year old cheated out of an ice cream cone. Things escalated and Elan became agitated by the situation, so that he pulled over and switched to sitting alone in the back seat with his friend driving.

I am ever so grateful that a third party was there because the next moments were so deeply mythical that I surely would not have trusted that they actually occurred without this witnesses' validation.

Elan told me "OK, I will give you a BOON. Only one. Think about it carefully – don't say anything until we're home." Now I had always been deeply enamored of the stories of finding a bottle at the beach with a genie in it, who would give one three wishes. I used to spend long hours thinking of what I'd choose as my wishes.

For many, many years, all worldly desires and familial yearnings had fallen away, until I walked around day and night, burning solely in the incendiary longing for liberation. Yet, since my Flight 93, I had been keenly aware that whether the actuality of liberation had truly transpired or not, it no longer mattered. The urgency of that yearning had evaporated. It is unseemly not to acknowledge what Grace has given.

Strangely, I had spent quite some time since then refocusing the laser of my intention. Because of that, immediately and with no ambiguity, I knew exactly what boon I would ask of him. For in my mind, there is only one thing anyone can ever share or give to another.

In the moment, I was boiling over with my hysteria and distress and I knew exactly what I wanted from him, who had actually already given me everything. So unhesitatingly and with no doubt I said, "I've already contemplated that. I ask to SEE, to KNOW and to UNDERSTAND the fullness of your state."

Elan became visibly distraught and responded, "But that would kill you!" To my shock, he meant it fully and literally.

He said, "What I'll do is give you back your state." And he did.

In that moment our relationship shifted. Some sort of protection from me on his part blocked the unity of connectedness that had been there previously.

As we arrived at my home, Elan went off by himself outside and I saw tears in his eyes. He said briefly something about not wanting to live if it were to be like this, and bemoaned his youth. He spent the entire night upset sitting up in a chair in his friend's bedroom.

I didn't understand, but think that the internal clash of the strength of his POWER collided explosively with the impulsiveness and rashness of his youth. How difficult it must be to balance those forces and live the semblance of an ordinary life, not quite clear on the extent of one's Power nor having a certainty of one's identity, but brimming with abnormal abilities.

Elan would no longer speak to me that visit. I stayed up all night writing different wishes, attempting to formulate more reasonable boons- to no avail. It was only much, much later that I decided that the boon I requested had been perfect.

I had not specified a time frame. If I received it immediately and it killed me, ah well, I have died, it seems, in all my lives. That life, in which his Grace descended upon me as I expired, was the most exquisite of deaths. Surely the insights that arose from that moment would not be wasted and must have had quite some impact on my subsequent existences.

Perhaps he would hold off the revelation of his beingness until my natural death, so that no loss of living would have occurred. Again, I'd have a lovely death and likely some ongoing level of his support in this life to prepare me for the fullness of the boon's promise. Another option would be that he'd show up in some other of my lives and I relished maintaining this connection throughout my various existences. All together, I saw no way to lose with the boon I had chosen. When he left, I told Elan that he is always welcome in my home, in every one of my lives.

I have since that time pondered deeply on what happened, with no clarity. Could such a beneficent energy actually kill a person? Is not God's energy pure love, blessing and grace? How could such a force as that ever cause harm?

Each person's samskaras, or karmic impurities, are positioned in the nadi system, or the subtle energy channels of the body. It seems to me that they must create an impedance similar to that of electric wires, which would prevent the easeful flow of energy or electrons in the body, so that frying one's circuits would be impossible? Yet this remains a theory, and many great beings whom I respect seem to believe in the potential danger of the energy that can be transmitted. In my mind, love's beneficence will always triumph with no ill effect.

I asked a British psychic reader I trust, Edwin Courtenay, about this, and he channeled the following as an answer to this question.

My question was: "I have a strong feeling that the belief in danger or in the power of the Christ or Maitreya energy to burn us is fallacious. I know many people talk about protection, but I believe that the natural body impedance to, perhaps literally, electron flows prevents damage. This impedance is likely governed by the impurities, samskaras (karmic blockages) and natural resistance of the body as a manifestation of the state of the being occupying this temple. I can't imagine why connecting directly to that Christ energy, to whatever extent I am able to, would not be more appropriate than meditations on someone externally, like a guru or teacher. It reinforces the notion that connection to the ultimate lies somewhere other than within. I know that I am Brahma the Creator, Vishnu the Sustainer, and Shiva the Destroyer of anything within the realm of what I will ever be able to experience. If I am in fact that divine force manifesting, how could that ever injure me? Is there an example that you know where too much Christ energy ever injured or destroyed anyone, or is this only an agreed upon fear of humanity?"

He responded as follows: *"My answer to that question would be that it's all about consciousness. Yes, the Divine is present within every particle of every human being and as such, the body and the energy system have a degree of intelligence, and as such, the body and the energy body cannot be harmed by that of which it is a part, the Divine.*

But the consciousness of a human being is determined by their karma and by that which they have brought with them into this life, and by their upbringing and their society and their religion and their education. That consciousness therefore is, to use an analogy, of a particular diameter, and therefore is capable of holding only that which can fit into its expanded space. When an energy enters into that expanded space that is too big for it or too heavy for it, the consciousness will collapse, or break apart, or fold in on itself, and this is how the Christ energy can damage an individual.

If the consciousness of an individual is not ready to receive the energy that it comes into contact with it, will be burned. It will be harmed. It will be destroyed. And when I talk about consciousness, I talk about self worth and self love. I talk about awareness of the Divine Truth. I talk about maturity of consciousness. It's much like teaching children. When children are young we give them levels of truth that they are capable of digesting and assimilating. If we gave them too much, it would overload them, or frighten them, or cause irrevocable psychological damage, and it's the same with the consciousness of an adult. If they're given more than they are capable of spiritually assimilating at any one point in time, it will damage their consciousness. Therefore we have to be gentle. That's why in mystery schools people are taught gradually the mysteries. They are unfolded piece by piece. Not because there is any kind of internal resistance to the student's own Divinity but because their consciousness, which is the framework of our understanding in this lifetime, expands slowly in accordance with the energy and information that it is given and the time that that consciousness needs in order to process and assimilate the information, that is entered into it.

A SHOCKING PREDICTION

For the next year my unfolding saga with Elan continued in ever more unexpected ways. After his Bay Area visit, I didn't speak with him for the next many months. I was very uncomfortable, because internally I could sense his annoyance with me throughout this period. The internal consciousness link with him had not been severed.

After a considerable time the relationship once again established itself. We then again entered a period where we spoke by phone frequently and at length. On one such occasion, near the end of a long conversation, quite randomly he said to me, "Oh, I'm so very sorry. Your husband will die soon."

My heart stopped. I could not believe that I had heard correctly, yet he repeated himself.

Now, the point at which I had gone off to the ashram for the summer was a low point in my marriage. We had had some wonderful years and had been married 18 years that summer. A set of compounded events had added enormous tension to our relationship.

My husband had retired from a long and totally satisfying teaching career, although he still continued to teach part-time, leaving full-time status produced an enormous shift in his influence in the department. His mother had just died, leaving him three ranches to maintain. We had 100 sheep and horses and he still irrigated about 20 acres by hand every weekend, six months of the year. He also mended all the fences and did all the veterinary work. When 28 tons of hay are delivered each year, he put them in the barn with hay hooks, lifting each 120-pound bale alone. It took him only about two or three weekends to accomplish this monumental task. He pruned all the 20 fruit trees at the ranch by himself, sprayed them, picked fruit, and burned the brush.

When his mom died, all of a sudden just the two of us were maintaining four houses and five properties. I could scarcely remember which needed toilet paper. We were renting out our old place until a buyer could be found. The huge new home had just been purchased. He had totally indulged me in the stretch of our finances that the acquisition had involved, but also was resentful of the burdens we had assumed in the process.

Our kids were just at that point where the sweetness of the younger years gives way to preteen and teenage angst. I was working full time, feeling hormonal shiftings that arrived quite early and stretching to maintain my meditation and chanting practices. One of our children was particularly unhappy with the move, which had been for better schools.

Likely, for these reasons our relationship had taken on levels of frustration, anger, yelling and unpleasantness. That summer I had considered leaving. I had discounted ever getting a divorce and was actually shocked to realize that I did not believe in divorce. My vows had been before God and I was committed to them no matter what.

Baba Jivananda used to conduct the marriage ceremony for some couples in Siddha Yoga, however I had heard that Uma-Guru decided not to do the same, since she found that Westerners were not always as committed to their marriages. So many of even these spiritual unions ended in divorce.

I had been unwilling to leave my marriage, but at the same time unable to drop years of frustrations, little issues, underlying anger and blame. Elan's comment to me about my husband's imminent demise cut through all of that with one mighty blade.

Although I could not imagine living through many more years of the negativities and little things that had built up, surely I could for a short time. Above and beyond that, for a short time I could see doing that without rancor.

And so I internally shifted my marital focus to a shorter time frame. With that shift, a miracle ensued.

Drawing in my point of reference brought me much more into NOW. Interestingly, I discovered that although it is easy to have a bad year or even a bad month, it gets increasingly less common to have a terrible week. Once you consider the time frame of days, a lot of them are quite fine. There are few hours that are truly bad; it's an exceptional minute that has any problem at all and unpleasant seconds start to be extraordinarily rare.

So instead of trying to live out the years of my marriage, I started to live out it's minutes and hours and to my shock they were really OK. After a while this shift of focus allowed the incipient bulbs of love, lying just below the surface to rebloom. After a time, the relationship I had with my husband regained a considerable degree of health.

This transition was not easy. For many years, I had been a member and group leader in Claudio Naranjo's SAT groups, which were connected with Sufi and Gurdjieff traditions among others. We worked in three or four month sessions usually with a number of major teachers at once. Claudio brought us teacher after teacher, guru after guru.

Through these groups I studied with Tarthang Tulku of the Tibetan Nyingma lineage, Dhira Vamsa who taught Vipassana meditation, Master Chu Fang Chu who taught us four months of Taoist breathing before starting us on Tai Chi movements. We were the test group for Bob Hoffman to develop his Fisher Hoffman psychological clearing

———

80

process. We practiced Sufi traditions doing the sacred dances. We studied in great depth for years the personality enneagram that was transmitted to Claudio through Oscar Ichazo of the Arica foundation.

A man and woman team was assigned to lead each of Claudio's SAT groups. I was paired with Hameed Ali, who later used the pen name A. H. Almaas, and was the founder of the Diamond Approach. On my very first night teaching with these groups, a sign was on our meeting door informed us to reconvene at Pauli Ballroom on the University of California, Berkeley campus to hear a talk given by Swami Jivananda. That was the first night I met Baba.

One of the most powerful tasks we were assigned in the SAT group of about 35 people of which I was a member, was a process called 'lines'. This was not the group I taught, but rather the one in which I had been participating with as a member for years. Our task was to be karmically clean with every member of the group. Over a period of many months, we set up appointments with every other person in the group, with the intention of having no left over issues remain between any of us, either as individuals or as a whole group entity.

Separate appointments were set up between every possible combination of two group members. At each of these dyadic encounters a candle was lit, representing the third force. Then each person spoke for a timed one-hour period with the other participant listening receptively, but not responding in any way. The process was then repeated with the roles reversed. Only at the end of the session did the two participants speak to each other freely. If the dyad had not achieved its goal, another appointment was made. The process continued until each set of people decided that they were clear. Claudio's first two groups had not been successful with this task, but group 3-4, of which I was a member, was able to reach the intended result. I learned through this process that only one person, myself, was needed in order to achieve the state of being in which I'm totally 'clear' with any individual.

The entire group then, each separately in a room of our own home, spent three days in simultaneous prayer. A bucket was used for excretory functioning; all food was placed in the room before the 3-day prayer began. Time was spent in long sessions of repeating certain prayers and mantras, said in particular postures, with short breaks between.

The entire process was very intense and during one of the many sessions, my past-life histories opened before me for the first time, almost always associated with various bodily aches. A pain might jump out of my arm bringing with it memories of a life as a farmer in the fields of France - ants crawling over me at a difficult moment as a priestess in Egypt – being a mother to 14 children in Poland – being a tough young guy with a knife – praying as a nun in a monastery in Europe – being a seer at Delphi. Life after life disclosed itself at this time, revealing that I had been man and woman, high and low, good and bad, spiritual and mundane.

The ultimate and life impacting lesson, which I took with me from this karmic clearing process of 'lines', was that to be totally 'uncharged' with someone, to forgive them entirely, has no dependence on the other at all. It slowly came to me, working with person after person, friends, enemies, ex-lovers or anyone – that it was totally up to me and me alone if I chose to be clear. And it was only in being clear that I could fall into the NOW to become aware of what was actually happening at this moment. Through this process I started to get early glimpses of the fact that I had no control over anyone else but myself, and that that was enough.

There is a magic in this process, for the only way one can ever forgive oneself is by forgiving everyone and everything that appears to be 'other'. This works because it is only projections of aspects of ourselves that are perceived in the 'others'. Truly, the only thing we are ever capable of discerning in all of creation are the aspects of our very own Self which we've attributed and distributed to all those folks, animals and objects 'out there'.

The other gift of this process was seeing how healing it was to allow someone to speak their piece, while giving them full attention. There was no necessity to agree in order to clear issues, only to be attentive and listen. That is quite sufficient. No one has to be right. No one needs to win. So somewhere, deep down inside myself, I knew at least as a concept, that it was possible to get clear with my husband, even with the seemingly endless litany of complaints, injustices, inequities and past hurts which my mind was expert at detailing.

The extraordinary agitation and upset that Elan's pronouncement of death had created, gave me the impetus to envision being momentarily clear, at least for what I perceived as a short time. Just possibly all the baggage might be dropped for a short while. Interestingly, once one steps through that door, the urge to re-shoulder those self-inflicted burdens evaporates.

There was another aspect of having death thrust into my immediate vision that arose for me. I had read with complete attention and fascination many, many years before, Carlos Castaneda's accounts of death sitting on one's left shoulder in his book, *A Separate Reality*, Simon and Schuster, 1971.

In it he says, *"If we were then in doubt about whether or not to take some action, we were to look to our left shoulder and see death sitting there waiting to take us. That would give us the stark reminder that we are human beings and we must act immediately lest death take us before we do."*

The anthropologist Carlos Castaneda's teacher in the book was a Yaqui wise man whose name was Don Juan. This Shaman, or Indian healer, said, *"We must live with impeccability because death is always over our left shoulder."*

"A detached man, who knows he has no possibility of fencing off his death, has only one thing to back himself with: the power of his decisions. He has to be, so to speak, the master of his choices. He must fully understand that

his choice is his responsibility and once he makes it there is no longer time for regrets or recriminations. His decisions are final, simply because death does not permit him time to cling to anything. . . . The knowledge of his death guides him and makes him detached and silently lusty; the power of his final decisions makes him able to choose without regrets and what he chooses is always strategically the best; and so he performs everything he has to with gusto and lusty efficiency."

I had practiced Castaneda's placing death on my left shoulder for many years. Each night before bed I had made it a practice to see if I could peacefully die that night. Had I lived that day well enough, without clinging to burning regrets or wrongs that hung in the air demanding to be righted? This was the measuring stick of my life each night. It was the lens that focused my intentions and energies. Death, sitting there on my shoulder, supplied the subtle magnetic field that allowed me to slightly bend my efforts for the better. I pursued this practice regularly for a number of years.

Now, many years later, there was death again, rearing its ultimate message that there is only NOW, and this time leading me through the needles eye, forcing me to drop the baggage of many years. Somehow, in totally believing in my husband's immanent death, allowed me to plunge once again into the love and enjoyment of each other, that I had thought to be lost forever. It was a very gradual process, but a profound one, which I believe is open to all those who have loved and then lost that love.

THE FATHER

The shock of Elan's decree, foretelling my husband's death, continued to boomerang in wildly unexpected ways. In a phone conversation with him one day, he told me of a possible visit to my area by both he and his parents. No specific dates were mentioned.

One morning, I was at the local ashram branch for chanting and meditating and was walking towards the main meditation hall. All of a sudden, I felt energetically compelled to simply stop dead in my tracks. I looked around, and there was a man sitting in an easy chair placed in the wide entryway. I walked up to him.

We looked each other directly in the eye and without a word, he took my hand and simply held it in his. Instantly, I knew who he must be, even though they did not resemble each other, and a short time later, as my friend Elan approached, there I was still holding his father's hand. Strangely, there was a perfect parallel, the connection of the hand, in that first moment with both the father and his son.

Our initial encounter was so very strong, that I invited his father to my house for tea, a talk and a walk. We spent an afternoon together pleasantly. At one point during our visit, his father randomly started to tell me a peculiar story about an Indian holy man.

He said there was a famous Indian saint, who had the

Siddhi, or power, to see into the future. One day a woman came to him for advice, because her five-year old child was ill. The saint said, "O woman, I am so sorry, but your daughter will die soon." Terribly upset, the woman ran home to be with her child.

Months passed. One day, the woman returned and told the saint that in fact he had been correct. Her child had expired as he predicted. However, she told him that he should never have told her this, as her moments with her daughter since had been fraught with anguish and despair.

The saint immediately knew that the woman was correct. Even if it is true, one is never to predict the death of another.   To repent for his error in judgment, the saint bit off his own tongue, causing himself to bleed to death.

This was the story Elan's father told me. It shook the fiber of my being. Whether there is any truth or not in the moral of the story was not the point for me. Rather I could not believe that his father chose to tell me a story involving someone making a pronouncement of death, as his son had just done to me.

I wondered whether he had psychically intuited that his son had predicted my husband's death without it being in his conscious awareness. I was certain his son would not have told him the dire prediction, which he had made. The synchronicity of his words was eerie for me.

My daughter had also met Elan's father on his visit to our

home. Shortly after this visit, she told me of a peculiar and disturbing dream that she had, where she had visited his father at an exquisite palace. There he had spoken to her and predicted that her father, my husband, would die soon. All these omens and interconnections left me profoundly ill at ease. Their bizarre nature left me unable to share any of them with any of the parties concerned or with anyone at all for that matter.

The next few years proved to be an agony in holding these strange crossed, interrelated tales solely within myself. I never told my husband, daughter, or the father anything of what any of the others of them had said. Much later, I related to Elan only briefly part of the story of which his father had spoken. Yet, for the most part, I sat alone with the fire of all this information and these tales for years.

Looking back, I see that I needed this internal conflagration to burn and purify the dross of my marital relationship. Sitting with the possibility of eminent death leads one to have a deeper appreciation for the little moments of life. Every situation merits a deeper care and a highlighted consciousness, because each interaction could be the last. Little annoyances can be tolerated more easily because their innate unimportance in the grander scheme becomes obvious.

One's major focus reorients to staying clear enough to feel that one has done one's best. In the end, the question which surfaces is whether a sufficient effort has been made to mold a relationship into all that it could be. When the angel of death finally knocks on one's door it will possibly be the honoring of human hearts that becomes the primary measuring stick of one's life.

The fruit of the process that ensued from Elan's pronouncement of death was likely what resulted in the survival and resurrection of my marriage. It allowed my husband and I to enter realms of beingness that would not have been possible without this cleansing.

I have come to believe that even when terrible circumstances transpire or painful pronouncements or situations, it is really always for our own expansion of consciousness. These life agonies are in essence contracted for in advance on a soul level. It is the set of lessons we have created for our Self and opted to undergo, so that we can progress towards light and truth, that divine matrix of all that is.

Learning and growth always involve an expansion into unknown regions. This process frequently, or perhaps always involves discomfort, unsurety and distress. No matter how hard these difficulties are they actually always lead us to a better place. Because truly, for each and every one of us, everything is always unfolding for the best – for the maximum and constant upliftment of our soul, all of the time, even when life seems to be at its darkest, even when confronted by the death of a loved one.

Somehow it is we ourselves who have designed these difficult paths for ourselves. There is an internal pull to undergo certain experiences even when we know on some level that they will not work out well. We often assume that it is just inexperience, or foolishness or errors that lead us into such predicaments. I think it is really much more. Our emotions, by which we are led into all of the situations and specifics of our lives, are God's leash that we have prearranged and contracted for in order to lead us unfalteringly through the gates and hurdles we've selected for ourselves. Eventually, more and more, we learn through these lessons to follow the path of least resistance.

As Paulo Coelho says in his book, *The Alchemist*, *"each one of us has a Personal Legend, the passion that calls to us as we lead our lives. The Universe conspires to assist those who follow their Personal Legend. It is a person's only real obligation, that which each one of us longs to accomplish. Yet no matter what one does, every person on earth plays a central role in the history of the world. And, when you dare to follow your Personal Legend, all the Universe conspires to help you achieve it. "* I believed myself to be following my Personal Legend in this revitalization of my marriage, through the fire of Alchemy. And in doing so, the Universe through these peculiar unfoldings certainly conspired to assist and support me.

There is a chemical principle called Le Chatelier's Principle, which describes how a chemical system at equilibrium, that is its position of balance, reacts to stress. In chemical terms, what is meant by stress is any new input of conditions. These conditions may be an increase or decrease of any reagent or an increase or decrease in temperature or pressure. Really just about anything new is what this model describes as stress. Within this context, Le Chatelier's Principle states, "*A chemical system will always shift in such a way as to reduce the new stress which is applied to the system.*"

It seems to me to be as true with people as with systems at equilibrium. It is the pain or discomfort, which we shift to avoid, that pushes us into situations of growth. And it is the comfort when we finally reach our own new position of equilibrium that we experience as the universe supporting us. This easefulness of flow in some direction allows us to link and to line with the divine intention manifesting.

There is a quote from Choquash, a Native American storyteller, which wonderfully captures the essence of all this...

"*The elders have sent me to tell you that now is like a rushing river, and this will be experienced in many different ways. There are those who would hold onto the shore... there is no shore. The shore is crumbling. Push off into the middle of the river. Keep your head above the water, look around to see who else is in the river with you, and celebrate.*"

So instead of moping in the river of my life, I chose to accept my circumstances. I found myself still in the stream with my husband, and after some time, I rejoiced.

THE GIRLFRIEND

As time went by, the theme of marriage again arose in a peculiar and unexpected manner. I wrote Elan a birthday card and whimsically recounted on it many principles I believed about marriage and some ideas on what it takes to maintain a successful marriage over the years.

Little did I know at the time, that he was contemplating proposing to his girlfriend and that I believe my musings to be based on picking up his thoughts on the subject, through psychical routes and even more, through having him literally live within me. On this occasion, as on many others, I came to realize that I was experiencing an ongoing input of his thoughts and feelings, without meaning to intercept them.

A few days later, I was speaking to him on the phone when he told me that his girlfriend, who he had casually introduced me to on one occasion, was in my area on a trip from her country and in fact was invited to a party at my house that evening. I told him that he must be mistaken, that I knew of no party at my house that night. He went on to tell me that it was a gathering that my daughter had organized.

Sure enough, as the day progressed my daughter asked me about having a group of people over that evening. I said, "Sure" and before I knew it, we had a group of about 25 of my daughter's friends and their friends, 15 of whom spent the night.

I knew many of them from the ashram and they invited me to join their merrymaking. We have a large 5-bedroom home with a substantial pool, waterfall and spa outside, as well as a small pond and waterfall inside.

Although my husband turned in early, I was having fun as well as acting as a chaperone and so I stayed up with them until the wee hours of the night. I didn't really get into a substantial conversation with his girlfriend until nearly 12:30 AM. I was more than curious about the nature of the woman that had set his heart on fire.

We made a substantial initial contact. She gave me my first Reiki session and I gave her a healing. We spoke of getting together over the next few days again, yet in fact, that never transpired.

At 1:38 AM, somehow I still remember the time on the clock I glanced at then, I decided that folks were settling in for the night and I started to go to bed. Just before I left, she asked me where in the house Elan had spent the night when he visited me.

I have one room of my house that I only use for meditation. It has many sacred objects from all stages of my spiritual journey, photos of many teachers I have studied with, water from many holy sites and a mattress covered with a llama skin I acquired in Peru. He is the only person that I have allowed to sleep there. I showed her where the room was and went to bed.

Much later, in a phone conversation with Elan, I discovered that another young man had found my meditation room that night and that he and Elan's dear one had spent the night there talking. They had fallen in love there, that very evening, in my meditation room, the weekend before the unrequited proposal of marriage. He was not happy. And I was utterly shocked to discover our karmic interconnectedness play out in this bizarre fashion yet again.

Elan and his love lived in two different countries from mine. How could such energies come together in my meditation room? These synchronicities of life are actually glimpses into God's intention, into the predestined nature of life's events. We spiral in with a certain electromagnetic swirl, so to speak, that we call karma, or destiny. Our freedom is in how we choose to react to those events, people and situations, which must ensue. I believe that this unexpected and unlikely conjunction of all of the lives involved in this incident, transpired in this way to soothe his feelings of rejection, by highlighting the destined nature of these events. It took me a long time to not feel in some way responsible for the pain this situation caused him.

Chapter Four:
Modalities of Creation

IN OUR MIND'S EYE

The link I feel to Elan's psyche is deeper than simply a psychic connection even though it is clear to me that I have been becoming ever more psychic over the years. Since my Berkeley Psychic School training, I nearly always know who is calling on the phone. Even before the first ring, I am often thinking of them. As their attention tries to contact me, just before the actual call, I experience that person as if they were energetically 'tapping on my shoulder'.

Sometimes over the years, the specificity of the input has been shocking. Once, in the Chemistry course I teach, in a lecture of about 60 students, I was discussing chemical resonance structures and I internally 'heard' a particular student thinking of a joke that I knew on the topic. Forgetting myself for a moment, I looked at him and said aloud, "Oh, that is a good one."

I proceeded to describe the mythical nature of the nonexistent individual resonance structures for chemical bonding as the equally mythical creatures of the dragon and the unicorn. I then compared that to the bonding structure, which truly occurs and is called a resonance hybrid, which combines each individual resonance structures' characteristics, as an equally real rhinoceros.

Realizing the wild leap of faith I'd made, in assuming that this was my student's thought and not my own, I asked him if in fact he had been thinking of that joke. He affirmed that in fact he had.

On a different occasion I was enjoying an afternoon grading papers at the outdoor Upper Level Café in Berkeley, California. I would often, before my married years, sit in this coffee house for 10 to 12 hours at a time grading my students' work, while sipping tea or coffee all day.

On this occasion, a young man at another table was talking to a friend, describing having just left a house he was considering renting. Immediately I could see the 'picture' that his mind's eye had created and recognized it as a place where I had previously lived. Wanting to test whether it was my 'picture' or his, I asked him about my perception and discovered that in fact it was in fact my old haunting grounds, which he had just surveyed.

On another occasion my husband and I were driving through a city I did not know, to deliver a lamb that had been butchered to specifications for a friend from work. My husband had inherited a sheep ranch and occasionally we would oblige friends with an order, even though neither my hubby nor I could tolerate eating lamb ourselves. My husband had been to this house before and although he had no idea of the street name or number, he believed that he simply might remember the house's location by passing by it.

So, we were driving around searching for it. I asked him what the house looked like and in my mind's eye, I saw in great detail what I believed to be the 'picture' of what my husband was visualizing. As we continued to check out the area, at one point I told my husband to stop. I had seen a few houses back, one that seemed to me to be a match to the picture in my husband's head. I asked him if we had possibly passed his friend's house a few homes back and in fact we had.

I had been able to spot the exact house by what must surely be an actual arrangement of perhaps electromagnetic radiation, that is to say light, which I perceived as a photo in his mind.

From these experiences I came to believe that there is a 'physical' reality associated with our internal thoughts, which connects, alters and interacts with the 'solid' matter of reality. When I remember something 'visually' it is as if I have a file cabinet of photos of each event in my mind, and am able to pull the visual facsimile of that event.

If I, as a psychic can see someone else's 'pictures', hear someone else's thoughts and feel their energy attempting to contact my 'consciousness', all of these phenomena must be organizations of energy, which are 'real' and hence will ultimately be measurable. Above and beyond this, they touch upon the heart of Bell's Theorem, by which the very act of measuring a system ends up changing it.

THE POWER OF THE WORD

There are many aspects to the interconnectedness of solid matter, energetic internal organization of picture thoughts, and the vibratory creative power of word and sound thoughts.

The 182 verse Sanskrit chant of *Sri Guru Gita*, had led me into the circumstances that resulted in my meeting Elan. Much of the chant is very poetic and uplifting. However, there were a few disturbing and hence mysterious verses to me for a long time, until a shifted interpretation of them arose for me.

The verses, which seemed peculiar to me, were these:

44. Sive kruddhe gurustrata
        gurau kruddhe sivo na hi,
    Tasmat sarva-prayatyena
        srigurum saranam vrajet.

If Shiva is angry, the Guru saves you, but if the Guru is angry, even Shiva cannot save you. Therefore with every effort take refuge in Sri Guru.

79. Harau ruste gurustrata
        gurau ruste na kascana
    Tasmat sarva-prayatyena
        srigurum saranam vrajet.

If Lord Hari (Vishnu) is angry, the Guru protects you, but if the Guru is angry, no one can save you. Therefore, make every effort to take refuge in Sri Guru.

101. Evam srutva mahadevi
         gurunidam karoti yah,
    Sa yati narakam ghoram
         Yavac-chandradivakarau.

O great Goddess, he who speaks ill of the Guru in spite of hearing all this falls into the most dreadful hell and (remains there) as long as the sun and moon shine.

I finally got the idea that the Guru is that inner power in each of us at our core, our highest Self. An external figure, who fulfills the role of Guru, is completely identified with the Self of all in such a way that they can assist one with aligning to that same internal connection.

But ultimately for each of us, an external Guru becomes unnecessary as that very same power is discovered within and our inner association with that power is strengthened. Then in fact no difference is experienced between the previous focus of one's attention, the external figure of the Guru, and one's inner Self. And in that identification, the interconnectedness of everyone's consciousness as and through the Guru or divine inner spark, the Christ force, the Maitreya energy becomes apparent giving concrete meaning to the phrase 'the body of humankind'.

These Sanskrit verses thus evolved to have a very real and personal meaning for me. What they came to signify for me was that if gods, or husbands or wives or children or all those outside powerful forces, get mad, the Guru, as my own inner Self, can protect me by my own choice as to what reaction to experience concerning whatever is occurring.

However, if the Guru, my very own Self, gets angry, maybe by having the thought "How could I be so stupid?" or "I'm just no good!" or some such thing, there is no protection internally from this continuing onslaught. One is in fact by one's own thoughts, either sending one's self to a waterless jungle of one's own self-disdain or to the realm of heaven on earth. It is always one's choice as one's own supreme and powerful teacher, or Guru. Guru means the one who leads from darkness to light. And surely we are each this for ourselves.

So in fact, by the internal vibration of thought, it is you who are Brahma (the Creator), Vishnu (the Sustainer) and Shiva (the Destroyer) of your own universe. I often toy with the idea that we are truly each of these gods in their fullness. Each day I expect and know the world will be here. I anticipate waking up and experience the existence of the world and myself even in the dream state, and so I sustain the Universe for and as the Divine.

So I am Vishnu for all that I can ever know and it is the power of my thoughts that totally sustain not only my universe, but also literally all of creation. And this happens through those internal words that go through my mind, all those things I choose to say to myself throughout each and every day of my life

It is said that matter is frozen sound, that is, frozen or condensed vibration of the subtlest thoughts. The words we repeat to ourselves in our heads all day and night and seem always to be present, except in deep sleep and some profound meditative states. We are literally creating the details of our physical self and surroundings constantly by the force of our thoughts filtering down and defining the specifics of our physical existence and environment. In the beginning there was the word.

It is as though our thoughts are born and manifest in the appearance of everyone and everything. This whole plane of existence is just the boomerang back of exactly and completely the thoughts activated by the emotions we bestow upon them reflected back to us. Send out anger and anger will return, even magnified. Send out joy and the joy returning to one will be increased as well.

This ultimate responsibility for all aspects of one's life can at first seem dauntingly overwhelming, that is until the juicy secret arises. Underlying the shocking realization that one is constantly creating whatever is manifesting moment-by-moment is the even more shocking realization that it takes no time at all to change it completely. Health, wealth, joy, satisfaction actually manifest the moment one can internally choose to see and bless oneself with these thoughts.

However, unlike the techniques of The Secret, this is not done by a specific feeling visualization of the result. Rather it is accomplished through deciding that one TRULY IS LIVING NOW in a beneficent world in which even those uncomfy weird things that might happen are the perfection of God unfolding moment by moment and each holds an exquisite gift, just that one needing manifestation in the moment for the perfect upliftment of the whole, that is for the highest good of everyone involved.

Allowing what is to feel joyous and perfect, often though using the door of gratitude, trusting that one is safe, protected, in the right place with the right people does in fact lead exactly that into instant manifestation.

Besides gratitude, my biggest door into this space is forgiveness of who is before me, so that I am not imagining subtle thought/vibrations/sounds of self-attack in my mind.

When I start making the phone call to the doctor with whom I am slightly annoyed, I know I will create exactly good further reasons to validate my belief so that I am right. One can either be right or be love. Never both. This is always a moment-by-moment choice.

So, when in a good moment of clarity, I realize I'm making a phone call from a space where I've already judged the other as someone not on my side, I readjust my thoughts. I forgive the other by removing my judgments from the past, entering into the present NOW. I see that one as my friend, my helper provided to assist my journey. At a deeper level, that one I have created by my own thoughts. Even the most difficult person is my own child, the product of my thoughts projected outward. I can forgive them their idiosyncrasies when I take the world less seriously and realize that they, as myself are a completely innocent being doing their best, just as I am.

Being projections of my inner state, as soon as I envision them as being safe, they will be.

Think of how many times a day, an hour, a minute we play scenes of dread, or worry. I was a girl scout, and our motto, "Be Prepared", actually asks one to play out all that could go wrong and have what is needed for each situation. Planning ahead is a form of fear and dread.

So what is the way out that guarantees a smooth and happy ride through life's vagaries? For me it is handing it over to Spirit, who can see the whole picture, what is the best for everyone, not just for the part of the whole that the separated me is. Whatever you might call this – Spirit, God, Love, Nature, Higher Power, Holy Spirit, the Christ force, Oversoul- there is a something connected to us all that can consider the good of the completeness of us. There is always a win-win position, which can manifest if one turns over control and trusts that this force is here and now and has heard.

As that force is so intimately connected and intermingled with what 'I' consider the 'I that I am', it cannot be other than with me always and it always hears and answers. It might not be the answer that the little 'I' wants, but ultimately it will be the win-win posture leading to the happiness of myself and of all.

So it is in surrender of control to 'I am that I am', to one's own breath being breathed by the Divine, to knowing that the next step will manifest the moment I trust to be shown, that easefulness then comes to me. Clarity comes when I realize that I don't know and that I can't on my own figure out what benefits all, without joining and extension into that mystery that will answer me.

All this ensues from the vibratory sounds my thoughts emanate rolling through my mind. And all this I can change, with practice, in an instant.

Breaking old patterns seems as difficult as the first time one attempts a two-wheeler. Surely it is impossible, until one tries and practices a while. Eventually a new second nature takes over, especially if one asks inside for help and guidance. What we really need to supply is not expertise, but willingness.

ANCIENT LANGUAGES AND MUSIC

The ancient languages have particularly extraordinary vibrations. Sanskrit, Aramaic, Latin, Hebrew, Tibetan and other ancient tongues contain sound syllables that connect one more directly with the extension and joining of love that we are.

In one three month period while I was living in India, I was assigned the seva, or sacred service, of changing the ashram's chant book from one form of Sanskrit transliteration to another. It was arranged that I study an hour a day with a Sanskrit scholar to assist my work there.

The previous three-month summer I spent at this Indian ashram, I had had a profound sound experience. One of the three major mantras, or set of sacred syllables, that Baba Jivananda taught was the So'ham mantra. It means 'I am that.' It is also the Sanskrit word for swan, which helps to explain why swans are considered to be a sacred symbol in India.

On my first free weekend at the ashram, I had planned to go into Bombay, as Mumbai was known at that time. However I was offered the seva of cleaning the 'meditation cave', where Swami Jivanada had done his sadhana, or spiritual practices leading to his enlightenment. It was purported to be the most shakti or energy filled site at the ashram and it felt to me to be an honor to get to spend an extended period alone in the embrace of its vibrations. It was not difficult for me to choose to clean rather than explore the city and I did so.

As I was cleaning I became drawn to the most sacred portion of the room, the puja or place of worship. There at the front was an altar with Swami Jivananda's padukas or sandals sitting on an ornate cloth. In India, a holy person's feet are purported to be the location where their holy energy flows most strongly out of the body. It is for this reason that a Holy person's shoes are worshipped as if they were actually the Holy one him or herself.

I went up to the altar and placed my head as is customary on the guru's shoes. The moment I did, I felt the walls of the room breathing in and out. I actually experienced them as oscillating all the while with their breathing. I heard So'ham. The walls breathed in on the 'So' and out on the 'Ham' and my body breathed with them. The experience continued with my spontaneously hearing 'So' with each in-breath and 'Ham' with each out-breath for the next year. It engendered some level of blissful joy in my being.

Eventually the next year, Swami Jivananda, Baba, gave a two-day intensive on So'ham. Happily I registered for it. During one of his talks, Baba described how to practice So'ham. He said it was necessary to breath in on the 'Ham' and out on the 'So'. I heard and felt the profound clunk of my mind realizing that I was doing it reversed.

Confidently, I knew from the depth and extraordinary level of the experience I'd had all year that I must be doing it 'right'. But, some doubt remained. My guru had just described the reverse process.

I went up in darshan line where individual questions were possible to ask. I shared my experience with him and then asked him if it was OK to continue doing the practice in the manner it had established itself in my being.

He said, "No." And with that, the mantra stopped repeating spontaneously in me. Twenty-five years passed during which Swami Jivananda, affectionately called Baba, died and Swami Chandra-prakashananda, also called Uma-Guru, became his successor.

Eventually I came to have a British, Indian spiritual mentor, Padma, who was versed in Sanskrit. I took a course from him on the sacred seed syllables of Sanskrit, which bring the unmanifest into manifestation. As he was lecturing, I suddenly had a deep revelation about Sanskrit.

Both Sanskrit and Hebrew start with the sound 'AH', much like a breathy 'Ham', and both alphabets end with a sound very close to 'So', or 'Sah'. It is as if both begin with the sound of the in-breath, 'Hah', and both alphabets end with the sound of the out-breath, 'Sah'. In between the inhale and the exhale is found all of creation. It is all the sounds of the letters going on between each inhale and exhale, from the moment of birth until their ceasing at death that create all of our existence through our thoughts. It took twenty-five years, but in the end I was gifted with a deep answer to my question as to why the mantra had to be repeated in accordance with the rules to manifest on this plane.

Most religions also have sound aspects using various sacred tongues. Often this is the deepest, most God connecting aspect of joined worship settings. In essence, this is another order of thought's creating. Here it is not words that have picture connotations in the mind that are birthed. Rather these vibratory patterns we call music are connecting bridges between various overlapping, potential dimensional spaces. This is why music is universally acknowledged for the joy, beauty and satisfaction it can elicit placing us in consciousness states we could not enter without it's vibratory keys for entrance and support.

I have sung all my life in semi-professional groups of many kinds. My first truly transcendental experience occurred during a performance in which I was singing Bach's *B Minor Mass*. At that time all performers, audience, all my awareness of anything but the sound vanished. I entered a realm of ego-lessness in which no individual sense of myself remained. The entirety of my awareness was the sound- the complete joy, fullness, and satisfaction of being in union with and as the sound with nothing else existing.

I have spent years studying sacred sounds and do find them a direct route to a surrender to the Divine Spirit. They provide a way to together enter the extension and expansion that Love is.

THE POWER TO CREATE

Our thoughts, either as pictures or words, create abundance or poverty, joy or sorrow, sickness or health. The source of the Power within is a manifestation of the pure love of the Divine, the unlimited POWER potential that we may direct along channels of our choosing. So we are in fact conduits for that pure Power of love, which runs and is the source of all of creation. It filters down through the matrix of our thought-webs into physical reality.

Although I usually surrender creation to Holy Spirit these days, for most of my life, I came to use a particular process to create whatever reality I wanted to manifest. I have used it with great specificity to get a job, my husband, to have children when I wanted, in the order, girl then boy, that I preferred. I used it to call into manifestation a particular house I wanted to live in and to get the position of interim Division Chair of Science and Engineering in my work place.

This method is a valuable secret. It has NEVER failed me - EVER- in creating what I thought I wanted in my life. Be careful, it works. It is a gift to each of you.

It can be used for anything, but for a moment let us consider it as applied to the issue of manifesting abundance in one's life.

Abundance is like a funnel. There needs to be a balance of giving and receiving. If there is a nonattachment to wealth, it flows through the funnel. There is always enough. If fear leads one to hold onto what one already has, that restricts the flow, only allowing so much to enter.

So what can you do? Here is a four-step process:

1. First visualize, like a photo, exactly what you are trying to create in YOUR life. If the photo is not quite right, "blow" it up into scintillating blue light and then re-create. Continue this process until the "photo" looks right.

2. When it does, ask two questions:

   A. Can I have this?

Listen to the first quick response of your Soul. If yes, continue. If no, "blow" up the picture and re-create it until you can answer yes on a soul level to the question, 'Can I have it?' (I guess I've been using digital deleting of internal pictures before it existed with cameras.)

B. Can I take responsibility for it?

Again listen for the first quick response of your Soul. This question is looking at how your creation might impact those around you as well as yourself, and whether this impact is acceptable to you on a soul level. If the answer is yes, continue. If no, blow up that picture and re-create it until the soul's answer to both these questions is yes.

3. Next, you must come to a place internally where it will be totally acceptable to you if you do NOT get this thing you are creating. Find that place of peace and acceptance of the Divine perfection of the unfoldment of your life, so that you are able to completely accept not getting this particular thing. (This is Nonattachment.)

4. The last step is to take the 'photo' you have created,-- that exact photo that you have said you can have and that you can take responsibility for---- and that you are ready to accept not getting as well. Now what you do is take it in your hands, throw it out to the world and forget it.

It will come back to you - in concrete reality.

THE HEALING

The ability to alter reality became apparent to me in an interaction with Elan that took place shortly after I had ripped the meniscus in my knee. There is a beautiful reservoir with paddleboats, canoes and fishing across the street from my home. I run there almost daily. I believe that the damage occurred when I continued to run with a mild injury.

After seeing my doctor, an MRI was done. Finally, I was sent to an orthopedic specialist who recommended arthroscopic surgery. I was using crutches and experiencing considerable pain during this period.

Elan called during this period, and when I described the damage to my knee, he asked me if I would like a healing. I said yes, not thinking that he could have much impact on such a distinctly documented physical situation. However, I was curious as to the flavor of his healing energy.

He was in another city and asked me to go near a window of my house and hold the phone in one hand, He started the healing and put down the crutches as waves of energy descended on me causing considerable shaking and trembling. Every few minutes he stopped and asked me if I was OK and if I he should continue.

I asked him to continue each time, as the force of the energy seemed to become stronger in each round. Then rounds of nausea arose and all at once the core idea, which caused the injury, became instantaneously clear even though we were not speaking at all during the energy transfer.

I clearly saw that as a child I had been angry at my knees for not letting me escape from my grandfather's unwanted advances. My inner psyche still held a grudge and so was punishing that knee, somehow forgetting our innate inner connectedness. It is not surprising to forget such a thing when it is just as simple to forget that the term 'the body of humankind' is a reality and not just a metaphor.

The shaking and nausea intensified round after round. Then all of a sudden, call waiting came on. I remembered that I had told my son that I would pick up his buddy at BART, the Bay Area Rapid Transit, near our house. So, dutifully, I ended the healing, grabbed my crutches and drove over to pick up my son's pal.

When I came home, I was profoundly exhausted. I went to bed immediately and stayed there for the next 24 hours. Most of that time I was trembling and nauseous.

Finally I realized that I was caught in the middle of my friend's healing and needed help to pop out the other side, I called him back and he worked on me further in the same manner. My body calmed down and from that point I no longer needed the crutches and the pain rapidly dissipated.

I decided to postpone the surgery to see if the condition might improve over time. Very gradually it did over the next year. Finally I returned to being able to run without pain, although not as continuously as I had. I am able now to sit in a lotus position for a short time instead of the several hours, which had been totally comfortable previous to the injury.

From this experience of Elan's healing ability for a concrete medically delineated problem, I came to believe that energy could impact our physical being at more profound levels than I had previously presumed.

QUANTUM MECHANICS

The manner in which one interacts with and hence selects one's conscious reality, can be described from the viewpoint of quantum mechanics. In this field, probability spheres describe one's location rather than a distinct point of reality within the matrix of space and time. One interacts with and thus selects one's conscious reality from many potential realities existent at any time.

If energy can be arranged, it can also be rearranged, and it is by this route that we can alter our physical reality, much as quantum mechanics predicts. It is through altering our emotional connection to a particular reality, that we are able to alter it.

Quantum mechanics is the field, whose emphasis is to describe the position and movement of electrons in any atom of any substance. An atom is the smallest discrete unit that still retains the innate characteristics of one of the approximately 120 elements, from which all physical substances in the Universe are composed. Atoms are very small. It would take about 10 million atoms lined up, touching each other, to make a line 1 millimeter long, about the length of an ant.

There are three basic building blocks out of which all atoms are made. Positive protons and neutral neutrons are about the same size and are tightly packed in a dense tiny nucleus at the center of the atom. The nucleus is so much smaller than the whole atom, that it only has a diameter that is about one hundred thousandth of the diameter of the entire atom. At a tremendous distance out from the nucleus, one finally comes to shells of tiny negative electrons. It would take 1,837 of these little electrons to weigh as much as only one of the protons or neutrons in the nucleus.

If the nucleus of an atom were the size of a closed fist then the first shell of electrons might be a mile away. If the entire atom were the size of a 10-story building, the nucleus would be the size of a sesame seed. If the nucleus were enlarged to the size of a period on this page, the entire atom would be about 5 meters, approximately the length of a full-sized automobile.

So, since only about one fifty thousandth of the volume of the atom consists of anything at all, what is the rest? SILENCE, nothing, the void of which Buddhism speaks. And since we ourselves are composed of atoms, it is only the tiniest bit of us that is made up of anything at all, other than that self same emptiness.

This pattern of small regions of high density of matter alternating with huge expanses of emptiness continues to the edge of the Universe. The planets with their distance from the sun are one of these regions. Our individual solar system and its huge distance from other solar systems of our galaxy are another. The set of galaxies, the Milky Way, of which we are a part, also has an enormous expanse containing no matter until the closest comparable set of galaxies, the Sea of Magellan. These many expanses of silent emptiness, no matter whether they are at the atomic or cosmic levels, are literally the most abundant components of the Universe.

This is the meaning of Quantum Mechanics. It describes the regions of electron density and regions of nothingness. The transitions that occur in an atom involve discreet jumps between energy levels and regions of electron density. It is like a stepladder, where a whole step is a possibility, but there is no way to take half a step. There is only emptiness part way and nowhere to put a foot down.

THE QUANTIZATION OF MEDITATION

I propose that all progress in areas of human growth and development involves quantized processes rather than a continuum of advancement.

A child's ability to walk, riding a bike, the world's change of consciousness on 9/11, pregnancy and for me, most major spiritual leaps such as seeing the internal flame and the kind of transition into joy that occurred for me on that flight to Denver are examples of quantized processes.

It seems that stages of meditation also occur in a quantized fashion. Over my decades of meditation practice there were distinct levels, which for me changed all at once rather than as a gradual continuum.

I started meditating when I had freshly moved to California and found that discussions of such practices arose more in general conversation than they had in other areas where I'd lived.

I was in a huge house shared by many other young professionals. There was a physicist in the house and we decided to test out the potential impact or affect of meditation using the scientific method. We decided to engage in a meditative process regularly for one month and then see if our set of observations led to any distinct conclusion concerning meditation.

The essence of the scientific method is to observe, take numerous pieces of data to check out reproducibility, to come up with a hypothesis, or guess as to an explanation for what has been observed, and most importantly to hold off on a conclusion until enough data has been collected. It is also important to continue experimenting to test whether that conclusion holds up with more experimentation over time.

We designed an experiment, where we meditated by sitting still and erect in a chair with our eyes closed, using an egg timer to demarcate a 10-minute period each day for a month. We decided to listen to the ringing in our ears as the meditative focal point, since we didn't know any mantras, or sacred words, and weren't familiar with breath or other usual meditative concentration techniques.

At the time, I was a chain smoker, and although I had tried to quit many times, I had never been successful. To my amazement, without any major effort, I quit smoking during that very month.

Although it was certainly a nonlinear cause and effect, I was certain that the meditative process had created a space where quitting became possible. It also was a useful process to pursue at those moments when my craving for cigarettes intensified, such as after a meal or at the intermission of a play.

During my initial years of meditation, thoughts, agitation and physical pains raged, so that a 10-minute session was a huge trial to survive. After many years of regular practice half-hour sessions became easy. Then came a variety of what was for me, quantized stages.

At some point over the years of engaging in daily meditation, the words comprising my thoughts stopped happening. I recall being shocked to discover that thoughts could maintain their flow without any words.

At another stage, which arose all at once after a significant time, I believed myself to be always falling asleep in meditation, often leaning over with my head on the floor.

It was only after this pattern, which I assumed at the time was a flawed practice, was firmly established years later, that I learned that this is a particular type of meditation Hindus call the tandra state. It resembles the sleep or dream state but is actually a true meditative process. It is profoundly restful and dream-like visions may occur.

It came to be my normal mode to dive into the tandra for many years and I became frustrated for quite a while by what I judged to be my inability to stay awake during my meditation period. This epoch ended abruptly when one day I was submerged in tandra and had a profound vision of a cobra.

Somehow, even from the depths of the state, I all of a sudden realized that I was having a classic vision of the Goddess Kundalini, who is often represented by a snake. This is a typical representation of the traversal of energy up the spinal column from its base to the crown of the head, since this transition if drawn would resemble a snake. It is due to this process that the medical profession is represented by the caduceus, showing the double intertwined snakes representing the two subtle energy spinal channels called the ida and pingala.

I realized that what I had been interpreting as a heedless quality, of being unable to stay awake in meditation, was really a profound state. As soon as I had this awareness, I popped out of the state blissfully refreshed. From that point on, my regular access to that realm vanished. That ended what had been a habitual experiencing of tandra.

Then came a number of years in which no thoughts arose for long periods of time. I would sit for meditation and then all of a sudden an hour would have transpired with no content save a feeling afterwards of being totally rejuvenated. I had one four-hour sitting with nearly no content.

There were also years intermingled where I was scarcely able to make time for meditation at all. One of these came after a very intense three months living in India. I allowed my routine to go on for a number of years without meditating regularly until very spontaneously it reestablished itself in my life.

The very nature of a quantized leap of an electron from it's ground or usual state to a higher or excited energy state is that it happens all at once. This transitioning only occurs if exactly the perfect amount of energy that corresponds to the gap between the states is shone on the system. For an advancement to a new level of meditation, I believe that there has to also be an exactly appropriate catalyst to initiate the change. This would also hold true for bounding into any higher state of consciousness or even a developmental milestone.

There are some fascinating corollaries that arise from the fact that only an input of a particular nature will result in the quantized transitioning. One of these is that although one may be exposed to many different teachers or circumstances for a long time, no permanent change will occur until exactly one's own transitional energy field is encountered, just as is true with the electron. Hence it may seem that no progress is being made for a considerable period, while really one is gathering experience so that at the moment of the impact from the appropriate wavelength, the transition will occur.

This is the moment of Grace that allows the fruition of all of one's self-efforts. This is why many paths to the Truth are needed and many religions are necessary to bridge one's consciousness to that of the Divine since each of our energies has its unique vibratory frequency.

At the ashram I attend, all the chants start slow, and then very gradually increase their pace to a vigorous level. I have for many years observed that when the chant hits an individual's natural body vibratory frequency, that place of their personal quantum jump, they spontaneously sway. In just the same manner, a string on a musical instrument will start to vibrate if sound of exactly the correct frequency is applied. It is also for this reason that a particular pitch is able to start up waves in a fragile crystal glass that at exactly its innate frequency can break it. The piece is chanted at all paces so that the resonant frequency of all the participants can be activated and thus each person experiences in their body an impact from the music.

Each time the flavor of my practice changed, it did so all at once and maintained that flavor for quite some time until the next quantized leap. I believe that most processes of spiritual progression are quantized.

Chapter Five: Inner Shifts Manifesting

AS WITH-IN SO WITH-OUT

The phrase "As above, so below' might refer to the astronomical levels of quantization between planets or galaxies with the vacuum of space in between, as compared to the similar kind of empty space existing between the specific electron shells present in every atom. It also refers to the Divine as being innately seeded in humankind as well. Each of us is a God-seed manifesting.

I believe equally valid is the phrase "As With-'In', so With-'Out'. This can signify that just as the entire external world is quantized, so is our inner realm. There exist spaces between distinct thoughts just as the space exists between electron shells or the sun and its associated planets. There are also a space or leap between different stages of meditation and truly speaking for all internal growth processes.

Another application of "As With-In so With-Out" manifests when we are grappling to modify some personality trait or what we have come to identify as a habitual pattern, which is no longer useful. The tendency one is attempting to impact can either be tackled externally or internally.

Either the internal sphere can undergo a lowering of entropy through, meditation, prayer, Self-inquiry, journal writing, or possibly through engaging in a therapeutic process or one could simply clean one's house or even a corner, order some papers, make one's bed daily, bathe regularly, or engage in some discipline, perhaps yoga, Pilates, or regular exercise and thereby lower one's entropy externally. A significant and 'permanent' weight loss or gain or a diet change is always paired with an internal shift in consciousness. Working on the external will impact the order of the internal or working on the internal will impact the external.

It is always the lowering of entropy or disorder, which is soothing to the nerves and the physical vehicle that we are. The lowered entropy feels soothing, calm, simple, easy or relaxing. Simplicity breeds an internal peace that accompanies the lowered entropy. At the other extreme, an increase of disorder internally is experienced as pain, discomfort, agitation, racing thoughts or disease, which is dis-EASE.

It is very clear to me that two of the most important spiritual shifts early on in my journey, were making my bed daily and tidying my room. I had little money when I first stepped upon the spiritual path, and paid for my early SAT groups by cleaning at Claudio Naranjo's printing press.

One of my earliest spiritual drawings is of a broom. It represented to me setting my world in order. Interestingly, at that time, I was able to establish making my bed daily, as a way of honoring the energy of the bed and its surroundings in the room as well.

ALIGNING WITH TRUTH

A secondary result of this cleaning process arose within me. Somehow honesty simultaneously edged its way into my life. I remember vividly the moment I aligned with the necessity of telling the truth rather than the "white lie".

I had repressed my childhood memory of an assault when those around me refused to validate my reality at the time. I thereby denied my own Truth in order to survive in my family for the ensuing decades, until it became safe and necessary to allow the memory to surface.

For me the ability to re-member occurred during grief counseling, years after my father's death. The perpetrator of the childhood attack had been a relative of my dad's, so that I felt my relationship with my father was in jeopardy if I allowed myself to remember while he was still alive.

Interestingly, when the recollection finally surfaced, my daughter was exactly the age I had been at the time. I think somewhere in my psyche, I felt I needed to allow the memory to arise in order to better protect my child from harm.

When the repressed memory came up, it took me many, many years to completely believe its validity. It was only after I physically visited the site where the incident occurred and saw that many peculiar details were in fact completely in agreement with my memory that I finally dropped my self- doubt.

The most troubling aspect of this chapter of my life was not the incident itself, but rather the truly terrifying realization that I could totally and entirely bamboozle myself. How could I ever believe my mind when it was capable of such a distortion for so long? I don't know that even now I can trust my reality.

This turning from a denial of reality, more than anything else, seems to me to be the heart of the spiritual path – an unending uprooting concerning the nature of one's Self and the world. In a strange way, we all distort our perceptions of our universe. I had done this in not allowing myself to make contact with what actually had happened to me, until that time that I felt powerful enough to protect myself in the remembering. I believe that we all do this in our identification as bodies and egos rather than stepping out of physicality into the united and undifferentiated matrix of Divinity that we more truly are. Yet this vision is no easier to drop than were the reestablishing of my blocked memories. And as one settles into the juice of NOW, this life's memories become undifferentiated from any other life's memories, all of them being equally unimportant in the fullness of the present.

THE SEARCH FOR TRUTH

Long before I came to the awareness of this life long denial of my own perceptions, that the repressed memory embodied, the search for TRUTH became the stated focus of my existence. I had become a scientist in order to observe and delineate what was True. It didn't take very long however to realize that science was not the definitive, unchanging Truth that was going to be capable of describing accurately the nature of life and the world.

My first major spiritual group was Claudio Naranjo's SAT. SAT stood for 'Seeker's After Truth' There is also a Sanskrit term SAT which means all that which actually exists, the matrix of everything that is. It is that which exists at all times, in all spaces and in all substances. It is forever unchanging and always pure.

Truth was not my strong point. Early on in life, I adopted a pattern of rationalizing my actions with lies or half-truths rather than aligning with honesty. I convinced myself that this was kinder in my interactions with others and also that it protected me. The repressed memory mentality is using repression of reality as a psychological shield against life's traumas. However the moment arose during my housecleaning phase, where the external ordering and cleaning of my surroundings, pressured me to clear up my internal space of all those "little white lies" and eventually led me to tackle the bigger ones as well.

The moment arose when I was teaching part-time at a community college in Oakland, California. The department chairperson of the Chemistry Department had asked me to give a lecture for his class. On the designated day I, for the first and what ended up being the only time in my teaching career, overslept thereby missing the lecture I was supposed to have given.

Many creative and extraordinary possible excuses, all lies, swirled through my mind with their usual abundance. But somehow, this became the pivotal moment of Truth in my life. I decided that no matter what the consequences were, and I did entertain a foreboding of ruining my potential professional life permanently, it was the moment when I must side with The Truth above all else.

So I admitted that I had slept through the lecture and I apologized for my lapse. Although he was somewhat upset by my slip, I realized that not only would the truth not kill me, no matter how awful it was, but that in fact the Truth was the only thing that could save me. It set me upon a path that was the only one of substance that really mattered, much more than all the ups and downs on the apparently important road upon which I seemed to be traveling. Truth, although I VERY often fell shy of hanging onto it, was the life raft in the wild ocean waves of circumstance.

THE WORLD AS A REFLECTION

This by extension could also indicate that all we assume to be separate and distinct from us, our spouse, children, friends, or the anger or love we may see as emanating from them, is only a projection of our own self.

Perhaps all Souls are the same identical flavor of vanilla, and we are just creating distinctions such as you and me, for lessons we need to learn. There is another verse of the *Sri Guru Gita*, which says that Maya, or illusion has been given the honor of creating the world. In a meditation on it, I experienced an explanatory vision.

I saw everything as the hand of God, with each of us as finger puppets not realizing our connection through the one body that we are. Those fingers closest to each other are best able to make contact. They might rub each other, either soothingly so our loving mutual divinity is felt or harshly, creating friction. In either case, our close proximity the one near the other, is felt and the growth of an increased awareness arises. It could be that those folks who push our buttons the most, actually are in a soul agreement to mutually assist in each other's awakening.

For this reason forgiving, even those who cause us the most pain, results in a magical Self-forgiveness for those aspects of our self, which we have projected as the other.

There is a Hindu practice of waving an Arati tray containing flowers, incense and a flame to great beings or to statues of gods and goddesses. The flame on the tray represents the internal light in the heart, which is often seen as on fire. For years, in my mind's eye, I would imagine all the people I loved the most as being very tiny so that they could be on an Arati tray I was waving to God, so that they might be blessed. Then I would place on the tray all those people with whom I was having the greatest difficulties. I would wave that tray as well, praying with equal intensity for blessings for them as well.

It is through doing this practice that I came to realize experientially, that as one absolves what appears to be difficult others out there, one is actually pardoning the rough nooks and crannies of one's own self. I actually believe that it is only our own traits and tendencies that we are able to recognize at all. If we don't have it, we can't identify it. So anything that seems to be an unpleasant aspect of another 'out there' is only as aspect of one's self that has not yet been exonerated. In this way, forgiveness becomes a prime doorway to the Kingdom (Queendom) of Heaven within. Every act of forgiving takes one closer to the acceptance and embrace of one's Self.

Forgiveness is also a quantized process. One might have to build up energy for the leap in consciousness for a long time, but once forgiveness occurs, a jump to a different energy level transpires internally with respect to the manner in which that individuals energetic imprint is stored within one's memory lattice. Forgiveness generates a lower entropic patterning. This is a more serene, less agitated storage of lesser amplitude. Amplitude is the height of a wave. This calmer wave will not disrupt other activities.

The memory of that person will be less 'charged' with this more tranquil processing hence using up a smaller memory region. This literally allows more freedom of interaction with that individual as well as with others of a similar signature who are likely stored in adjoining regions.

WHAT THE BLEEP

There is another interesting aspect of classical quantum mechanics, the study of the electron shells of atoms, which considers that the electron is more like a cloud of charge and mass rather than a distinct particle. The reason this is true is that the electrons cycle about the nucleus of atoms at about 10^{16} cycles per second (that's a 1 followed by 16 zeros). Therefore, it is impossible to know exactly where the electron is at any moment because it's zipping around so fast.

Heisenberg described this inherent, unavoidable uncertainty in the speed and position of the electron. Both can't be known exactly at the same time. So the electron is more like a smear of charge and mass that is described as having a particular probability of being located any possible position, even though we can't accurately know exactly where.

The movie, *What the Bleep Do We Know*, explores the principles of quantum mechanics by applying them to states of consciousness. It has given me a theoretical explanatory framework for my simultaneously living in multiple realities/places/times. The probability sphere model as depicted from the quantum mechanical perspective, rather than the distinct location model of the world has given me a theoretical framework for finding my consciousness simultaneously in different people, as has been my reality with Elan since that flight to Denver.

The movie uses material on quantum mechanics, specifically the wave vs. particle models of the electron, to explain the wild array of possibilities of reality from which we choose and lock into, based upon our biochemical predilections and hence our "patterning". It also offers potential ways to break this biochemical cycle.

The overview of many realities is simply taking the quantum mechanics wave or probability sphere perspective, rather than the locked-in one-reality, cause and effect, linear time frame, which mimics the particle vision. Or at least this is what the movie conveys to me.

Shortly after I viewed this movie, *What the Bleep Do We Know*, an opportunity to put its' principles to work arose.

I had heard about a very powerful and particularly clear channel in England named Edwin Courtenay who channels the Ascended Masters. Although I had not wanted a reading from anyone for many, many years, trusting my own perceptions over those of strangers, I had listened to a friend's reading and was very impressed by the clarity, usefulness and specificity of what I heard. I decided to pursue the matter.

He did my reading long distance from a few questions and

pictures of myself and of my family. The night I received the reading from Edwin, before I even heard it, I had a strange irregular heartbeat for many hours all night accompanied by shortness of breath. A week later, I had an echocardiogram that the doctor said showed a possible valve chord rupture and some other valve problems.

I worked with the concepts in the '*What the Bleep Do We Know*" film on how to simultaneously live in many possible probability versions of reality. I accepted anything that might happen....death, open-heart surgery, etc. A friend told me to "Trust my Heart" and that became my mantra, my sacred phrase.

I am of Jewish extraction, and the most sacred Jewish holiday of Yom Kippur was approaching. On Yom Kippur, God is supposed to seal one's fate for the next year in the "Book of Life". The 10-day period between Jewish New Years, Rosh Hashonna, and Yom Kippur are a time of introspection and refocusing ones life direction. Jew's say to each other at this time "L'Shonna Tova Tikasevu". It means may God inscribe you for a blessing in the Book of Life.

So, on Yom Kippur, I received a call from my doctor saying that he didn't understand it but that he received an amended report saying I didn't have any heart problem. I felt that I had consciously changed reality by totally accepting any outcome, while being open to other reality possibilities, as the movie had described.

Another aspect of the movie intrigued me by its

synchronicity. In reading the movies final credits, I was amazed to discover that one of the people in it, William Tiller from the Stanford engineering Department, was a man I was going to do research with, on the measurement of subtle body fields, right before I became pregnant with my daughter. Where the molecular level overlaps what I see reading chakras and auras and doing healings, is where there is great excitement for me, but it is difficult to find anyone who has depth on both sides of the issue (metaphysical and scientific), as well as a common language base on both sides with whom I'm able to discuss these matters.

SCIENTIFIC PURSUITS

I spent a sabbatical leave contacting and engaging in discussions with scientists on the knife-edged interface of metaphysics and hard-core science, among them, Gary Zukov, Fritzjof Capra, Linus Pauling, and William Tiller.

For much of my professional life, I have had unrequited dreams about being involved in the development of instrumentation to measure subtle body fields for earlier medical diagnoses. It has been a secret intellectual passion.

A friend of mine, from Claudio Naranjo's SAT groups, said he could alter a scanning tunneling microscope at cryogenic, that is very low temperatures and accomplish that goal. I was tempted to pursue the matter, but I needed people to work with and someplace to put it.

I have a Masters degree and four years of doctoral research experience in Chemical Physics at the University of Chicago in cryogenics, that is low temperature studies. I worked on a project that involved the quantized, or distinct energy levels, of vortices that formed around alpha particles projected through a cell containing superfluid liquid helium.

Alpha particles are the nuclei or core portion of the atoms comprising Helium. Helium becomes a liquid at 4 degrees Kelvin, or Absolute, temperature. If cooled further to 2.2 degrees Kelvin, a superfluid forms which has less friction and appears to defy gravity by crawling up the walls of its containers. It is fascinating that Absolute zero, 0 degrees Kelvin, is the lowest possible temperature, seemingly a natural limit of the Universe. One cannot travel faster than the speed of light in air, WARP ONE. WARP three means three times the speed of light, in Star Trek terms. In much the same way, it is thought to be impossible to be colder than Absolute zero. I also developed techniques to measure amazingly cold temperatures very close to Absolute zero of about 20 milli-degrees or $0.020°$ Kelvin.

My advisor, Lothar Meyer, had assured me that I would be finished within six months. Then suddenly and unexpectedly he died. The Chemistry Department asked me to start a new project with a new advisor. There was one man who could have taken over the research I was working on since his group was pursuing not so dissimilar areas, however I was told that he would not accept a woman in his research group.

It was one week to the day later that someone broke into my locked apartment in the middle of the night assaulting me. Within the next few months my grandmother, with whom I shared a bedroom from the time I was six until 12 years old, died. In my shell-shocked state, and given the flavor of the time, with respect to women pursuing scientific fields, I never thought that I could appeal the decision to exclude me from that research group based on my gender. I therefore never published my research.

On my last Sabbatical Leave, while taking courses in my field, I came to read about the Nobel Prizes awarded in Chemistry and Physics over the last number of years. I was taken aback to find how exactly parallel my research had been to the work done by Alan Osheroff of Stanford University, who won the Nobel Prize in physics in 1997. He had been at Cornell while I was at Chicago and published his award winning research two years after I was to receive my degree. Though it certainly didn't look like it at the time, as is often the case with basic research, this area had implications with respect to the Big Bang theory of the origins of the Universe.

ONE'S DESTINED PATH

It is useful when one's life has had profound upheavals to search for why one might have created such a scenario, knowing that everything that transpires is actually a lesson the Divine, as and through one's self, paints into our existence for our ultimate upliftment. This moment in my life was a quantized shock point, which shifted me suddenly to a different geographical region, to a different associate base holding a different focus and to a different career. It was as if God yanked me out of that life by the fine strand of hair that Brahmans in India have and then lose during the ceremony they participate in to become a swami or religious renunciate in Hinduism. This shift exemplified a quantum leap to a new level of existence

I decided to vacation in California and was shocked to find a full time college teaching job in a week. I decided to lecture for a short time until I could recuperate and discriminate as to the best path to pursue. Eventually however, each of us can come to the startling realization that our perfect and only possible path is the one upon which our feet actually tread.

So, I never returned to finish my degree. However life unfolded along a different vector. I can now look back and see that many gems became available in this transition. My credentials would have placed me in a high-pressured publish or perish world, not conducive to either family life or spiritual pursuits. Trying to understand the suffering I had endured, which resulted in this move, led me to embark on a spiritual path ultimately leading to more profound satisfaction than any worldly endeavors ever could. California had a wealth of spiritual teachers passing through and in residence. I studied with many of them and came to settle with my guru, Baba Jivananda. My husband, who hired me for the job I came to hold, was there waiting for me. And far down the road as well, was meeting Elan.

Abdy

Chapter Six:
Entering The Sacred Conduit

THE HANDING OVER

As time went by Elan started attending energy sessions given by someone named Abdy, who made occasional visits to the city in which he lived. Elan often called me immediately after these events. The energy he had just experienced seemed to rub off on me as if it were contagious. I experienced heightened states of awareness and bodily shaking (kriyas) on such evenings. Sometimes they continued all night. I was intrigued by the intensity of my reaction.

On one occasion, I was unable to sleep all night due to many different levels of agitation, shaking and energy flows. I spoke to him the next morning and surprisingly discovered that Elan's experience of the previous night had been exactly identical in flavor to mine.

Finally, in one conversation, Elan told me that I was supposed to meet Abdy in on March 8, when he came for his monthly visit to that city. I asked if I could stay at his place since I knew no one else in the area. He agreed and I made travel arrangements. A brief time before that fateful day, he rescinded his offer due to various circumstances in his life. I told Elan that in that case I wasn't coming. I didn't want to stay alone nor try to figure out transportation to the site where the sessions were being given. So I backed out of the trip.

Elan insisted that it was crucial to my sadhana, my spiritual path, to meet Abdy on that very day. I stubbornly refused to go without a place to stay.

A week ahead of his intended visit, magically, Abdy ended up switching his plans. He decided to give a session in my area on the very day that I was told that I must meet him. In this way, the Universe supported the prediction, allowing it to manifest. Whenever one aligns with the Passion of one's personal destiny, that which we are able to accomplish in our lives to satisfy our personal fulfillment and hence necessarily the fulfillment of all beings in existence, then the entire Universe conspires to support us.

This marked the end of my intense ongoing communications with Elan. He met a new love and launched into various all-consuming adventures. We have had a few more conversations and occasional interactions, but the relationship organically evaporated as he, perhaps consciously, handed me over to Abdy for the next chapter of my spiritual journey.

THE FIRST SESSION

The night before my first session with Abdy in San Raphael, California, on March 8, 2003 was the first time I saw his picture. I found his website, www.abdy.info, and was struck by his eyes. I woke up the next morning staring directly and intently into them as I emerged from a very deep sleep. Later that morning, another friend synchronistically gave me a CD of some music, which I later discovered was played during his sessions.

Abdy

After work, I drove 1 ½ hours through rush hour traffic to get to the location. Immediately upon entering the space of the session that evening, I was enveloped by the meditative stillness of the room. The musician, Galalisa Star, whose CD I had been given, was present and chanted live. She bounced her voice off a heated Native American drum producing one of the purest tones in any singer I had ever heard. Much of the time, her voice was indistinguishable from the pure tone of a musical instrument, having the quality of a flute. She performed in this manner acapella, without instrumentation, while Abdy worked.

One by one, Abdy motioned to people around the room to come forward; he touched them and they fell back gently and were assisted in lying on the floor. Most everyone remained motionless for a very long time, sometimes for hours. A few people moved in unusual and sometimes yogic postures, while one engaged in a beautiful slow motion 'dance' around the room.

Abdy motioned to me to come to the center of the floor. He touched my head and throat. I was dumbstruck as I instantly, as if propelled to warp speed through a tunnel of light, entered an internal realm where none of the usual thought processes operated. This instantaneous relaxation from the normally treaded pathways of my mind left me aware of, but giving no weight or significance to my surroundings or those in it. The sweet fulfillment of the inner realm flooded my awareness leaving me in a state of 'suspended animation' with a sense of feeling completely satisfied and nourished. There was no hint of lack. I said to myself, "This must be Heaven."

I lay motionless for nearly two hours. At the end of the session Abdy spoke to us. From the state I had entered, I was able to hear his words from a different place so that they penetrated into profound recesses of my being and impacted me strongly.

Later the continuing afterglow of the state that arose from his touch along with his words, led me to write the following, which for me encapsulated what I had heard him say and what I took from the session:

Each of our lives is truly perfect. There is nothing that can be changed. Our destiny has been planned from the moment we originated, so truly there is nothing to do. Who you meet, marry, etc. is already mapped out. Take a deep breath. YOU CAN RELAX into the very fabric of your life. You don't have to struggle. There is no way to be wrong. There is only the choice of how to react to what is happening. Relax into the gift of the exact life God has given you. It is your own perfection. It is your perfect seva (sacred service). Feel God breathing you - each and every breath. Each struggle, each situation, each person, the hard and the easy, is the exquisite perfection and exact flavor needed for the constant upliftment of your soul.

That first session, created a permanent change in me. This philosophy initiated a shift in my perceptions that has helped me to accept and to not blame myself for the invariable crises that arise in a working mom's household of two teenagers, a husband, a cat, 90 sheep and a horse.

One profound affect of my session with Abdy was to initiate a deeper acceptance, which is more complete all the time, that my spiritual path isn't some high place apart from the realities of my life. Rather my full and perfect destiny exists fully within each step I take - with my family, my co-workers and all those people with whom I cross paths. That realization, which continues to grow and deepen through my conversations and encounters with Abdy, lets me ever more fully experience the joy and wonder inherent in even the most mundane and difficult of situations.

For example, a while after this first session, I was injured by one of my students in the college chemistry class that I teach. The state workers compensation organization for months refused me a counseling session that I felt would be useful since the incident had left me uneasy and nervous in my classroom.

A five-hour evaluation was mandated to determine whether worker's comp would cover any counseling. I spoke to a friend who was a judge in this system who told me that one is more likely to receive treatment if the situation is viewed as an isolated incident in a person with a healthy life.

From having worked with and listened to Abdy, I knew that somehow there was perfection in the entirety of all that had transpired, including the attack. So the day before the scheduled evaluation, I decided to practice retelling my life's story to myself, not in the dramatic way I usually do internally, but from the position that even the most difficult of my life's circumstances were just minor incidents in a basically whole, satisfying and productive life. I also realized that it would be just fine whether or not I received the counseling I believed would assist in allowing me to set aside the assault more easefully.

I returned home from work the night before my scheduled evaluation to a message on my answering machine telling me that the worker's compensation claim manager had cancelled the evaluation and simply decided to grant my request. Interestingly, my mind has refused to return to the old, more dramatic version of my life's tale, because somehow I came to realize that this new healthy internal version of my life was in fact closer to the Truth.

No matter what our circumstances, we have total freedom in their interpretation. A traumatic incident can be viewed as a verification of the potential danger from others and the unfairness of life. The same incident might be considered as a learning situation that one has on a subtle level created for oneself in order that a lesson might be learned. One might interpret the whole incident as a way that the world has unfairly squished one like a bug. Conversely, the very same circumstance can exemplify how one's inner strength and deeper discriminatory abilities came to be solidified. It is in our perception of events that freedom lies.

When I left that first session with Abdy, I discovered that my friend, Aubrey, whom I had brought to the session, knew the organizer of the event. On the way out the door, the organizer said that they would like a larger house for Abdy's next visit. Aubrey said, "She has a larger house", pointing to me. I never would have thought to volunteer my house, yet as soon as she said it, the idea was immediately appealing. That offer led me to interact on a more ongoing basis with Abdy and hence began **yet** another remarkable connection of my life.

There were two more three-hour sessions the next day. I returned and stayed for both of them. Unbeknownst to **me** it was Abdy's 39th birthday. I approached him before **the** session and offered him the use of my home for a **session** the next time he returned to the area.

MOUNT SHASTA

We started speaking fairly often. It was a great joy to **me** to discover that we both had Chemistry degrees and a language base to discuss scientific aspects of **the** energetic processes transpiring in his sessions. More broadly, he also provided overviews and models for **the** evolution of humankind and the earth itself as a whole, at this pivotal period of human evolution. Not only did **he** share many ideas with me, but he also sent me a **large** number of channelings and writings from an assortment of spiritual people and groups from around the globe.

One email that Abdy sent me was from an entity named Kryon, channeled through Lee Carroll. It catalyzed my interest in Mt. Shasta. My daughter was in school in Arcata, California about five hours west of Mt. Shasta but I had never before been there.

I hadn't been off on my own without my husband and/or kids for even one day since 1994. That year my husband let me take a pilgrimage to India while he watched the children. This time I drove my daughter up to school at Humboldt State University. Before driving home, I found I had a rare 24 hours to follow my inner spiritual directives, as I had always been able to do in the many years that I lived alone before having a family.

I dropped my daughter in Arcata telling her that I wanted to find a group to meditate with at Mt. Shasta and that I wanted to see the mountain. She had teased me as I left Arcata by saying, "There goes mom looking for the psychic people."

I drove like mad Sunday August 17, 2003, neither stopping for lunch or dinner. I felt like I had a date with destiny. I also really wondered why I didn't simply stay by the beach in Arcata. When I skip an encounter with the ocean it is more than strange, especially since I knew no one and nothing at Mt. Shasta. Astrologically, I'm triple water. My sun and moon are in Cancer, with Pieces rising. Ordinarily nothing soothes me more than being by or in the water, whether I'm in a tub, in a boat or especially by the ocean.

I arrived in the small 3,000-person town of Mt. Shasta at the base of the exquisite 14,600 ft. snow covered peak and drove through town wondering where to go. I was seeking a community where I could spend the night and meditate.

As I drove through the main street in the town, I came upon a health food store that was still open. I went in and immediately realized that it was nearly their closing time.

I walked up to a customer and asked her if she knew the

area. She looked at me strangely and asked me if I meditated at Uma-Guru's ashram. It turned out that she recognized me from my participation with a group that helps lead the chanting there. She invited me to stay with her in her tent on the mountain. I considered it but declined. I felt certain that there was some community I was supposed to find that I belonged in for that evening.

I tried to talk to a checkout clerk in the store but he was too busy. So I went up to an Asian man who was helping to close up the store and asked him whether he knew of a meditative community in the area where I might be able to stay for the evening. He referred me to an isolated Zen monastery down the freeway only a short distance away. I followed his directions and found myself at an isolated exit with no stores or houses - just wilderness.

I took off and with some difficulty arrived at Shasta Abbey on the top of an isolated peak overlooking Mt. Shasta. I entered through a gate and asked the female monk I encountered whether I might spend the night. She said to wait while she found the guestmaster of the Abbey. I remained at that spot enjoying the grandeur of the mountain's expansiveness that lay before me.

To my amazement, the next person to walk by was a colleague of mine from the state community college at which I teach. Not only were we fellow instructors, but she was also one of the ten women in a group, which had been meeting at my house each month. I had known that this friend was on retreat, but I had no idea where. I was surprised to discover that she was a participant in an advanced Zen meditation retreat, which was just beginning that day. She went off to join the opening session instructions.

The guestmaster arrived shortly thereafter and I was invited into the monastery. We walked through cloistered arches along an outdoor walkway, which led eventually to the guestmaster's office. I occupied the proffered seat. After brief pleasantries I made a request to pay for lodging for that evening. However, I was informed that there was no room for me to spend the night, not even in my colleague's room.

Somehow I did not feel moved to depart immediately and no one asked me to. Time passed. I completely accepted that I couldn't stay, but the monks and I seemed in some suspended state. I felt a viscous, honey-sweet energy embrace me. I found that I couldn't leave. The monk suggested various regular lodging facilities in town. None resonated with my heart's longing nor the certain community connected vision that had pulled me to this town.

Eventually the energy palpably shifted and another monk entered the room. He gave me the phone number for a retreat site, apparently magically located right across the street.

I called the number he provided and set up a room for later that evening. There were only two rooms that could be rented. I had shared with the monks my desire to meditate with them and they allowed me to stay for their meditation and scriptural recitation, which opened the advanced retreat that evening.

My meditation was very strong. I became the mountain. There was great effervescent activity in my crown chakra, which seemed to reflect something actually happening in the mountain. It felt to me like the activity was that of the "5-dimensional beings" who were described as the guardians of the mountain in the channeling which had initially catalyzed my in this spot. Mt. Shasta is thought to be an energy vortex associated with the root chakra of the planet. During the meditation, I felt within me the tip of volcanic effervescence associated with this peak.

Later in the meditation I felt a physical/energetic shift in my body's magnetic center/posture that seemed to reflect deep in the mountain's magnetic center. It seemed to be reinforced/transmitted/magnified by the meditative energy of the advanced meditation retreat participants around me. I believe that this was one reason why I had been permitted to remain for their meditative program. It was one reason why I was there.

It was almost dark after the session. The site the monks had found for me was a house directly across the street from the monastery, BUT about one mile straight into the woods down a dirt road. It was so dark that I kept driving off into the trees. I had to keep getting out of the car to see if I was still on a path. Finally, I consciously aligned with my magnetic center and eventually found the place. I was the only guest and had a private separate guesthouse with a kitchen, two bedrooms, a bath and sauna. Each room contained meditative music from a large variety of spiritual traditions. There was even a small trampoline. Great, holy energy deep in the woods. The place was called Wellspring.

The night was eventful. There was one other time that I previously had experienced the kind of unremitting pulsating energy all night that descended upon me at this time. The other episode had been decades before – when I followed my first internal 'psychic message', which led me to an Indian village and ruins in Tepotzlan, Mexico.

On this particular night at Mt. Shasta, I probably slept no more than one hour all night. The energy coursed through me as if I was plugged into an electrical circuit I literally shook with energy most of the night. My nearly constant imagery was of holding Abdy's feet as I actually had during one of his sessions in London. A group including myself had gathered around him at the end of that event and had given him a healing. All through the night the energy from his feet streamed through my hands into me and out my feet, which were pointing towards the mountain. I felt that he and I were a unit together somehow activating the region and setting something up for the future.

The next day I awoke without an alarm and arrived just in time for the 5:30 AM meditation and recitation session at the monastery. I was fortunate that the monks allowed me to join the advanced meditation retreat participant's for this portion of their morning program.

Afterwards, I sat on benches along the porticoed arches

of a walkway lining the site. I rested there at the monastery and reread the channeling that Abdy had originally sent to me which had piqued my initial interest and drew me to see this place for myself. New aspects of it highlighted for me.

As I breathed in the crisply clean air surrounding me in this pristine environment I was transfixed by the stunning vista of Mount Shasta's grandeur that lay before me. Even in these last days of Indian summer, the top of the broad and gradually ascending mountain expanse was covered by snow. It was hard to believe that I wasn't simply looking at a panoramic postcard's picture of perfection. After lingering for a time, I felt the mountain beckoning me to visit and I could not refuse.

I drove up the mountain as far as cars could travel. I was nearly to the snow. At the point that most vegetation stopped I started hearing a cacophony of subtle spirit voices all speaking at once, but they ceased before I could make out anything distinctly. I climbed up even further and meditated near the top just below the snow level. Then I drove back down and started my journey back to the Bay area.

It was a profoundly interesting journey, having been gone from my family for a mere 20 hours. I found it a metaphor for all the journeys that we make looking for Truth outside of our own selves and our own lives. In searching for "the psychic people", I kept running into my own life. I bumped into people who already knew me and even a very close friend. I thought that no matter where I look, trying to find something exotic, I seem to run into my very own self and my very own life.

COSMOLOGICAL PYRAMIDS

This wasn't the only time that a few words from Abdy would fling me into some new direction or lead me into a deep state of heightened awareness.

As I talked with him on the phone, even briefly, I often found myself falling into profoundly deep states. Occasionally I would simply hold the phone in silence – and the energy of the connection no longer required words.

On a number of occasions, after speaking with Abdy casually, I found complete scientific or cosmological theories arising in my dream state or downloading into my conscious awareness all at once in my waking state.

The first time this happened was one morning just as I was waking up. It was not the usual feeling of remembering a dream, but rather a sense that all of a sudden I knew a whole bunch of information that I not only did not know the moment before, but had never contemplated in my whole life.

I received a vision of the nature of interconnected functioning on the planet of those beings who were in more evolved states of consciousness. Their energetic contact formed three larger bodies affecting the entirety of the globe, just as all our individual cells form the whole of our living body.

The energy form of this networking generated three pyramids composed of the consciousness of those involved. This multi-human structure appeared to be in constant flux as to who was in which position and with whom they were interconnected.

It most closely resembled the equilibrium characteristics of a crystal lattice in a saturated solution, that is, a solution that has as much dissolved in it as is possible at a particular temperature. In this kind of a solution, some individual molecules pop off the crystal lattice while others are re-precipitating by finding a spot in the crystal where they fit exactly. Hence, they are able to link up to the solid when they have the geometry required to fit exactly into a vacated hole in the lattice.

In much the same way, individuals attach to the three planetary pyramids of energetic consciousness at times when they are able to contribute some aspect of their beingness that is useful to the whole.

When one thus attaches to this three-dimensional pyramid, one becomes a member of numerous three-fold operative cogs, which act as gears to impact the world in some way. Some one on the outer pyramidal edging would have only one person above them, whereas someone closer to the interior might have three. There are also attachments to those below and to one on the same plane.

This theory purports that it is three-membered units that are causative impacting cogs or gears of the energetic world. All this I received instantaneously in my dream-like state.

I was deeply intrigued by this import of information. I wanted to talk to someone about the intensity of the strange downloading that had occurred and quickly felt compelled to share it with Abdy. When I called him and explained to him the theory and how it had arisen he was quite surprised. He told me that the theory was in fact his theory and that he had only ever told it to one person, interestingly only days before I 'dreamed.' it.

He had shared this theory at a private lunch with only one person – Elan, the very person who had led me to meet him and with whom I'd had so many catalytic adventures. It was even clear to me immediately that Abdy, Elan and I formed just such a triadic cog.

Much later I came to believe that two members of each group carry some aspect of opposite energies with the last member existing as the third or resolving force. The candle had served this function of the higher resolving third force in the dyadic process I had experienced during the 'lines' karmic clearing process of the SAT groups. The third-force person of the group operates from a higher consciousness base. No matter what gender the individuals are, one of the other two likely carries a polarity of predominantly masculine energy with the other imbibed with predominantly feminine energy.

The higher aspect of the feminine energy is the embracing presence of allowing everyone and everything, including oneself, to be, exactly who and what one is. It is also the knowledge that each one, both oneself and others are perfectly innocent. It is knowing that everyone one is always doing one's best, including one's own self.

The higher masculine principle is having that inner courage to venture forth and dare to shine one's own truth.

An aspect of the hypothesis that arose for me touched upon the relationship between Divine, societal and individual's energy. The shift on earth involving dropping the patriarchal hierarchy structuring of society and replacing it with a uniting of the masculine and feminine is evident. One sees it with the push for allowing women to function in the role of ministers and priests. One sees forces to shift the chattel status of women in some societies and the fight against genital mutilation. Women politicians are increasing along with women in the positions of college Presidents and Chancellors. A woman occupying the office of the President of the United States is becoming a conceivable reality.

Although I was the first woman hired in the history of my college's Chemistry Department, we eventually became seven women and three men. On the other side of the spectrum, two children, a seven-month old and a six-year-old girl, were occasionally present at our Chemistry Department meetings, both brought by their fathers.

The unfoldment of a joining of the masculine and feminine polarities within each of us is occurring reflecting within and also on more cosmological scales. The Christ energy of the Divine Father, which has molded societies for thousands of years, is uniting with the Magdalene Flame, the ancient and long removed Divine Feminine Goddess energy, prominent in ancient Lemurian times.

This same Union is also the one unfolding within each of us. There is an ancient three-fold flame, the original Trinity, within each of our hearts. There within can be found the pink thread of the Divine Feminine, the blue strand of the Divine Masculine and the resolving golden flame of the Holy Spirit, Maitreya or Christ force. The transformative power of St. Germaine's violet flame is due to its perfect balance of the Feminine and Masculine.

The internal union of these forces is facilitated for individuals, societies and the planet by these many three member units of the three pyramids. At some cosmic moment of human unity down the road, these three may merge into one large planetary pyramid of high human vision supporting all existence energetically. These were among the complex array of ideas that descended upon me from 'the dream'.

I found interesting correlations with this theory in a scientific magazine called Astronomy, which I happened to peruse at the Chabot Space and Science Center where my son was a volunteer. I discovered it in an edition, which focused on Mars in November of 2003 at the time that Mars was the closest to the earth in 60,000 years.

The magazine discussed the fact that the magnetic field of the earth was changing direction, although not varying in intensity. It described that in fact at other times, perhaps in 50,000-year interludes, the earth's magnetic poles have reversed and have had little impact on the existence of life on the planet.

This time the article was predicting a polarity shift into three separate pairs of magnetic poles. It discussed that life would not be deeply impacted by this shift except in three ways. The aura borealis would be present over much of the earth, planetary navigation modes could no rely on the earth's magnetic field and solar storms would be deflected and attracted to the planet in quite different patterning than at present. When I read this article, it seemed to me to match up with the kind of three-fold pyramidal structures, which I had envisioned in my dream.

This dream experience led me to reminisce about my favorite scientific dream in which Kekule formulated the structure of the benzene molecule.

Benzene, a common solvent now known to be a carcinogen, was first isolated from a whale oil byproduct by Michael Faraday in 1825. By 1834, its molecular formula was determined to be C_6H_6, but its actual structure didn't fit the many possible models that could be drawn. It wasn't until 1865 that Friedrich August Kekule, a chemistry professor at Ghent, Belgium and at Heidelberg and Bonn, Germany, proposed a satisfactory structure for benzene, which arose for him also in a meditative dream. The following is his personal account of his dream as described in John Hill's *Chemistry for Changing Times*:

"During my stay in Ghent I resided in elegant bachelor quarters. My study, however, faced a narrow side-alley and no daylight penetrated it. For the chemist who spends his day in the laboratory this mattered little. I was sitting writing at my textbook but the work did not progress; my thoughts were elsewhere. I turned my chair to the fire and dozed. Again the atoms were gamboling before my eyes. This time the smaller groups kept modestly in the background. My mental eye, rendered more acute by repeated visions of the kind, could now distinguish larger structures of manifold conformation: long rows, sometimes more closely fitted together, all twining and twisting in snake-like motion. But, look! What was that? One of the snakes had seized hold of its own tail, and the form whirled mockingly before my eyes. As if by a flash of lightening I woke; and this time also I spent the rest of the night in working out the consequences of the hypothesis.

Let us learn to dream, gentlemen, then perhaps we shall find the truth. But let us beware of publishing our dreams till they have been tested by the waking understanding."

Until Kekule's vision, chemists had only thought of having chains of carbon atoms, but this insight which was dream inspired, led chemists to propose rings of atoms as well. Although I enjoyed my dream model arising so completely in all its complexity, methods to test such energetic ideas have not yet been devised. Perhaps society is on the brink of such abilities at present.

Abdy has often spoken to me of the power of the dream

state. In fact he says that it is not that we sleep at night to be available for our life in the waking state, but rather that we live out our lives in the waking state so that we are prepared and able to enter into the more powerful and expansive existence of our dream state. It is a time of leaving the corporeal body identity realm and, at least in deep sleep, connect with Source and our joined unchanging identity as ONE. So it is not surprising to me that Kekule was able to develop his proposal for the structure of benzene from that more influential realm of dreams.

This was not the only time that my contact with Abdy led me to new scientific explorations. From my contact with him, completely new scientific clarifications for metaphysical processes arose. These invariably sprouted from my mind dwelling on some very few but particular of Abdy's words. These bits of core concepts were like spiritual seeds that were planted and which then sprouted into full bloom at a breathtaking speed.

ELECTROMAGNETIC EFFECTS

A new scientific theory arose in me when my husband and I celebrated our 20th wedding anniversary with a trip to London. Just after I booked the trip, I discovered that Abdy would be giving a session in London at just that time. I arranged a bed and breakfast inn quite close to the flat in which Abdy was staying. Upon entering our hotel, we were touched to discover that Abdy had dropped by before we arrived, filling the room with fruit and flowers.

Abdy's London session was on August 3, 2003. Long before I came to England, he had told me that the heart chakra of the planet was centered in the region and that it would open the day of our session. Although this was an intriguing idea, I never expected a blatant outward manifestation of the process to be apparent.

The energetic power fueling Abdy's events comes not from Abdy himself, but rather from the location itself. He is the key or catalyst that unlocks the energy of a particular place. He opens the portal to a region's innate subtle strength and allows it to cascade down on all those present. He also works on each individual present in a more concentrated manner to bring about healings, alignments, realizations, transformations and advancements, as they are required.

The Spiritual Hierarchy as channeled by Edwin Courtenay has said: *"Abdy works with the Christ energy, which is a bridging consciousness that aligns the consciousness of man to the consciousness of the Divine. The power that Abdy anchors, that he is conduit for, aligns people to the presence of the Divine, to the Divine's mind, to the Divine's heart, to the Divine Spirit wherever the person needs to connect to at that particular moment in time. It can activate the Christ Light within."*

It was also at this session that I became aware of how Abdy uses the totality of the unity of all the group participants to create an overall effect. This in turn impacts not only those taking part, but also the planet earth itself. It is for this reason, I believe, that he does not do individual sessions. It is also why it is generally true that the larger the session, the more powerful the effect on both the participants and the locale.

It was at this gathering that I first realized that Abdy places participants in his sessions in patterns on the floor treating them as one organism, as well as tending to each person individually. In this session he arranged all the participants in a large particular formation, which resembled what is often called 'the flower of life'.

It was the day after my London session with Abdy that an extraordinary heat wave hit all of Europe. It was very intense and went on for months. Temperatures in London for the rest of our trip were near 100 degrees Fahrenheit. Later I thought that if the planet's heart chakra had in fact opened, this heat wave easily might be a manifestation of just such a process.

After the powerful weekend session, I kept trying to see Abdy again before he went off with a group to Devon to give a further set of sessions. He had invited my husband and I along. However, my husband had never before been to Europe. We travel together infrequently and only for short periods of time due to his responsibility for single handedly maintaining our 100 sheep, thoroughbred horse and three ranches. So we decided to stay in London and see the sites instead.

Although we were staying only a few blocks away from Abdy, every time I tried to call him or to see if he was home, I missed him. Over and over again I found it impossible to even reach him on the phone to talk. I became quite frustrated in not successfully connecting with him during those last few days in London.

This was a notably unusual occurrence, since I ordinarily find myself in the right place with the right people at the right time. So I asked myself why this time had I somehow lost my ability to make connections? The answer I got was that I usually operate from the "magnetic center" in my body and it leads me to know where to be. It is my spiritual core. I found that I was off in two important ways during those few days after the very powerful gathering that had occurred with Abdy. My magnetic alignment had shifted due to the session and as well, I was experiencing the earth's magnetic shift from my new British positioning on the planet. Besides all this, the huge energy surge emanating from the planetary heart chakra opening, which heated up England and France to tropical levels, had been affecting my personal orientation as well.

The following explanation came to me, when I asked myself why I had not been able to connect up with Abdy.

All electromagnetic radiation (light) has an electrical and a magnetic component, which are vectors perpendicular to each other. Those who operate completely from three-dimensional physical reality rather than a more energetic orientation, align themselves and orient themselves completely with the electrical component of their own energetic (light) field. It is harder to be flexible from this orientation. If one instead operated entirely from the perpendicular magnetic component of one's field, one would be a total spiritual being operating from higher dimensional realities.

In some systems it is postulated that there are actually 12 possible potential dimensions of consciousness. Time and sometimes light through its speed are said to relate to the fourth dimension. In some postulations in physics the fourth dimension is represented by a vector of the imaginary number i multiplied by time as well as the speed of light. So as the term en-LIGHT-enment implies, one's interaction with and consciousness of light has to do with one's spiritual state and perceptions of the world. In conversations with Abdy, he proposed that a person's relationship to one's intension and to one's emotions are some defining aspects of higher dimensions of functioning.

Abdy speaks of the emotions as the glue that binds the higher soul energy to the body. The emotions are also "God's leash" which allows us to be drawn into those destined aspects of our existence, so that we are enticed into living out that life which is pre- designed for each of us. As more and more of one's higher energy is drawn into this physical three-dimensional realm of the body, the emotional glue is contracted and "squeezes out". That is situations might arise which illicit a burst of anger, anxiety, fear, hatred, love, attraction or some such emotion. As the soul moves in more completely, these emotions are expelled and must be experienced during their removal.

As they exit through their expression and through one's experience of them, one's Soul descends ever more completely into the three dimensional reality of the body. The more this process ensues, the more completely is one able to manifest the energy of the Divine through the vehicle of one's own unique Self. Hence there is an intimate relationship between one's dimension of consciousness and emotion.

Beings in higher states of consciousness remain more and more in a state of emotionless calm where much of the emotional well has been experienced, accepted and expelled. In a sense the emotional preference for one of any number of sets of opposites such as love and hate, good and bad, joy and sorrow has been obliterated by the acceptance of allowing things to unfold as they must unfold in any case. In our realms of physical existence this idealized level of functioning cannot exist while still, speaking, interacting and functioning in normal ways. So there are degrees of moving towards this high state of existence by which 12 different levels of consciousness can be delineated.

Assuming that in fact 12 possible dimensions of reality do exist, and dividing the 90 degree difference between the electric and magnetic fields into 9 equal segments gives 10 degrees in each portion. These 9 are equal divisions of the 90 degrees between normal three and 12 dimensional reality.

So this leaves 10 degrees between the electric and magnetic components for each dimension to define each of the other levels of consciousness between the 3rd and 12th dimension. The state of one's consciousness is dependent upon the degree that one orients one's functioning between the intuitive (magnetic) component and the (concrete-rational) 3 dimensional reality of the electrical component. Transitioning between each dimension must be quantized process, that is, a jump rather than a gradual and continuous transitioning.

Now, when I attend an Abdy session, the magnetic component of my orientation is shifted by the ferromagnetic effect of Abdy. By this I mean that Abdy in his function as a conduit of the Christ or Maitreya energy, is acting as a powerful magnet, lining up the personal magnetic fields of those individuals with whom he contacts. This shifts those individuals to a new place leaving an imbalance in their energy field, that is to say a lack of perpendicularity between their electrical and magnetic components.

Hence one becomes disoriented and momentarily falls into holding onto that magnetic component, losing the more physical body awareness and detaching from one's electrical component, which grounds a person into their ordinary three-dimensional existence.

Now a choice opens up. Those vectors must relax down to a normal perpendicular orientation from this 'excited state' one way or another. Either one brings back the magnetic component to that 90 degree orientation, in which case, one has had an experience of the 'other' but returns to one's normal awareness, or one can choose instead to reorient the electrical component to the new magnetic position in which case, one is permanently changed.

That change is profound. It has literally shifted three-dimensional reality allowing diseases to be healed, weight to change, metabolism shifts etc. One's body becomes actually transformed and changed over time. This permanent shift to a new magnetic position results in a deeper, more spiritual orientation and allows one to operate from a new dimension of consciousness.

To some extent this effect also occurs when one travels, especially long distances. The earth's magnetic field, being in a different position than one's normal geographic alignment, actually does an 'Abdy' on one, thereby altering the individual's magnetic component. That is why people experience jetlag and the disorienting shift that occurs with long distance travel. It is also why travel is so mind expanding and often permanently alters one's perceptions. After a trip, one can realign with either the magnetic or the electrical component to re-achieve perpendicularity, resulting in a permanent or nonpermanent shift in the dimensionality of consciousness.

If the earth's magnetic field is due to the alignment of paramagnetic minerals undergoing unpaired d-electron transitions, and if the magnetic poles come to be off from the spin axis, by only a few degrees, planetary magnetic realignment shouldn't be so hard for the light workers of the energetic pyramids to achieve. That is, it may be possible with a great number of individual's personal magnetic fields aligning due to their intent, heart-felt emotional alignment, spiritual development and spiritual activation, to actually subtly and slightly alter the magnetic orientation of the planet as a whole. This would

167

impact on some level all beings living on the planet at the time.

In addition, this process could be hastened from an external source of light, such as that produced by an increase in solar flares. These flares do introduce new magnetic fields, which alter planetary communication systems as well as creating increased aurora borealis patternings.

The magnetic center of the body is the same as the lower dantien from which the bodily chi of Taoist theories originates. I think of my magnetic center as being a few fingers below my navel deep inside my belly. I can see that extra imbibed, ingested or decorative paramagnetic metals could have an impact on one's magnetic center. Chinese herbalists provide patches that pull out magnetic metals that have been ingested.

Early on in our interactions, Abdy suggested that I replace my older mercury amalgam dental fillings with the non-magnetic white polymeric material that has come to be used more commonly. The purpose of this exchange was to remove artificial and unnecessary internal magnetic fields generated in the body from the magnetic spiritual re-alignment process as well as divesting my body from the biological toxicity of mercury.

GURUS

Abdy is not a Guru. With gurus I have known, I feel their energy enter me and touch that sacred internal space, activating it, and thus putting me in contact with my essential nature. They leak energy. Objects, clothes, shoes that they have worn still retain some of their energy and the Guru's disciples consider them to be sacred.

With Abdy, I feel no energy other than my own. He has told me that what he holds during a session is 'no intention'. He knows that everything is unfolding in a perfect fashion for each person and that there is no need to direct the Christ energy that flows through him in any way. It is this divine force that is his "boss", and he is just doing its' bidding. So in all matters, it is the energy that directs him rather than he who directs the energy.

When he works on me, I experience only the fullness of that divine energy that is already me, activated and expanding. He only needs to interact once with an individual to act as the catalyst that he is. Even if a person believes that nothing has occurred, the appropriate unfoldment for that individual will gradually occur over time.

Yet, I believe that all Gurus, to some extent, have stronger magnetic fields that create the possibility for the individual to achieve that permanent or temporary shift to a new consciousness through a reorientation of their magnetic fields. I believe that this is achieved by clearing out the karmic impurities that cause the body's impedance or resistance to an electrical flow. The fewer of these blockages that exist, the stronger will literally be the flow of electrons through the vehicle of the physical body. A moving charge always creates an induced magnetic field, so the clearer the guru's body, the stronger will be the field. And the stronger that field is, the more it can affect and act to align the magnetic fields of those who come into proximity with that Guru.

It is also possible to draw Divine energy into oneself directly without a transformer of that high vibration in the person of someone vibrating from a higher dimension of consciousness. That Light energy can then itself initiate a process of raising one's consciousness.

Chapter Seven:
Pilgrimage Preparations

TIMBUKTU

I had a leave from work in the fall of 2003 and besides tending to my family, my goal was to go anywhere in the world that I must in order to have another session with Abdy. He was taking two trips back to back. The first was to Timbuktu and the second to Israel. He kept telling me I should come along. I did not have the time nor the resources for both trips. I also had no inclination to go to Israel, as well as a deep underlying fear for my safety there. So I started the set of immunizations needed for travel to Mali, where Timbuktu is located.

At the last moment, logistical issues for the group going on the Mali trip mandated a shift in the proposed scheduling dates. With this necessary change of plans, portions of the two trips overlapped.

Abdy backed out of going to Mali opting to take only the Israel trip. When I first heard the news, I simply decided to back out of the pilgrimage. Abdy repeatedly suggested that I join him on the trip to Israel. He said that it would be very powerful.

Finally I told him that I felt terror at the thought of going to Israel. He said, "Don't worry. The worst that can happen is that you'll die." Immediately, I laughed. Somehow his words instantly evaporated my fear and allowed me to opt for the journey. The trip was called 'Journey to the Heart'.

The next day, I had the seva of dressing the statue of Bade Baba in the Oakland ashram. One of the very few quotes that has been attributed to Bade Baba is, "The heart is the hub of all sacred places. Go there and roam." As I stepped into the gazebo that morning which houses his 'living statue', or murti, I internally heard the statue say to me, "The heart is the hub of all sacred places. Go there and roam. Journey to the heart." Over and over I heard these phrases. They gave me the immediate confidence that in fact I had made the right choice to embark on this journey.

The next day I signed up and paid for the Israel trip. When I told Abdy I was going, he said he had known that I would for the previous three days.

And that began for me what was possibly the most amazing journey of all my lifetimes. The last thing Abdy said to me before I left on the trip was, "Well Sundari, your life is about to change." And so it was.

THE DANTIEN

I had learned many years before to listen to that internal directive that led one to be at the right time, at the right place with the right people. Not that the reality of this isn't always true, but to be aware of it is deeply soothing. I associate the ability to be at the right place with an 'opening' of the instinctual belly center. This is also known as the Kath, in Gurdjieffian Sufi terminology, while Taoists call it the chi of the dantien, or belly center. It is literally the magnetic and gravitational midpoint of the body, about three fingers below one's navel, deep within. It seemed to me to be the place in me from which the decision to go to Israel with Abdy was made.

I had studied Tai Chi for a number of years with Master Chu Fong Chu, who Claudio Naranjo had brought to teach us in SAT. Claudio's genius was in bringing together the right teachers with the right people at the right time. I met about 25 gurus of one sort or another in just 3-4 years through being a part of this group.

Master Chu did not teach us any movements until we had practiced Taoist macrocosmic and microcosmic breath circulation for three months. When we finally did learn the movements, they were always accompanied by particular breathing patterns enhancing the building up of one's chi, or innate body energy. This pranic (breath) energy was an aspect of the power within, which could be used for longevity, healing, martial arts defense or one's orientation and interactions with the world and other people.

After just a few months of practicing this Taoist breathing practice, I had my first concrete experience of what I at the time called 'the other realm', that is to say the sphere where energy becomes as real as a brick wall. I experienced a welling up of internal force fields of energy, which were so strong that my lips, fingers and feet became paralyzed, sometimes for hours. Although tinglings were familiar to me previously, this level of energy was unfamiliar and awesomely powerful.

I found that my Tai Chi practice impacted my teaching as well, so that I became less defensive in interacting to questions from my students, which appeared to me to be aggressive or attacking. I learned to yield to the question while adhering with a focus of attention, that acknowledged the question, while ignoring its implied 'threat'. This is the very technique taught in Tai Chi, appropriately yielding and adhering, used in the physical practice of the movements, each of which is an interaction with an "attack' made by an opponent.

Exercising the breath in this controlled manner also opened my belly center and led me to give myself the freedom to follow my instinctual center, my kath or dantien belly center. This new orientation, in which I was being directed from within, crystallized at the same time that a comet called Kahoutek was approaching the earth.

GUIDANCE WITHIN –TEPOTZLAN

I was innocently reading an article in Reader's Digest, which described the January 8th day that the comet was to be closest to the earth, and that it was likely to be seen best in Mexico. Suddenly, in that moment, there appeared an internal bulletin board within the vistas of my mind, which lit up with the message – 'You are to go to Mexico on January 8, the day Kahoutek is closest to the earth'.

I was taken aback by the visual specificity of this, my first internal message. It would have been easy to ignore, especially due to the fact that I had previous responsibilities already laid out for that day. I was teaching organic chemistry at The College of Marin, in Kentfield, California, and the final exam was scheduled for that day. I could have just ignored those inner realms, but somehow I knew that I had reached a juncture where the decision to align with the power of the instinctual center had become a possibility. I decided to trust that place deep inside myself.

I approached my class and to my shock, they all agreed to a person to take their exam a day early, opening the possibility of following the inner directive. It is said that when one aligns with one's personal legend, the Universe conspires to support you. And so it did for me.

As part of the SAT groups, we were asked to listen to a tape made by a Sufi, Rachad Field. It was about an hour long talk. As I was listening, two items from the discussion highlighted brightly on the inner blackboard of my mind. One of them was that if one meets a Sufi master, the appropriate gift is a pot of honey.

The process of the transformation of pollen to honey, of the coarse to the fine, is a representation of the possible internal transformation, the spiritual journey itself. It is parallel to the alchemists transmutation of lead into gold, all of which reflect back to that place of Heaven available to us all within. It is why the Naqshbandi Order of Sufism, variously known as the "Brotherhood of the Bees", uses the symbol of the bee, as an entity, which is capable of managing this conversion.

The discourse touched upon a description of the ley lines of the earth. These ley lines are natural linear energy patternings aligned along the earth's surface. The Chinese science of feng shui also recognizes that certain powerful currents and lines of magnetism run invisible through the landscape over the whole surface of the earth.

Rachad, in his discourse that day, spoke of many power hubs where these ley lines crossed each other on the planet. Stonehenge for instance was one of these. Such junctions were places of spiritual power noted for their stillness. I believe such places to achieve their power from an overlapping of the nodal points of many electromagnetic waves of all magnitudes running through them. A nodal point is the place where a wave crosses the zero point. That position is located half way between the crest or high point and the trough-or low point of the wave. The greater the number of nodes that are present at a site, the deeper will be the affect upon someone at that location.

Many positions on earth were mentioned that day, but only one of them lit up in the inner realms of my awareness. It was Tepotzlan, Mexico, an Indian village of about 1200 in the mountains, not so terribly far from Mexico City and Cuernavaca. I immediately knew that Tepotlan was where my internal guidance was directing me to go on that day

Kahoutek was closest to the earth. I also knew that I was to find a Sufi there and bring them a pot of honey.

At the time, I was transitioning between houses and staying for a number of months with my friend Aubrey, her husband and two children. Also living at the house at the time was Rabbi Zalman Schachter-Shalomi, who taught us some Kaballah, or sacred esoteric Jewish teachings, nearly each day, and Don Gatch, a shaman. A shaman is a member of certain tribal societies who acts as a medium between the visible world and an invisible spirit world.

Aubrey had a counseling practice and one day as I walked through the kitchen, I found a young man waiting for his appointment with her. He was in the midst of mental breakdown, but well enough to have a semblance of a conversation. I casually mentioned to him that I was considering a trip to Tepotzlan, a village in Mexico. He looked at me strangely and in an automaton-like voice stated, "There is a brujo (sorcerer) in Tepotzlan named John Cooke." Immediately, my internal board lit up yet again and I knew this was the person I was to find. A moment later he said in a peculiar tone, "I think I have given you a message." And he had.

I was at a peculiar junction along my path. All the messages I was getting seemed bizarre to me. In spite of this, I chose to follow and align with my koth, my body's magnetic center, which the Taoist breathing had somehow activated. I listened to the vision and the direction I was receiving within.

Since my organic Chemistry class at the College of Marin to a person had agreed to take their final a day early, the journey became possible. I bought a beautiful ceramic pot and filled it with the most exotic honey I could purchase.

I gave the final on the arranged day, graded it for many hours and was just barely able to submit my final grades that day. Early the next morning, I flew from San Francisco to Los Angeles, then to Mexico City. I took a bus to Cuernavaca and finally a taxi to the village of Tepotzlan. I arrived at sunset on the day the comet Kahoutek was closest to the earth, just as my internal directive had indicated. Interestingly, Kahoutek ended up barely visible and a dud as far as the world was concerned. For me however, it was the moment of learning to trust my inner light and voice, so it did shine for me brightly, just not externally.

It was about 8 PM and I had never been to Mexico and didn't speak Spanish. I looked at the village square with quaint looking couples strolling and wondered how to proceed to find the brujo. After walking up to a few of them and saying, "Hombre, John Cooke?", I realized from their puzzled looks that this was not going to work. So, I went to the local Inn, seeking a phone book. There were scarcely any numbers listed at all and none of them belonged to a John Cooke. I decided to book a room for the night.

I was given a small separate hut apart from the main building of the Inn and sank into bed, savoring the strange smells and décor of the place. Before I could drift off into sleep, energy started palpably surging through my body. It came in even stronger waves than I ever had experienced before from the Taoist breathing practice. It didn't stop all night. Then dogs started barking in packs and in my fear, it sounded and felt like a march of people, animals and energy through me all night. It was a conscious state that I experienced between waking and sleep lasting all through the entirety of the night.

In the morning, I arose and went out to see the town. It was market day and I had never before seen the colorful array of foods, clothing and goods that met my eye. I wandered and sampled a while, not able to converse with anyone. Gradually the magnitude of what I now viewed as my foolishness in having followed my internal directive grew in me. I began to doubt my own sanity in having given any credence to what I had earlier assumed to be signs. Gradually the idea arose that perhaps it would be better to return to Mexico City, where I might find people to talk to and perhaps interesting museums to see.

I went back to the Inn, packed my suitcase and brought it down to the bar for something cold to drink before I left. There I encountered the first person, who could speak English, the bartender, Vincente. We had a pleasant conversation and just before I was about to leave, wildly, I thought to ask him if he had ever heard of a John Cooke in the area. To my surprise he said that there was a strange man in a wheelchair some distance away that he thought had that name. I asked him how to get there, and he gave me a map of a trail through a valley between two mountainous regions that ran along a brook and eventually

179

came to what he thought was John Cooke's hacienda.

Excitedly, I grabbed my daypack and placed in it the pot of honey, my Tarot deck and my journal. I had been doing readings using the Waite Tarot daily and I never went anywhere without my journal.

The trek took about an hour, at which point the path crossed the stream and I became confused about which direction to go. I sat a while contemplating what I should do when a sweet young couple with a bambino came along. Again I inquired, "Hombre, John Cooke?" This time the young woman responded, "Si, Si." (Yes, yes) She handed the baby to her partner, took me by the hand and led me down one of the paths a ways until we turned a corner.

There was a stunning hacienda with a road approaching it from the other direction. A car was parked and a British looking man perhaps in his 50's with a neatly trimmed goatee was in a wheelchair near the vehicle. I walked up to him inquiring, "John Cooke?"

"Yes", he said to my amazement.

Not quite sure how to proceed, I stated, "I got a ...um.........message to see you, and I've brought you a pot of honey."

He graciously accepted the honey and said, "Thank you. I'm off somewhere just now, but do come back tomorrow for lunch."

I accepted his offer and hiked back to the Inn for another night. The evening passed pleasantly and this time I slept well, exhausted by my journey and trek.

The next day I returned to his villa, this time easily finding my way. A maid showed me inside and directed me to an interior patio and garden, typical of the architecture of that area. There he was with an elegant woman, about his age, who had a similar look to him about her eyes. I glanced at them, but my eyes quickly became transfixed by the huge symbol covering the entirety of the round table about which they were seated.

It was an enneagram. Amazingly, a goodly portion of our studies in SAT, Claudio Naranjo's groups, had centered around very extensive studies of this esoteric system, which delineates the functioning and flow of the personality self, including interactions with other types. This system is purported to have been transmitted to Gurdjieff during his spiritual pursuits in the Hindu Kush Mountains of Afganistan. The personality aspect of the system originated with Oscar Ichazo, the founder of Arica, whom I've met along my journey, and through him, during a 40-day retreat in Chile, to Claudio Naranjo.

I had been co-leading one of Claudio's groups with Hameed Ali. Hameed later came to call himself Almaas, and teaches a group named the Diamond Path. The enneagram study encompassed 10-30 hours of my time each week for a number of years. It was very intense, elucidating hidden nooks and crannies of one's self and allowing a profound and dynamic map depicting one's functioning patterns in numerous circumstances. We signed secrecy contracts every three to four months agreeing not to transmit or teach this oral tradition. No books had been published on the topic at that time. I have shelves of documents on the system, many still secret, on my bookshelf.

So I was taken aback by the profundity of the synchronicity of finding this symbol covering the table at the house of this almost mystical John Cooke, whose origin for me was the inner message of my very own interior landscape. There was nothing more central in my leisure pursuits at the time than my enneagram studies.

I looked more closely at the table and discovered that it also contained a Tarot deck I had never seen before, which I later learned had been created by John Cooke through channelings he had received when he had been living near Carmel, California years before.

At this moment in time I knew beyond a doubt that there was no other spot in the entire world that could have any greater significance for me. My own instinct, my own power within, my own inner voice was indeed to be trusted above all else. My breath-activated koth, or instinctual body center, had most definitely led me to be at the right place, at the right time, with the right people.

I sat down. John introduced me to his sister, Alice Kent, of Kentfield, California. By chance or more likely destiny, it was the very city in which I was teaching Chemistry. I later found out that the town had been named after her family, an old Hawaiian sugar family, and that her primary residence was only a few miles from my college. I ended up visiting with her many times over the next number of years.

After these introductions, John looked at me intently and spoke to me in a slow and deliberate manner. "The night before you arrived, I had a dream," he said. "And in that dream, a total stranger came to my house bringing a pot of honey and oysters, the best of the land and the best of the sea." He paused and proclaimed, "You've forgotten the oysters."

He proceeded to teach me the enneagram of the Tarot, which I have taught on occasion after having received permission to teach the enneagram components from Claudio. I returned for three days getting to know John and learning from him.

He told me how he had been a dervish in North Africa. He had fought there and returned with a friend retracing their previous routes. Along the way he was graciously welcomed into a village and feted for three days. The tribal leader had recently died and his wife, the wise woman of the village along with her son, who was destined to assume leadership, asked them to stay. Little did John know at the time that he was fulfilling a prophesy of 20 years by his very presence.

John's friend decided to leave with their jeep, but it was agreed that he would return in two weeks. John studied and learned many esoteric teachings from the woman and her son. They later proved to be of great use to many people whom he encountered along his path.

The day before his friend was to return, the woman asked John to go into retreat with her son into a cave for 18 days. John felt that he had absorbed as much as he could at that point and refused. The crone became irate and shook her fist under his nose, cursing him. That night a high fever came upon him and he became increasingly ill. His friend did not return until eight days later. He was then transported by jeep to Tangiers. However, by the time doctors treated him, he had permanently lost the use of his legs. He bore his infirmity well, bearing no bitterness towards anyone.

The most important thing I retained from this experience was not the information that I had been taught, which was certainly rich, but rather the very fact that there actually was a John Cooke in the village of Tepotzlan and that what he had to teach me made sense in the framework of my journey through life. This experience was my quantum leap into trusting my inner messages. It was the moment I knew that my body's magnetic center was awake and alive and could get me to the right place at the right time with the right people, by focusing on the messages from within.

A few years passed. A time came where all at once I knew that John was going to die. I was inwardly certain that I had to pay him one last visit, and that it must be undertaken very soon. I sent him off a letter that I would be coming, which in fact never reached him before I did.

I purchased another special pot of honey and took it to

Baba Jivananda to bless, telling him that I had a friend who was dying. And then I arranged my trip. Somehow the Sufi, Reshad Field, whose taped lecture had originally led me to Tepotzlan, heard that I was about to visit John Cooke. I was told that John's Sufi name was Rasheed and that Rashad and John somehow had been searching for each other for 23 years. Rashad asked me to meet with him before I went.

At our meeting Rashad handed me a psychic, invisible line. He told me that I must maintain a conscious awareness of the line throughout my journey until I reached John Cooke. I was then to hand it to him. I took on this task, never bothering to question it's validity, purpose or sanity. I did this task well, somehow managing never to drop my awareness of the line until the transfer.

When I arrived again in Tepotzlan, I immediately hiked to his house, breaking the heel of my shoe on the way.

I arrived at his door, hobbling a bit, taking him by surprise. I felt quite pleasantly startled to find him looking so well, and very foolish in assuming that his death was eminent. I fulfilled my task by transferring the line to him, and experienced an immediate relief from the burden of the undertaking. Until that moment of transfer, I didn't realize how much weight I was experiencing from the endeavor. Today, I ponder the possibility of placing new planetary ley lines of energetic connections and wonder if in fact I was successful in doing so at that time.

It was a light-hearted and joyful visit. His son was visiting from Morocco and he and I connected strongly at once. There were ancient and sacred ruins in Tepotzlan, which were difficult to access high up a steep mountain path, where one had to climb through areas of huge boulders finally arriving at a grating to climb through to the sacred site itself.

John's son and I joined five young Mexican boys who were his friends. We spontaneously decided to make the trek late one day. His son and I wore fairly long Moroccan robes. We spent a long time climbing up but it was worth it to sit in the powerful energy of the ruins. The view from the top was exquisite leading us to dally.

When finally we started down, it was nearly dark. I became concerned for my safety. I didn't know how I could pick my way through the boulders. The young Mexicans went faster and faster, telling me to just let go and run. Boldly I did. I never stopped rapidly running all the way down, my feet hardly touching the ground. I was in a deeply altered exhilarating state. Later I knew that I surely had experienced the "gait of power", an instinctual way of 'feeling-running' in the night of which Carlos Castaneda had spoken in his books. When I relooked at the terrain the next day, it was inconceivable to me that I had been able to run at all.

I left John and his son looking very well and I decided I had been completely in error concerning his eminent passing. Within two months however, vessels in an ulcerated area of his arm burst and he died. Somehow in this window Rashad Field must have visited with him,

186

because much later Rashad wrote a book about John Cooke and his death, called *The Invisible Way*.

This whole period of time demonstrated for me the power of the opening of the dantien, koth or belly center. It gave birth to the incipient realization that truly all of us are always in the right place at the right time with the right people.

This center is literally the gravitational core of one's body in exactly the same manner that the earth has a gravitational center. Gravity exists between any two objects that have substance or mass that can be measured.

GRAVITY

The Law of Universal Gravitation is as follows:

> Every object in the Universe attracts every other
> object with a force directed along the line
> of the centers for the two objects, that is
> proportional to the product of their masses
> and inversely proportional to the square of
> the separation between the two objects.

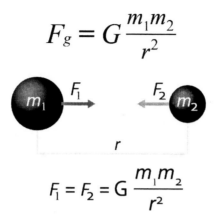

$$F_g = G\frac{m_1 m_2}{r^2}$$

$$F_1 = F_2 = G\frac{m_1 m_2}{r^2}$$

F_g is the gravitational force

m_1 and m_2 are the masses of the two objects

r is the separation of the two objects

G is the universal gravitational constant

This means that any two masses, m_1 and m_2 are attracted or pulled towards each other, not only planets and suns, but even you and me. When I pass a car on the freeway, I notice on the average a slight tendency for two cars approaching each other to get ever so slightly closer. The 'r' on the bottom is how far apart the two things are from each other, no matter what they are. So the farther apart the cars are, that is a bigger 'r', the smaller will be the gravitational pull. The smaller the 'r', the closer the two planets are to each other, and the larger will be the gravitational effect.

To align with and impart consciousness to the dantien, that true gravitational hub of the body, is to activate the instinct that leads one to be aware of being in the right place. The gravitational pull of our bodies for each other, along with the subtleties of each individual's electromagnetic or light field, that is to say their aura, are what scientifically allows and constitutes that which we call karma or destiny.

Just as wars, storms or earthquakes on a planet don't alter the manner in which the entire planet traverses through space, so are we unable to alter the flow of our destiny. We come in with a certain swirl just as surely as the initial big bang kicked off all celestial bodies on their unalterable courses.

However many situations can develop in response to our planet's traversal through space – droughts, El Nino conditions, hurricanes. In the same way we have the freedom as to how we will feel about what is ensuing as we live out the situations of our lives.

Abdy speaks about prayer in an unusual way. He says that it is not really God to whom we pray to make something happen, but rather to ourselves to be aware of what is about to ensue. The purpose of prayer is to activate our awareness of something approaching. This is important so that we will not miss being conscious of it when it finally spirals into our existence. It is prayer that sharpens our focus onto some particular realm so that our consciousness will not miss a shift or nuance in that aspect of our life.

My experience of finding John Cooke in Tepotzlan was the moment I knew that my body's magnetic center was awake and alive and could get me where I needed to be, by focusing on the messages from within. It was such a remarkable and specific match of surprising internal information matching external circumstance, that it forever after allowed me to trust and honor the power of my inner Self to lead me along a perfect path for my highest good.

This scientific attunement to the electromagnetic aspects of the center of our own force field needs to be interpreted by the body. It is the subtle physics of the forces involved that are then transformed through one's physical body channels, which act as an electrical transformer, into a different kind of signal, which can be more easily interpreted. The input might thus manifest as thought, visions, emotions or intuition, which can then lead one to the exact spot that is already mandated by the fields. In this way, we live out our predetermined karma or destiny. Thus, there is no way to be wrong.

Chapter Eight: Israel

JOURNEY TO THE HEART

I entered into the journey to Israel to do a session with Abdy. I knew nothing of the group, Jon Marc Hammar, also known as Jayem, who led and organized the pilgrimage, or anyone in it.

I felt intimidated when I discovered that I would be the only Jew at the gathering. I had been raised Jewish and still belong to a Temple. However, I had not had significant connections with Christianity. After seeing that our journey would take us to many famous sites of the New Testament, I realized that I needed some pre-trip study.

I had been in Bible contests as a child, but only on the material contained in the Old Testament. I started reading the New Testament but realized that I couldn't finish it before the trip began. I reverted to some books, which presented an overview of the material, but saw that they too were more than I could digest in the time I had. I even in desperation used a Cliff Notes synopsis of the New Testament.

So, being so unfamiliar with New Testament history left me unprepared for what transpired immediately after paying for the trip. I was deeply taken by surprise. From the moment I signed up I became consumed by past life memories from a life lived with Jesus and the certainty that this was a "class reunion" of sorts for those who had been together at that time and place. I knew that I had decided to book this trip centuries ago. I still find it more than amazing that within the 50 of the group, as far as I know, there was a general assumption with us all that this was so.

I have not had a connection in this life with Jesus Christ until the day of the Harmonic Concordance and lunar eclipse of Nov 8, 2003. Interestingly, that was the day Jon Marc Hammer's CD of the Lord's Prayer in Aramaic arrived. I had ordered the recording because the group was to do a series of daily meditative exercises before the trip began. Listening to or chanting the Lord's Prayer in Aramaic was part of the process. I was one of the last to sign up, so I was excitedly awaiting its arrival to try to catch up with the group process. As I listened to it the ancient words of Aramaic washed into the fibre of my being.

The next day while I was chanting a long Sanskrit chant at the ashram I attend, Jesus appeared before me in tremendous Light. It was not possible to distinguish his features, because the luminosity predominated. It shone from his entire body, but especially from his head, and I was reminded of the religious art depicting halos. There was an internal recognition that I had known his energy before during that life I had lived in his presence 2000 years ago.

Then quite unexpectedly Jesus stepped into the physicality that I occupy – my very body- and filled it completely, taking up residence. I felt permeated throughout by the most wonderful, cradling, soothing heat nurturing my very essence. We merged on a molecular level and this union created a profound shift in my worldview in subtle and not so subtle ways.

I knew that I had received the ultimate gift of the Lord's Prayer after hearing it just that once in Aramaic. I had received far more fruit than I ever could have imagined from the trip even before it began. Within about a week, I knew the Lord's Prayer in Aramaic by heart.

I left for Israel by way of England on November 20, 2003. Abdy and I were to meet in London and travel together to Tel Aviv. He gave sessions in London, Belfast and Dublin in the days preceding the trip and our attempts at phone contact left a wake of missed voice messages.

I had hoped to travel with him to the airport. The night before our departure, I was staying at a colleague's house in London and I had not told Abdy its location. Abdy called, but my hosts wouldn't wake me. I arose very early the next morning for the hour journey to Heathrow Airport, having no idea where Abdy was. However, I knew I'd find him on the plane. I got on a London Underground train car at about 5:30 AM. To my utter shock, after about three minutes, Abdy walked up to me, and we rode the remainder of the way to the airport together.

ABDY'S ISRAELI SESSIONS

Upon arriving in Tel Aviv, Abdy and I easily found the largest portion of the group who had traveled through Frankfort, Germany. The Australian contingency, who had arrived earlier in the day, had returned to welcome us. A number of participants had arrived days earlier. Although I knew only Abdy and a few others from the London session of his, which I had attended, there was an immediate comfort and ease in this group. There was more of a feeling of the intimacy of a family and no flavor of being strangers.

Besides the power of the sites we visited, the chanting we did together at those sites, and the amazingly open hearts and still minds of the group members, what is most memorable for me are the energy sessions, which Abdy conducted.

The new moon and solar eclipse of November 23 was the day of the closing of the Harmonic Concordance. The group had a full and long day of swimming in the Dead Sea, hiking, chanting and meditating at the Qumran Caves, where the Dead Sea Scrolls were discovered, and finally spending the evening with song and dance around a bonfire overlooking the Dead Sea while lightening flashed throughout the sky for hours without rain.

When we returned to the hotel, Linda, from Kauai, gathered together those of us who still had the energy, to add our meditative input to the creation of a sacred blend that she started preparing at the initiation of the Harmonic Concordance in Hawaii on November 9th. After a lovely ceremony, she asked that we sit in meditation and allow our combined energies to flow into the blend. I sat in a full lotus on the floor in meditation very close to the center table on which rested the coded (sacred energy imbued) water she had brought, along with other sacred objects donated by others in the group.

Abdy was in a chair sitting behind me. After a short time I entered into a deep meditation. All at once, I was jolted in surprise to feel Abdy grab my head in a vigorous and swift motion resembling and sounding like a chiropractic snap. My head shifted up, face to the ceiling, and back at a strange angle. He leaned me backwards unto his leg and still I maintained my meditation posture at this seemingly impossible angle. After a while I righted to vertical.

From the moment he touched me, I dove into the now familiar, profoundly deep energy state he elicits, not laying down this time, but in my meditative posture. Later, others told me that he worked on a number of people that night. Nancy, our photographer, was taking pictures and told me that she was struck by the trust I have in Abdy and his energetic work to allow this manner of his work, which I believe was not characteristic for him. I sat motionless in that state, being aware of and hearing all around me but completely disinclined to interact, content in pure awareness, until perhaps 3AM in the morning, a few hours later.

Abdy gave the first large group session at the Nof Ginosar

kibbutz on the shores of the Lake of Tiberias (Sea of Galilee). I remember that the group seemed to relax and unite more deeply after this time. Later Abdy said that this was a session for the individuals.

The most powerful session of the trip was the one Abdy gave the Thursday night we returned to Jerusalem from the Sea of Galilee. Actually that day was the most profound of the trip. It was Thanksgiving and Jayem, Abdy and a yoga instructor of our group, Elizabeth, had led the group through five hours of a ceremony in which each of us was baptized in the Jordan River.

It was only after the trip that I realized that the group's five-hour Baptismal ceremony in the Jordan River very appropriately occurred on Thanksgiving Day.

The night before, a Sufi Sheik from the town near Sefat, had come and led Zhiker (Sufi chanting or devotional prayer) with us. He had answered our group member's question by saying that now is the time to lift all the veils and allow the light to enter everywhere. It is time for all to be revealed.

At the end I went over to thank him and he grabbed my hands and told me that out of everyone there, he was most happy to see me.

When he grabbed my hands, a transmission occurred, such that I was up all night with kriyas (shaking) save for perhaps an hour. All through that night an ever-growing inner directive to speak to the group before the Baptism arose within me somehow generated by the encounter with the Sheik.

I asked Jayem for permission to speak that morning at breakfast, and he OK'd it. I was in a deep altered energy state up to the time I spoke.

Elizabeth, upon anointing us at the Church of Beatitudes, had whispered in my ear, "Be the voice of the feminine Christ," and I prayed that I might be so in speaking to the group at that time.

The night before the baptism, a woman in the group named Rosemary, had asked a male group member to request permission for her to speak to the Sufi. She had approached the Sheik on her knees to ask her question. She described a dream in which she wanted to comb Mary's hair, but Mary's veil prevented it. Finally the veil came off covering all of Israel and Palestine. She asked what her dream meant. The Sheik had answered her question by responding that now is the time to lift all the veils and allow the light to enter everywhere. It is time for all to be revealed.

The subservient position, in which she had approached this holy man, had highlighted for me the manner in which the female energy has deferred to the masculine in the patriarchal age that has predominated these most recent millennia.

I commented that now at this second window (eclipse) of the Harmonic Convergence a nodal point existed. The nodal point is that of the masculine predominance coming to be

balanced by the descent of the feminine goddess energy, so that the amplitude of the difference of our male-femaleness is at a minimum. It is at this null that our issues of masculinity/femininity can most effectively be healed.
.

I first addressed the women. I said that it is now a time to bring all secrets to the light. It is no longer appropriate to speak in secretive whispers, ashamed, "I've been raped". So I said that if now or in any life you women have been molested, raped, beaten, or forced into subservience and perhaps even forbade yourself from remembering these things, NOW is the time to bring them into the light and be healed. It is the time to forgive those who've hurt you and in so doing to forgive yourself. It wasn't your fault.

It surprised me when I spoke to the men of the group that I focused on the pain of men having been aggressors towards women and also those who witnessed these things. I said the following to the men.

If you've had to be macho to prove yourselves, if you've denied your heart and gentle nature, if you've been the aggressor – killed, battled, attacked, made war – raped, beaten – or have used your maleness aggressively – or if you have witnessed and thus acquiesced to male aggressiveness, NOW is the time to bring these to light and forgive yourself and be healed.

And if your Soul has residues of these gender discomforts that you have brought to the level of bickering and hassling in your marriages, partnerships and interactions –

NOW is the time to forgive and thereby be forgiven.

Lift the veil.
Let the all-pervasive God light of the Universe,
Let the universal God light of this group,
Let the Divine light of the flame of love that is your own
heart and being,
Cleanse and wash you pure,
So that as we enter this new age we can be purified and
truly start anew,
In our own Light, and in our own Love.

This is what I chose to say before we were baptized. A few others also spoke. David Schock, from our group related the following:

"I personally went through a major encounter in Israel with the relationship between and the divine drama of masculine and feminine within me. I feel that the harmony of the two, personally and globally, will be the hallmark of the "new age". This comprises the end of the perception of separation, of differing interests.

One concern I feel called to speak about at the Baptism is the importance of the masculine finding and staying in a place of awareness of it's own innocence, as the feminine Christ emerges more fully, both as an appropriate thing in itself, and as a form of not enabling feminine projection. I have found that men can often, in their own desire to serve the emerging feminine, take on more of the responsibility for women's anger and blame, than can at times be Holy, or accurate. My feeling is that we, men and women, are EQUALLY innocent, and have also been equally immersed in the illusion of guilt, that is, we have engaged equally in acts, which the egoic mind would consider to be mortally guilty."

We then, each of the 50 of us, approached Jon Marc (Jayem) and answered questions he had put to us on what we chose to be de-vested of in the Baptismal ceremony, on what purification we intended for ourselves. Jayem created this sacred Baptismal portal as we all became mesmerized by the awesome mystery of five hours of baptism.

As I watched, it seemed to me that Abdy, who along with Elizabeth, stood in the river for the entire time, was doing a separate energy session with each person who he baptized. Afterwards I talked to Abdy asking him and he said that it was the first time he had done his sessions holding intentions. Each of us said what we wanted the ceremony to mean, what we wanted to divest ourselves of before we entered the river. Abdy said that during each baptism, he took each individual's intent as his own as he allowed the energetic process of his sessions to transpire.

When it was my turn, I asked to have all thoughts, feelings, actions, words, which were not in alignment with God's to be washed away, as well as anything preventing my body from being a Temple of God.

I chose complete immersion and remember dissolving into the pleasant coolness of the Jordan River. I asked a fellow group member to collect water from the river at the moment of my Baptism and presently have it sitting on my puja (altar) in my meditation room.

As I viewed the beautiful CD of music and photos from the trip that our official photographer, Nancy, produced, I came over time to be perplexed by a picture of one woman, whose identity I could not figure out. Abdy was holding her arms upward in a 'V' and she looked in a transfigured state with an up-raised head.

Eventually, I studied the woman's features. One day, while looking at myself in the mirror, I raised up my head and noticed a similar feature to this woman, an unusual formation of the nostrils. After studying her hands, I found similarities to mine as well. Eventually I asked the photographer, and was shocked to discover that it was ME. The moment of the Baptism was so profound as to created a look I had never seen in myself. It explained to me why more and more over time I am led to stretch my arms upward, in just the manner of my Baptismal moment.

When first I read about the trip's agenda, it was the baptism that made me most uncomfortable. Certainly as a Jew, I couldn't imagine engaging in this process. However between the signing up for the trip and the baptism, my very foundations shifted in such a way that the process was most natural and honestly in tune with the depths of my Soul. I could not imagine a truer Baptism than that which transpired in the Jordan River with Abdy being the instrument of the baptism.

It was only after the trip that I realized that the group's

five-hour Baptismal ceremony in the Jordan River very appropriately occurred on Thanksgiving Day. The most powerful session of the trip was held later the very same day at the Knight's Palace Hotel in Jerusalem. In doing this session, the group shifted the energetics of the planet as well as the region.

The group returned that night after having left the kibbutz on the Sea of Galilee, after the long 5-hour baptism to our hotel in Jerusalem. It is this same hotel that the pope stays at on his journeys to the Holy Land. Although very tired, Abdy told the group that those who chose would reconvene to do a session for Jerusalem, the crown chakra of the Planet, that same evening. He asked us all to hold no intent.

I was helping to set up the room for the session that evening and was surprised to find that our meeting space had been given out to another group. It was only a half-hour before those, who still had the energy, were to reconvene. I was told that there was a choice of a long, narrow room adjoining the dining room or a small open space near a bar-like area. Abdy came and looked and picked the long, narrow room, which was apparently infrequently used and dirty. The staff quickly cleaned it and group members brought down pillows and blankets for the floor so that lying down was a possibility. At the last minute, one of the staff informed Abdy that the space he had selected had walls, the lower half of which were actually the original walls of the old city of Jerusalem!

I was one of the first to be touched that evening and

immediately fell into a profound and uncluttered state of mental suspension. I lay for a while on the floor in an expansive state of peace. However, as the floor space was limited, Abdy soon pulled me up and placed me vertically against a wall of the room. There was no perturbation of my internal state during this process. The sense of horizontal and vertical felt identical in my body, the lying on the floor or against the wall. Although I watched those around me in the room and Abdy as well as some other group members working the energy, the depth of my state remained unchanged.

There was a slight protuberance in front of my face in the rock wall. I placed my forehead, my "third eye" or ajna, 6th, chakra, on that spot and was stunned.

What I saw was like a peephole, which allowed me to watch a 'television show'. As soon as my head touched the wall, tableaux of life in old Jerusalem, perhaps during the time of Christ, appeared before me as if they were actually occurring on the other side of the wall. They were simple scenes – the market place, children playing in the street, common life actions from an ancient time. Each time I raised my head the picture would cease. Each time I placed my head on the wall a new view of life in the old city would instantly be there. That continued for the rest of the session.

At the end we all came together spontaneously near the center of the room, with Abdy at the center, physically merging into one heart of pulsating, breathing love. Our bodily borders were blurred for me – I felt and was and became ever so many bodies touching together in the purest, most abundant, infinitely satisfying Union of Spirit and Being. I have no idea how long we remained together in this melding.

Gradually in silence and with great ease, we gently dispersed, each of us into our own room. There was no feeling of separation. Perhaps that moment was the apex of the merging that has truly forged this group into one living, breathing organism on some subtle level - One Heart of Love.

Later I asked Abdy how powerful the vortex of 'joined energy of no intention' that this group had produced had been. He commented that the energetic vortex created by the group had successfully extended out even further than the City of Jerusalem into the adjoining countryside.

The last group session Abdy conducted was that at Ibrahim Abu El-Hawa's house on the Mount of Olives near the University. Ibrahim allows peaceworkers of every religion to live free together for any length of time in this house he maintains.

Abdy was scheduled to give a session on one of our last nights there after a visit to Bethlehem in the West Bank. Our group ws one of the only tourist groups to visit West Bank at that time and the line of vehicles attempting to exit and return to Israel was long and nearly not moving at all.

As time passed it became clear that there was no

possibility of arriving on time for Abdy's session on the Mount of Olives. I was sitting behind Abdy on our bus. After the realization that it was getting very late for his commitment, I watched as he somehow shifted into a deeper relaxation and acceptance of the perfect unfoldment of what was happening. Suddenly our bus was pulled out of the long line and moved to the front. Before I knew it we were on our way. After dropping off some of the group at the hotel. The rest of us together with Abdy arrived at Ibrahim's house for the session.

The house was very small with almost no floor space. There was no equipment to play the music he usually uses during a session. Abdy started chanting strange sounds and notes of unusual, neither eastern nor western, tonalities. Occasionally he sang in a very exotic and ancient sounding language. It felt like a "Soul language". When I later asked him what it was, he told me that he didn't know but that he often chanted it during his sessions, although seldom aloud. As Abdy touched them, people went into various states, some sitting, some lying down. A group of the residents seemed intimidated watching the process and went downstairs for tea. I followed to give them someone to talk to about what they were witnessing.

After a bit Abdy came down and worked on me. First he touched my head and throat. I was instantly far into the depths of my being. After a bit, while I was lying there, Abdy returned and pulled on my left large toe resulting in a painful cramping in my foot. Yet I was able to remain completely relaxed. Still later he returned, and pressed his hand on my upper chest near my neck in such a way that I felt as if his fingers had actually penetrated into my chest cavity. I coughed a bit and became instantly VERY COLD. I ended up having something like a chest cold, but not really. It continued for many weeks. There was a raw sensation in my throat and a little cough. Yet I knew it wasn't really a sickness. It felt as if it were a physical purification relating to my having had smoked decades before.

For the fourth time in the session Abdy returned to me. Then all of a sudden he grabbed both my big toes with one hand and swiftly held me upside down in the air hanging by my toes. I was so deep into the energy that even though my calf was cramping like mad and I was therefore in considerable pain, I could totally relax hanging there upside down. I never opened my eyes from the first moment he touched me. Abdy set me down and after quite some time I noticed that I was warmer. After a long time I thought that perhaps he had placed me between two people. Only after the session did I realize that he had placed me actually in contact with another member of the group. The other group member was also so deeply into that profound state that neither of us realized that we were touching until the end of the session.

Night after night after I returned, I found myself hanging by my toes upside down in my dream state, All night long as I hung there inverted, the Lord's Prayer in Aramaic flowed seamlessly through my sleeping state. I felt myself the embodiment of the Hanged Man card of the Tarot. Later, someone told me that some of those crucified during the time of Christ were in fact crucified upside down and since this trip to Israel, I believe that I could have been one of them.

There were two more sessions that I saw Abdy conduct in Israel. One was in the upper room of St. Mark's Church on the second day of our stay, when the entire group was chanting, praying and meditating with the nun, Jostina, at this profound site of the Last Supper. Although Abdy did not touch people, I watched as he leaned against a far wall working the energy, although not in an obvious manner, during the evening.

The last session I saw Abdy give in Israel was in the West Bank, in Bethlehem. The group had stopped for lunch and souvenirs at a gift shop of the Kando family, friends of George, who was our Palestinian tour guide throughout the trip. He also became a member of our group and even brought his wife to our last formal dinner and closing circle. At the tourist shop, the Kando family had generously given a free lunch to the entire group. Just before we left, Abdy had the group hold hands and form a Star of David formation. All the employees of the store were invited into the center of this formation. We thanked them, chanted the Lord's Prayer in Aramaic and then Abdy touched each of them. Over and over around Abdy, I watched him honor every person he encountered in an identical fashion. Bus driver and tourists, shop workers and those they serve – these usual and automatic distinctions evaporated in the one heart of shared humanity of us all.

THE WESTERN WALL

Some of my most powerful individual experiences of this journey involved the Western (Wailing) Wall.

When we first went up to the wall at sunset on Saturday our second night of the trip, Rabbi Eliyahu McClean, a Rodef Shalom, or pursuer of peace, led a Havdalah service as Shabbat ended. He traveled with us throughout the trip,

After our ceremony we approached this ancient site of prayer said to be the walls of the original first Temple in Jerusalem. I placed my head on the wall. It acted as a magnet pulling an etheric grey smoke out of my body through my forehead and hands into the rock. Then up out of the wall came the pain of Jewish suffering throughout all ages – the six million slain in WW II, the Spanish Inquisition, the loss of the Temple – tears flowed and my heart opened sending peace and blessings to all those trapped in suffering. Then the tears became thoughtless and wordless as a vision of the 'Holy of Holies', the Ark of the Covenant in the first Temple opening on the Jewish Day of Atonement, Yom Kippur, arose, leaving me in wordless awe.

Later, while I was meditating in the Essene caves overlooking the Dead Sea at Qumran, I found myself spontaneously starting to pray for peace. Almost immediately I realized that this wasn't how to plant the seeds of peace in Israel. What came to me was an experience with Rabbi Zalman Schachter-Shalomi, with whom I'd lived in a group house in Berkeley long ago.

My daughter and I both needed Hebrew names at the time of her Bat Mitzvah. Reb Zalman told us each to meditate for a week on what quality we would each like to imbibe. She decided that she wanted to align with inner peace so he gave her the name "Shalva" – inner peace. That is what came to me at the Essene caves – that each of us in the group (and the area) who could completely come to a place of inner peace and forgiveness would plant that seed in this region so needing peace. I shared this with the group. Synchronistically, I also discovered that the rabbi we were with that night around the campfire (Rabbi Ochad) as well as Eliyahu, the great peaceworker who traveled with our group, were all students of Zalman's.

Later back in Jerusalem our group joined with a weekly peace vigil overlooking the Western (wailing) wall. Each person passed a rose quartz heart-shaped rock which Felicity, a poet from England, had brought along on the trip, and spoke their individual wishes/blessings for peace.

Then we were asked to meditate for peace. As I started meditating, everything which was not at peace in me arose and collided with the peace attempting to establish itself within. For each one of these, item-by-item and person-by-person, I somehow found that place of forgiveness and hence peace within, through choosing to release each grievance.

At the end of the meditation I saw a golden white light

emit from each of our hearts and come together laser-like at our joint center. One part of the united beam rose vertically and another shot out horizontally like an atomic bomb blast wind covering the region and the globe in peace. I had successfully found that place of peace within myself.

The group scattered for lunch, but I couldn't. Instead I went to the women's side of the wall and again placed my forehead on it for 45 minutes. The women around me engaged in their usual cacophony of weeping and praying. From the moment my head touched the wall, I was in a serene state of total and profound inner peace.

What transpired amazed me. Gradually I noticed that the women closest to me had stopped weeping and had fallen into silence. As time passed more and more women ceased engaging in the clatter of praying and crying. After about a half-hour I realized that the only sound I could hear anywhere was that of birds chirping. The inner peace I was experiencing had spread to the other women and to the wall itself.

Unlike my first experience of the wall, when its pain had overwhelmed me with tears, this time I was able to somehow give the gift of inner peace to the wall and leave its seeds in that place. It seemed to me that this moment was the fulfillment of some ancient personal assigned seva (sacred service) that had led me to this place at this time.

Our last group roundup of the trip with Abdy was very powerful for me. We each shared what had been most important for us during our stay. Abdy spoke to us for a while and then gave each of the 27 of us gathered there a flower- purple for the women, yellow for the men. We sat for our meeting under the glass pyramid ceiling of that room.

At a seemingly random moment in his talk, in a voice that for me connected to the ultimate origin of universal Power, Abdy channeled a Force directly to us. His voice was like nothing I have heard before or since. Its impact penetrated to the core of my very molecules. Much later I thought that it had perhaps been a DNA activation for the people. Months later Abdy commented to me that it had perhaps been a DNA activation for the planet.

When we broke at about 10:30 PM I was filled with energy. The hotel staff was waking us up at 1 AM for breakfast and the 2AM journey to the airport. I knew it would be useless to try to rest. The intense energy of our farewell meeting left me unable to sleep.

I wandered through the hotel for a while and finally found another group member, David Schock, up and about and willing to walk around the city. We strolled for an hour or so through the mainly deserted streets, shops and rooftops of the old city. Moonlight shone on the amazing beauty of curved arches, narrow walkways and the alluring angles of the old city.

Finally we found ourselves at the Wailing Wall, which was surprisingly crowded for that time of night. I went alone to the women's side and placed my head on the wall.

Immediately, I again saw the Ark of the Covenant from the first Temple. However this time all four sides had flung open and tremendous light was streaming forth on all sides. Multitudes of people were dancing and singing in exquisite joy around the Ark. From each upper corner of the Ark a ladder rose upwards. Down each of these ladders angelic and other celestial beings descended. Gabriel was blowing his horn. When I later shared this vision with Reb Zalman Schachter-Shalomi, he told me it was Jacob's ladder.

I felt that the Universe was pleased with this group's work and with our sessions. I left the wall and before I knew it, I was on my way home. What a powerful vision had been given to me to seal the trip.

I was so surprised when long after our journey, Felicity from our group sent me a picture, which exactly depicted my last vision at the wall. It is called *Ark of the Covenant*, by Devorah Curtis, "Thou shall be the living Ark of the Covenant" from the Academy for Future Science.

Over a year after the trip, I saw a tarot deck called Sacred Geometry by Francine Hart. The cards grabbed me. One particular card jumped out at me, number 47, which is called 'Together'. It depicts a woman and man, standing inside a three dimensional Star of David (Merkabah) with energy spirals at each of the six points of the star. Instantly, a whole bunch of information downloaded in me and I said to myself it's not right, one of them needs to be inverted. And instantly I knew why the energy had directed Abdy to place David and I as he did in the session on the Mt. of Olives, why only we two had individually chosen to speak at the baptism and why it was we two who spent the last moments of the trip together at the Wailing Wall.

On the Mt. of Olives, David and I in our strange placement had become for the group the physical manifestation of the wholeness of masculine/feminine in the form of the inverted triangles of the Star of David. Much as in the body found in Dan Brown's Da Vinci Code, he and I were literally laid out in that form - his legs apart, mine together, our heads linearly opposed in opposite directions. We looked like the three-dimensional Star of David representing the masculine in the point of one triangle and the feminine in the inverted point downward. This posture is also reminiscent of the "blue star" or "blue pearl", the true Merkabah vehicle that is the transmigratory conveyance of transport of the 'Soul essence' between bodies after death.

Even before the trip began, the entire group had been asked to daily practice a meditative visualization of the Star of David being superimposed upon our bodies. Both David and I were led to speak of aspects of masculinity/femininity at the Baptism. Our 'physical union' as the Star of David, that same symbol, which the entire group, each on their own, individually created before the trip, was an extension of the essence of the group's purpose of anchoring the divine masculine and feminine forces at the last spot where they had existed incarnate on the planet previously, in the beings of Jesus and Mary.

David and I somehow found each other, apparently randomly, when we went to the wall together at that last moment in Israel. We were the representatives for the group to seal and anchor, through our connection to the forces that exist in that place of the Wall, the group's energetic and successfully united female/male energy with the Divine.

Years later, I went to a little gathering led by a person, who had met Abdy in Australia. His name was ZaKaiRan and he works with energy and sound. His session was pleasant, but fairly unremarkable, until the end when he toned to each person a strange language that seemed to trigger an immediate response from the level of my DNA. I could not help answering in kind very loudly in what seemed to me to be the same language. There was no option internally. I knew immediately the proper response to his initiating phrase, that it was Lemurian (which I would not have thought I knew before then) and that I had heard Abdy chant it that night at Ibrahim's house. Yet, it went far beyond the Lemurian and really keyed into my DNA. Since that catalytic moment, I walk the reservoir near my house and sometimes more and more of it bubbles up and out of me.

Occasionally other folks walking hear me, even though I am very far away and am not being loud, because it projects and grabs others in a very abnormal way. There are many sounds in it that I have never heard or made consciously before. Pips exuding from all my cells at once and 'shooting up vertically', and deep flappings in the middle of my chest sounding unlike any other sounds I have known.

I had once before felt this DNA seeding at Mt. Shasta, at the same time Abdy was opening the earth's root chakra at Uluru, also known as Ayers Rock, in Australia. There was a break in an ongoing snowstorm on Mt. Shasta at the time, and I drove partially up the mountain alone. Soundless, wordless voices directed me to stop at a particular meadow. I felt that the fifth-dimensional beings of the mountain, the Telos, Lemurians, came to me, entered me and placed some message directly in my DNA.

VIGNETTES OF ABDY AND THE GROUP

There were two small incidents with Abdy that made a particular impression on me.

Abdy and I were shopping in the market of the old city of Jerusalem on one of our first nights there. After a while we realized that we had become disoriented in the winding streets and neither of us was readily able to relocate our hotel, the Knights Palace Hotel in the Christian quadrant of the old city.

We asked a pair of military police for directions. At that time, the police I encountered were usually a very young man and women paired up in this country of universal conscription and mandatory military service. I was amazed on one occasion to see one of the rifle-toting young girls in her military uniform with little pink bows lining the back of her hair. This particular pair said it would be easier for them to show us the way than describe it. We followed them and then recognized where we were.

However, at that point the police encountered a man who was somehow incapacitated, perhaps by drug or alcohol usage, or maybe just mentally incompetent. Although we could easily have gone on our way, Abdy motioned me to stay. He simply stood there until the somewhat delicate situation resolved and the energy was such that I knew he was a large part of the resolution. Over and over, I saw Abdy care evenly and equally, with a great detachment and a great compassion, for EVERY individual he encountered.

In another incident, seven of us, including Abdy, were having dinner in a small outdoor café on one of the last days of the pilgrimage. It was the end of Shabbat as well as the end of Ramadan, and crowds were milling in the streets.

A Russian man was at an adjoining table and, as many other people had throughout our visit, he became intrigued by the unique energy of our group. "What is this group?" he said in broken English. We all looked at each other not knowing what words to use to define ourselves.

Finally Abdy said, "Peace group." The Russian looked puzzled and said, "For or against?" Abdy said "For." The Russian, showing his mettle said, "I am against!" Abdy without a pause said, "Good." The Russian thought we had missed his point and becoming ever more animated, perhaps looking for a debate or fight said, "No, you don't understand. I am against peace." Abdy smiled and said, "Good. For peace is good. Against peace is good."

I knew that Abdy meant it. If one truly believes that the unfoldment of the Christ energy is manifesting perfectly, then energetically all aspects of any situation are necessary, because they would not exist if they were not needed in some manner for nurturing this physical universe. From this viewpoint all of those involved, the peace workers, the insurgents, the wars and the terrorists are somehow each critically needed for the unfoldment of Universal energy, to achieve some cosmic goal beyond the scope of our vision.

Somehow the Russian knew that Abdy and our group were not kidding him. He realized we meant what was being said and he fell in love with us on the spot. He followed us around for at least a half-hour after we left the restaurant.

THE *COSMOPOD* OF LOVE

One evening at the Nof Ginosar kibbutz on the Sea of Galilee, six of us from our group found each other wandering and joined to go to the waters edge together. We decided that we would throw into the water at that Holy site, those subtle qualities that we chose to expunge from the fabric of our being.

This reminded me of the Jewish ceremony before Passover when one gathers all leavened bread crumbs and tosses them into a body of water or burns them to purify the home. This removes the chametz, or leavened items from the dwelling, rendering it pure for only matzoh, the unleavened wafers called the bread of affliction, and used during the exodus from Egypt. Jews escaping from Pharaoh's slavery had no time to tend to the breads leavening, or rising, and could bake these wafers on their heads as they rapidly left pharaoh's lands. Even today, various synagogues hold this Taslich ceremony of tossing out the crumbs. This means leaving old baggage behind.

So the six of us joined closely in what we called a hexapod, the six-pointed/sided form we together constructed from ourselves. With the full attention of the group, each person gathered some pebbles into their hand. One by one we named each pebble after one of our inner demons and threw these pebbles of imaginary impurities into the Sea of Galilee under the stars in the early hours of the morning.

The Star of David was the symbol of our trip and the shape upon which we had meditated before the journey began. We were the living embodiment of this symbol and started to call ourselves the organic cosmopod of love. A strong bond was forged which has for most lasted through the subsequent years.

Another profound moment occurred at The Church of the Beatitudes. There, two women of our group, Elizabeth and Diane, were each a pillar of equanimity and calm, as they whispered different individual profundities into our separate receptive ears, while anointing our foreheads with oil as we stood with closed eyes in a circle. I was shocked by one of the indications I received. It was, "Be the voice of the Feminine Christ!". Although it seemed bizarre to me at the time, the meanings have unfolded and continue to deepen over the subsequent years. Looking back, that moment seemed to be an initiation into that energetic.

I've not forgotten even one of those who made this pilgrimage - the color and flavor of each and everyone of them are forever indelibly etched on my soul and for that I am eternally grateful. As someone on this trip has often said – we have a GREAT GOD! And above and beyond that, we, each of us together and apart, living that one Great Heart that we are, are that Great God manifesting.

BLESSINGS BROUGHT FROM HOME

Nearly everyday I walk at a beautiful reservoir across the street from my house. One of the regulars who walked there, was a lovely woman named Lee. When I let her know about the trip to Israel that I was about to take, she asked me to write blessings on a piece of paper and place it in the wall for those whom I see on my walks at the reservoir.

That started for me a profound series of contemplations before the trip. I eventually wrote two identical copies of this blessing. One I placed in a basket to be sent to India and burned there in a Shiva temple. The other copy is perhaps still there in a crack of the Wailing Wall where I placed it

Blessings

Bless me, O Lord, so that I may always ride the wings of
God's intention and purpose.
Make service, blessings and love
The pillars of my existence.

Let my every thought, word, breath, deed and feeling
Be in God's service
And be a blessing to the world
Now and throughout all eternity.

Let Trust, Gratitude, Forgiveness and Love
Fill our beings.

Let health exude from every molecule of my body
And let me maintain a healthy body weight
And eat in a balanced and harmonious fashion.

Bless my family.
Let them value their bodies and Selves
As the Temple of God
And come to know their True Value.
Let them experience
Their own perfection and strength.

Grant them health and happiness, contentment,
satisfaction, abundance and love.
Grant us all righteousness, wealth, pleasure and liberation.

Blessings to my mom and dad,
And all my ancestors and descendants,
To all those I have loved and all those I have disliked,
To those whom I've hurt and
To those who have hurt me,
To all those I have encountered and
To all those I have yet to encounter,
To those easy folks and those difficult ones.
Blessings to all those teachers I have had
And still have yet to know.

Blessings to all those dear souls where I worship,
At school,
At my children's schools,
To those with whom I've sung, walked, and meditated,
To relatives, to friends,
and
To all those living on this planet now and always,
To all beings everywhere
Throughout the Universe,
Throughout all time.

Bless this pilgrimage and all on it.
Let us all be sustained in and as God's Light and Love.
Let us manifest the Divine Will
And live out God's plan
As our very own Self.

Chapter Nine:
Entering Planetary Service

A CONDUIT FOR CHRIST ENERGY

For the next few years I was in communication with Abdy nearly weekly. Long ago Abdy talked to me, at a time when he was going to do a session at my place, about how the "gift" sometimes arises when he has worked in the home of someone. I remember that Abdy told me, "You know Sundari, people can catch the ability to give these sessions from me, when I do them at their place".

I was intrigued by this remark, and even more so when it came to happen almost as he had predicted.

Although he had scheduled a session at my house, he wasn't able to get into the country. The session at my place was cancelled. However a few of those intending to be there came to my house anyway and demanded that I work on them. I heard in their request Spirit's demand for me to step into this role. It was a huge leap to dare to do so, but my heart's longing to align with service gave me the boldness to do so.

I searched for a personal modality to create the energetic space for being a conduit for the Maitreya or Christ energy, which flows in these sessions.

My friend, Edwin Courtenay (http://www.ipssissimus.co.uk/ or www.edwincourtenay.co.uk/), the brilliant psychic of great clarity and specificity, who I periodically consult with through receiving channeled readings, discussed the Maitreya energy in this way:

"The Maitreya force is a great and cosmic power, a consciousness beyond description or compare. One of the first three Souls created by the Mind of God as a bridge, to connect mankind to its divine source. It exists within us, within all living things, within all things that have known life as a spark of energy, waiting to be kindled into a flame that will guide us back in time towards the light. It is our beginning and our end, our home, our Source, that of which we are a part. The Maitreya is power then and wisdom. It is compassion and kind truth, enlightenment and empowerment through the recognition of our divinity as conscious beings and co-creators here within this physical universe, this physical world. It is the power to awaken, to enlighten, to catalyze and alchemize. It is the force that opens the eyes of the slumberer, that encourages them to awake to the truth of the presence of the Divine in the world around us, and in our selves. It is the light of God, the Holy Spirit, the sun, the streaming rays of the Divine. It is the awakening force of love and light."

For me the flow of the Christ or Maitreya energy came to involve using my voice to step into the critical space of alignment. Although this differed from Abdy's methods, those attending said they "got it" and even called Abdy later tell him so. People in these sessions often lie on the floor for hours in a suspended state, aware of all around them, but with no desire to do other than just be, sometimes for hours. Everyone said they experienced a lot.

I realized that I could do this work, but at first it didn't seem to be comfortable transmitting in this way. My mind felt unable to embrace a space outside of doership and time. It took many years of practice for me to center in the place that Abdy lived in during his sessions and which I had often asked him to describe to me. When I queried him as to his thoughts during these sessions, he told me that the only thing for him was to have no intention.

I spent much time contemplating what no intention meant. For me, it eventually involved trusting the energy to do its work. I was led to touch people in particular ways and to trust the innate intelligence of the energy to do what was necessary and appropriate without my needing to figure out, analyze or interpret what that was. That is to say, I gradually learned to 'step aside' and to feel that I was not doing anything but rather 'showing up' to be used as a servant of the Divine.

In one reading, years later, Edwin Courtenay described the Maitreya, or Christ energy channeled through the conduit I become in these sessions in the following way:

"Part of the teaching work that you will do will absolutely involve initiations, Christ like transmissions, Yes! Similar to what you did before and similar to what Abdy does, but also fundamentally quite different. They will be more specific. They will be more specific to the different

workshops, retreats, and pilgrimages that you are guided to run. So if you're doing something in Egypt, the transmissions will be very much to do with the working with the rays and energies of the ancient Egyptian deities. If you're working in specific places, the transmissions will be about working with the harmony of the sacred geometry of those spaces; attuning people to those sacred geometries, to the keys that are held within the dimensional matrices of those locations. So where as Abdy is working with a single thread of light, the Christ light, you will be working more with a tapestry of color, and you will be plugging into the different threads that are associated and connected to the different people, and to the different places. So it will be individual attunements for the people to the varying different expressions of the divine light that they need in order to grow and evolve, rather than being attuned or fed by the same stream of energy."

Giving sessions was a huge stretch for me. It was an enormous step to start touching folks and letting them fall back to be caught and laid on the floor. There were globally four other people I knew, who also had started doing similar sessions after having received them from Abdy.

One of my greatest gifts is to connect people. I started an email networking between us so that we could share our experiences stepping into this work and the side effects we experienced in doing so. The incredible similarities of our processes were remarkable.

Even before I met Abdy, my friend Elan, who was one of

the earliest to enter into doing this energy work, would call me immediately after his sessions with Abdy, and I would 'catch' the energy and shake all night. It happened to him too. For a year or so when I connected in this way, I couldn't sleep most of the night due to the fairly constant shaking of my body for hours on end. Sometimes I would go up to my meditation room so as not to keep my husband awake.

This shaking didn't upset me and was actually pleasant in its' own way. Although it kept me from sleeping, I didn't worry about it and found over time that I ended up as rested as I might have been from a normal night's sleep.

I also discovered that when I am linked to Abdy, a session, or the Christ energy directly, I hear that energy audibly as a pleasant high-pitched shimmering scintillation sound. The amplitude of this sound increases the stronger the energy field I feel myself to be in. I often hear this as well coming out of and going into sleep.

I was amazed to discover that all of us entering this work were having the same kind of experiences. Although we each used different methods to connect with the energy and step aside, the effects of that energy on us were remarkably similar. Here are some of their accounts.

Elenor's account was as follows. "It came as a surprise when Abdy said 'when are you going to get up and start doing this work'. I started with a group of people who came together for a meditation. They gave me permission to 'practice' on them. When I started I quickly realized that

227

something happens to me. I enter another dimension and it felt like I always knew what to do."

Kathy shared this. "Yes, I do the same format as Abdy. Sometimes I only look into someone's eyes and they fall back. I can do it one on one and sometimes it happens when I am doing a counseling session.

I remember not feeling worthy when Abdy said to do it, so I had this one on one conversation with God. God's reply to me was...'I am not asking you to DO anything, just show up...I will do the rest'. It still did take courage just to 'Show up', if you know what I mean. Kathy is not there when I do this work. I am in such an altered state that only God is present. I know what is happening at the time but as soon as the moment has passed, I am no longer in that dimension.

Once when I tried to do a massage using this energy, the person couldn't get off the table for one and a half hours. It was another two hours before she could get into her car to drive home. I had to help her walk to a chair on the deck. She was totally in bliss and said that the trees and sky were actually talking to her. So that is when I knew I couldn't do massage any more. That is the best I can explain it.

Also things happen to me during the night. Sometimes my whole body is pounding...releasing energy for the universe. I get up and put some music on and have a session to myself. If my partner is around, his body goes 'off' as well. I just accept that I can enter this state whenever the call is there. (Not my will but Thy will)."

Another friend wrote: "I also know the sound you described. It happens to me too. That sound always has my undivided attention, like it knows my real name and instantly releases my mind and I am one with all."

Here is another description from Elenor. "It takes me to a space where I flip my identification from this body, mind story of myself, to an expanded sense of frequency of energy, in which my mind goes abstract. The energy begins to flow outward from an infinite source somewhere within. It flows through my hands and heart and very powerfully out the top of my head, like a volcano really - whoosh!! With this energy movement there is a sense of all that is not that, going skywards out of my head so that I come to a place of equilibrium in which I have no boundaries, and am one with everyone in the room.

A sense of completion goes with this, like there is nothing I could add to it to make it better, or improve upon it. It just is as good as it gets. When I 'work' with 'others', the energy moves through me to wherever I am given to place my hands and gradually activates the energy field of the 'other', so that they seem to 'fill up' until we are the same mind in the same frequency.

When everyone in the room is 'fizzing' together, it is like a vortex whirls upward taking all that is 'not that' upwards and away, like a huge centrifugal cleanup. Then the 'frequency' seems to become finer and finer. Finally we are all just totally silently, at peace in that place of 'completion' Yum! Love it!

The only challenge in the role is to stay out of my own way so to speak, and let spirit work. I think that is what I am getting better at. It certainly takes the worry out of it. All I have to do is turn up and remove my mind from any attention to the identity that I'm not in truth. After that it's up to Spirit/God to make happen what That wants to make happen. I'm learning to trust the process."

Another friend's account, Maurice's description, was as follows: "In regards to my process and experience while doing a session, it is difficult to describe, however, I will make an attempt to do so. You see, each experience is unique and what flows through me each time is different. My initial impetus is to align myself with Source, and I divest myself of any thoughts of directing the process. There is a recognition of staying in the heart, and through thinking of this connection, staying in relationship to God. I feel a physical vibration flowing through me. What 'usually' happens next, is that, Source/God will start to move my body in specific ways to bring about the healing that is necessary for that individual. In some cases various sounds and mantras emanate from my being and they are targeted at areas on that person(s), to create the necessary shift in body, mind or spirit.

Though I don't like to use labels regarding what I do, I am aware that it is connected to being a 'Rainbow Bridge.' I view this as an energetic 'connector' living in various dimensional realms simultaneously and hence capable of 'bringing Heaven to Earth.'"

It was through the mutual support of sharing our experiences that I gradually felt bold enough to hold sessions at times other than Abdy was giving them. Slowly the voice of Spirit became louder, so that what I was being told to do and when I was being told to do it became internally undeniable.

METAPHYSICAL-SCIENTIFIC INTERFACE

Over a three-year period, I often called Abdy, nearly weekly, wherever he might be around the globe giving sessions. He postulated that these sessions open planetary vortices of light, which assist not only the people involved, but also that global region where they occur. This in turn supports the evolutionary advancement of our planet.

Abdy and I both hold Chemistry degrees. Together, we'd hypothesize theories about the nature of the unfoldment of the planet. I felt that I had been waiting all my life to have these conversations. One of my strongest passions lies at that metaphysical/scientific interface and there are not so many folks, who I have found to play with at that junction of the analytical right brain and intuitive left-brain perceptions.

I had spent a part of one sabbatical leave, meeting with scientists exploring aspects of this junction. I visited with Linus Pauling, Fritzjof Capra, Gary Zukov and William Tiller among others. I found that even when both sides of this scientific/metaphysical interface were strongly present, mutual language base was needed on both sides of the interface to engage in meaningful conversation.

For me the ease of communication with William Tiller was most satisfying during the time of the sabbatical and I was planning to do some research under him. He was working on magnetic cages in order to more effectively measure subtle body fields. The development of instrumentation to measure subtle body fields for earlier medical diagnoses had always been my secret intellectual passion.

Tiller's work aligned with what I had contemplated for years. It was during my days as a healer with Berkeley Psychic School's Monday night Healing Clinic, that I came to know and 'see' that there was a perturbation in the body's energy matrix long before the disease or tumor or illness reached presently detectable levels. Slight molecular shifts occur during the initial pre-creation stage of tumor growth. They generate subtle electromagnetic field shifts capable of detection, through the magnetic field alterations and perhaps even from the 'cellular sound', which is altered during disease as well.

It seemed obvious to me that if I could see/sense/feel these changes, which eventually lead to a full-blown illness or condition, then this should be measurable. Far earlier detection of the energetic dis-ease could be developed fairly easily during the initial stages of illness, long before the condensed nature of the disease manifestation eventually develops into grosser forms. Discovering this mutated and what I see as 'darkened' energy, which eventually can progress to become locked into the body's physical manifestation, perhaps as a tumor or immune system illness, opens new possibilities. Far earlier and more successful treatment could lead to a better prognosis. Treatments could be less invasive and less severe as earlier detection becomes a possibility. Protocols for treating pre-dis-ease could thus be developed.

EARLY DIAGNOSES INSTRUMENTATION

At some point, many years after this sabbatical, a friend of mine from Claudio Naranjo's SAT groups, Josh, had founded a company, Atomis, producing scanning Tunneling (STM) microscopes, which are capable of detecting individual atoms.

Josh informed me that for a rather low cost, which I could afford, he could alter a scanning tunneling microscope at cryogenic temperatures and accomplish my goal of building an instrument that would actually be capable of measuring such subtle body fields. Synchronistically, I have in my background four years of research experience at the University of Chicago in the low temperature cryogenics that the project would require.

As elated as I was at first to hear this, I eventually realized that I needed a group with which to work. With two young children, a college teaching career, a husband, spiritual and music pursuits, I realized that I didn't have the energy or time to was unable at the time to figure out a practical way to undertake this project on my own.

233

continue pursuing my dream of effectively measuring pertinent subtle body fields with diagnostic potential, while maintaining the rest of my life.

A lifelong dream of mine was to work on instrumentation to measure subtle body fields, allowing earlier diagnosis of body problems, such as cancer and AIDS, and hence allow more effective treatments and prognoses.

I did not speak to Abdy about this particular scientific passion, yet our conversations allowed me to indulge my deep urge to use solid scientific principles to explain, elucidate and expand on spiritual matters.

INDONESIAN TSUNAMI SERVICE

I attended various energy transmissions with Abdy whenever I was able. I also found that I could virtually 'tune in' to his sessions by listening to the same music he uses in those programs while I lay on my own floor or bed, in a similar manner to his methods, at exactly the same time as he was conducting them. In this way I received a similar energetic, deeply reminiscent to the way his sessions impacted me.

I attended one of Abdy's sessions in Los Angelis, one in Vancouver, Canada and eventually Abdy and his partner came and stayed with me while she was pregnant with their first child. Abdy gave sessions both at my house and at the college where I taught. Interestingly, a strange phenomenon arose at the college right after his programs there.

There had never been a problem with the squirrels on the large campus of 25,000 students. Yet for the first time ever, for a four-month period after Abdy's sessions, they became aggressively wild, with the squirrels jumping onto people's feet as they walked along the campus paths. Gradually after a time these attacks tapered off, never again to return. I imagined that the squirrels might be sensitive to the newly opened vortices of light and shifted magnetics, but eventually they adjusted to the change.

I didn't see Abdy for the next year and a half, although our nearly hour conversations each week still transpired.

Then came the Indonesian tsunami of December 26, 2004, which killed 230,000. I was deeply moved by the biblical magnitude of the event with the enormous loss of life. I could feel the rumbling of the planetary waves.

I view myself as one of the planetary caretakers. I shine light daily on the earth, it having actually become my heart. When I look inside there it is, the pristine image of the planet where my heart should be.

This internal image originated on the very day that I became a conductor, they call it a caretaker, at the ashram I have attended. This was also my guru's initiation, or Divya Diksha Day. I conducted six lead chanters, harmonium, mridang and tamboura players in an OM Namah Shivaya, Bhupali raga chant celebrating this event.

Short 10-15 minute meditations were common after most of the ashram's chants. In some day or weekend programs, hour-long meditations might occur. A unique, and as far as I am aware, unprecedented programming of a 169 minute meditation, followed the chant which I conducted on that first day in my role as a caretaker.

A profound state of peace along with a feeling of being in 'suspended animation' settled upon me after conducting the short chant. I didn't move for the duration of the 169 minute meditation, which followed. I rested in a nearly thoughtless, imageless, peaceful internal realm.

As the meditation period approached its end, my inner screen came alive. As I watched, my heart metamorphosized into a perfect, gleaming, exquisite replica of earth rotating, suspended in space. My heart had become the planet. It remains so to this day.

It took many months before I finally realized that on my guru's initiation day I had also been initiated, not only as an official caretaker at the ashram, but also simultaneously, as an official caretaker, one of the 36 for the planet. The earth's heart and mine became one. Since that day the most satisfying aspects of my life have become those in which I am doing my planetary work.

I take this work more seriously and feel what I am doing in this role to be more significant, satisfying and joyous than most any other aspect of my life.

THE 36 PLANETARY CARETAKERS

For a long time, I wondered if the ideas that had come to me about 36 planetary caretakers was just an internal fantasy. It was again time for one of my periodic readings with Edwin' Courtenay from England. He is the only one I trust not to direct my thoughts toward some particular future, but to reflect on the present in such a way and with an amazing specificity that opens new spaces in relationships and supplies information, which has often been beneficial in situations which later unfold.

Here is his channeled response to the following question I asked him on planetary caretakers.

My question was: "The day that I became a conductor, they call it a 'caretaker' at the ashram I attended, was also my guru's initiation day. That day I felt as if I were initiated as one of the 36 planetary caretakers. I spend considerable time daily in maintaining and sending light to Gaia, the planet. What can you or the Ascended Masters tell me about the 36 planetary caretakers, if there are such?"

His answer was: *"The mantle or role of the thirty-six planetary caretakers has been handed down from generation to generation to various people in different cultures and periods of time. It is a role that encourages those individuals who are bestowed with the title and power, to become custodians of particular rays or frequencies of energy that are used with intention, in* order to stabilize the planet's present evolutionary phase and to encourage the planet to continue to move forward in its evolutionary cycle. There are many planetary caretakers who work in different ways aligning themselves to different intelligences, forces or powers from the angelic to the elemental. There are those who work with divas of color and sound, those who work with higher expressions of divine consciousness, and those who work with subtle forces for which the world at this moment in time has no name.

The energy that you principally work with, as one of the 36 planetary caretakers is light - light seen and unseen, the light of the inner planes, the light of the mind, and light within the conscious sphere.

The mantle of a caretaker of the planet is something, which is at this present time bestowed from one individual to another by the highest spiritual planes. Some of the 36 caretakers are unaware of their status, but do the work that is asked of them invisibly by Spirit, through an unconscious impulse. It is a mantle, which is bestowed upon people because of the previous incarnational experiences that they have had, regarding those areas of specialty, which they are drawn to use, in order to aid and assist the planet. You have worked with the principles and powers of light many times before and it is because of this, that in this lifetime this mantle has been bestowed upon you."

I spend a considerable amount of time, usually 1-1 ½ hours daily, maintaining and sending light to Gaia, the planet. On a typical day, I might tend to 40 planetary locations, by virtually seeing myself at these sites, shining out from my heart in all directions. I do this work daily, during a solitary walk I make at the exquisite reservoir near my home. I hold no intension, much as in the energy sessions, but allow my purpose to be directed solely by Spirit.

Near the end, I connect each day with all 8 billion hearts on the planet and watch all beings become aware of their heart flames being alight.

I have received the next day, newspaper validation for some of the subtle global work I've done. Since a workshop I did with Tom Kenyon, I view my planetary light work from just outside the Milky Way. I judge the strength and distance of the energy impact emitting from my heart from that vantage point. The more I ground myself to the spot on earth that is being worked on and to the core of my body and heart, the more effective the shining seems to be, jumping upwards and outwards in quantum steps.

My work on Mt. Fuji has gone on daily for about 2 years. It is strange and unique compared to most locations involving more simple 'shinings'. As soon as I connect to Mt. Fuji, by seeing myself located there, a very thin, dare I say infinitely thin line/column of very white light forms. It connects central sun to central earth through that Japanese planetary site. Then I maintain that luminous line to ground myself, as I do work on four African sites, with only internal impetus guiding me to do so.

I always extend my arms the length of the African

continent, calming the Saharan winds by centering at the Dogan Mali Timbuktu site, all the while maintaining the Mt. Fuji infinite light column awareness. Just after the 2011 earthquake, tsunami and Fukushima nuclear disaster, this column has broadened to light being projected in all dimensions. I twice received, to my shock, newspaper confirmation of the efficacy of this work.

At the point when I was whimsically working with the Saharan winds in Mali, I had no idea that any reality supported my planetary imaginings. However, I chose to drop that work for a few days, after doing it regularly for many months. The next day in the newspaper, I read that an American serviceman in Mali had been killed when the strong Mali wind blew over his tent. Later that week, I read in Newsweek Magazine about a new simple cooking stove had been developed for Mali, which was not impacted by the strong winds in the region. Until I read those two accounts, I had no idea that strong winds even existed there, although that was what I was led to work on.

I work in a similar but somewhat different manner in Dafur. Just before unrest in Mauritania, I started working on that region, and in Cameroon, exactly before my niece was assigned to a Peace Corps stint there. I often notice shifting major events in a region after it adds on to the areas on which I'm directed to focus. I trust that the light of shining itself, without further intention or direction, has the innate intelligence to shift energies for the greatest good.

When I was preparing for the 2003 Israeli pilgrimage, the

group was doing the preparatory two-dimensional Star of David contemplation in our body. I had trained myself, through solar flare reports, to recognize when they were occurring by their emotional impact on me. One day, I was out walking and knew a flare was occurring, but had forgotten about it. I felt it overwhelm me. I noticed the moon was at about a 40-degree angle to the sun. I spontaneously used my arms along with the moon's gravity, to redirect the force of the flare towards the moon. I continued this for over an hour. As the energies rushed through my body, they turned the Star of David visualization I was doing, spinning it into a three dimensional Merkabah, which has been with me ever since.

The next morning I was reading a newspaper and to my shock found a brief article commenting on the solar flare. It said, that although severe disruptions in planetary satellite communications had been expected, the energy field from the solar flare had been mysteriously deflected from earth for unknown reasons!! I've saved the article.

My mother lives in Ohio. I have worked on Ohio, connecting with and using my mother's heart to boost the energy in that region. I tend to follow with Washington, DC, using President Barak Obama's heart. After doing that for a few months, I was surprised, in real life, to be able to get my mother and two of her friends front row seats to a town hall meeting with President Obama at a high school 15 minutes from her home!

My best friend from high school has a son who books President Obama's speaking engagements around the world.

Her son thought that his mother and I went to that high school, although we went to a nearby rival high school in fact. That is why he booked Obama there. It was actually the school his mother always wanted to attend, so he thought she had done so. It came to me one day that the juxtaposition of my mom and President Obama in my energy work created that same juxtaposition in reality, whereby she was actually able to meet him.

After working on Rome for a while, where I centered my shining at the Vatican, the priest molestation scandals came to light. Just after working on Greece, riots transpired in that country. It almost seemed at times that shining light on these places led to powerful transformations in 'real life'.

It seems important to me to not have a particular outcome in mind when I work in this way, but simply to shine the heart's Light with love, and the transformation most needed for the greater good of all simply occurs. This works since light has intelligence, a far greater intelligence than I could ever hold. That energy itself can perceive the greatest good of all, where if I "try to do it myself", instead of surrendering to a greater intelligence, my life and work do not unfold as easefully.

For these reasons I, as a scientist, have come to believe in the efficacy of planetary visualizations and how enormous anyone's effect can be in sending light and blessings. When for a time the complexities of my own life didn't allow time for both my networking and this planetary work, I clung to the planetary work as most dear to my heart. It feels to be my sacred duty, beyond any other, and I do know I have the gift of the capacity to truly make a difference on a very practical level, as do we all. I am so grateful to people, who catalyze larger groups of us to do more potent group planetary work together. The butterfly effect of our truly being connected to everyone and everything is very real.

TREE TALK

I often seem to simultaneously exist in multiple dimensions of consciousness. I have the normal flow of life's vagaries involving job, family, money, health, and relationships. However, I am getting more detached from this three-dimensional realm all the time, because far juicier experiences are transpiring simultaneously. There are sounds, light, talks with gods and goddesses, discussions and assisting of those in transition, that is those who have died and are now, 'on the other side', that capture and hold my attention more than the 'normal' 3-D realms. I also have a particular tree that 'speaks to me' every day as I walk the reservoir near my house.

Along the route is a wise old pine tree that I sometimes merge with energetically. The tree seems to connect me to the earth's core, to planetary events, and to Gaia's, our planet's, needs.

At times my energy, especially my heart energy, has sunk deep into the tree's roots, to the center core of the planet while I am hugging this tree. It joins with other energies

243

there - and expands out forming one huge golden heart around the planet.

One day, in communing with this tree, I felt the earth breathing. I breathed in 'I accept' and breathed out the 'Love of God." Its undulating pulsations were beneath my feet. Before then, I never knew the earth breathed. I held my breath to see if it was me breathing, and it wasn't. I wondered if it was pre-earthquake undulations, but I think it was just breathing. Later I could no longer feel it.

Now I saw a merged heart at the earth's core made from the joined love of the tree and me with all of nature, grow to a size a bit larger than the earth, bathing everyone and everything in a much more powerful golden light than any of us could create individually, radiating outward from the very heart of the entire planet.

Each time I repeated the exercise with the tree, I felt a wave of golden energy bathing me from my feet up. Each time there was a time lag before the golden light reached me. It left me in awe. The tree and I were in oscillations of loving each other.

Whimsically, one day I asked this tree for advise, and it told me to 'connect with my roots and feel my head touch the sky.' What ancient wisdom, I thought. Another day I again dared to ask it for advise. It told me 'feel the nutrients flowing through you.' It's a wise tree.

Discreet as I've tried to be, at least for a while, regular walkers at this reservoir came to spot me communing with this tree. Sometimes they'll call me the 'tree lady'. At some point I gave up caring whether or not I was noticed while communing in this way.

One day Becky, the 5 yr old daughter of a reservoir regular, approached me. She inquired as to what I was doing with the tree. I told her that I was listening to what the tree was telling me.

She immediately became agitated with what I guessed to be irritation and a bit of anger. "Trees don't talk", she told me and walked away in disgust. I was surprised and delighted to see her a few weeks later snuggled up against that self-same tree listening intensely.

After the Indonesian tsunami, I was on one of my walks and placed my forehead on a knot of the tree. It became a viewing port, much like my experience of placing my head on the wall in Jerusalem. Immediately, my tree let me connect to the tsunami region and hear the cries of those affected and see what was transpiring there.

Somehow it did not disturb me to hear and see this, but it did plant a seed desire to assist in some way.

Abdy had been traveling the world giving sessions and though we spoke weekly, I hadn't seen him for 18 months. After a time he announced a pilgrimage to Bali, which was the easiest place to go that had some proximity to the affected region. The purpose of the group was to work with the energetic vortex of the area. I interpreted this as extending the group's energy to assist in a subtle re-stabilization of the region after the biblical level of destruction and loss of life that had occurred.

I felt inspired to journey with Abdy's group of 90 to Bali. My scheduling was difficult and it necessitated giving chemistry lectures the day of my departure and the day of my return. Yet, the tree demanded that I go. And I always listen to 'my' tree.

Chapter Ten: Bali

PARTING WAYS

I helped Abdy register all the United States participants on the pilgrimage. I collected monies for him and did his banking in the states. I believed us to be in a good supportive space with each other.

However, from the moment I arrived in Bali our relationship was askew. It was as if the vortex of chaos and destruction that had so recently been operative in this region worked its destructive energies on us as well. In hindsight, I think the universe mandated a separation between us, so that I might grow further into the independence of my own being and power. But during the trip it was excruciating for me to live through the rift that was rapidly approaching.

I had spoken to Abdy just the week before Bali and all seemed normal and well. Yet, my first encounter with him in the lobby of the Bali Nusa Dua Hilton was strange in that he seemingly did not recognize me.

The first evening of the program all 90 of us gathered in the hotel's ballroom. Abdy asked us each to share why we had come on this pilgrimage. He looked around and said, "Sundari, you start."

So, I spoke of my alignment with believing myself to be a planetary caretaker and how my guidance and the calling from 'my tree' had led me to come on this journey.

Without a second's pause, he yelled out at me, "You're a liar!" I was shocked, and in the moment doubted my reality, both about my motives and about what was transpiring. Abdy said I wasn't in Bali for the planet, but to get his attention.

I felt deeply hurt, as he was one of the very few I had shared with, concerning what I envisioned as the new caretaker role I could assume. He knew that over the previous few years I had come to believe myself to be one of the 36 planetary caretakers.

It was just before the trip, that I had received my reading with Edwin Courtenay, which had validated the planetary caretaker role. I did not dare ask him my secret inner wonderings about the possibility of being one of them. To my surprise, in the channeling he unbidden identified me as one of these caretakers.

True or not, Abdy's calling me a liar about my deep yearning to serve the whole, which had come to be of more importance than any other aspect of my life, felt significantly invalidating to me in an arena of my existence that was giving me the greatest juice and joy.

After very deep contemplation, which continued for years following the trip, I came to know that I was not lying. When someone calls one a liar and it isn't true, it seemed to me that there is nothing left to say. I came to slowly realize, with more and more pain, that this was to be his interaction pattern with me for the entire Bali pilgrimage.

In EVERY encounter with Abdy, from the moment I first saw him in Bali right up to the end of the trip, I felt that he interacted with me as if I were ONLY my ego. The constant reflection of that from him felt more than I could bear. At every opportunity he delineated in great detail, sometimes with a tone of disgust, my foibles.

It is always true that each of us, moment by moment, can realize that, in fact, each person is doing his or her best. Even the burglar, the alcoholic, the murderer and yes one's own mom, dad, brother, sister and child is in fact doing their best. Once this is deeply acknowledged and realized, it's easier to accept everyone as they are, and without having a goal of changing or fixing them. It is a moment-by-moment choice to align with the other's light rather than their ego or imperfections. And it's never too late to re-align with that.

When all one chooses to see and acknowledge is the others' light, then they are able to live up to that and align with it, because we learn who we are in the world by the reflection we receive from others. This becomes contagious, because once we choose to see the perfection and light of the 'other', we are able to see that in ourselves as well.

So, the trip continued for me with an ever-increasing abyss between the mentor I cherished and me.

I experienced the sessions as chaotic, with everyone working on everyone, and Abdy's usually powerful work diluted. During one session, one woman and I were interacting silently in the depths of profound eye gazing. Abdy pushed the two of us together tumbling us into each other. I fell onto her and a muscle in my groin was injured. It wouldn't dissipate entirely for a number of years.

I approached Abdy to discuss this incident a number of times. He refused to speak to me about it at that time as well as in an email I sent to him after the trip.

Another wedge that drove me from my previous space of trust arose from another injury on the same trip. At one point I fell in the lobby of the hotel and while I was still lying on the floor temporarily in pain from exacerbating the previous injury, Abdy said, "You are doing that Sundari, to get negative attention." He walked away without helping me up.

It would have taken a lot to get me to detach from Abdy, as my spiritual mentor, and to step more fully into my own power, knowledge and wisdom. I needed to stand on my own feet. So much later, I came to recognize that a separation had to occur. However, at the time, I simply felt a level of abuse occurring, that I was not able to accept. I chose to severe our ties. After the trip, I did write Abdy about my concerns, but he never responded.

Over the years I emailed him a few times, but did not hear back from him. Five years passed until our paths re-connected again, this time from a different level of spiritual equality.

I deeply appreciate the profound connection we had and all I learned from him. His love for humanity and his service to the world is all consuming and beautiful. His work as a catalyst for clearing, healing, attunement and ascension is not in doubt in my mind or heart. I am ever grateful that I have 'caught' from him the ability to give these sessions and for all I gained from our time communing.

I always believed that our path together was not yet complete. Interestingly, another aspect of our interconnectedness arose during the time period that followed, when we were not yet communicating directly again.

I followed his journeys and travels after our split. On one occasion he was back in Jerusalem giving a session. I decided to lie down for it, put on the music he uses during sessions and virtually tune into the energy, while it was occurring. I had done this many times before and at times it was as strong for me as actually being there.

I readied myself, put on the music and lay down. Instantly I received the inner directive to go to Jayem's website. Jayem, Jon Mark Hammar, was the person who led that first Israel pilgrimage Abdy convinced me to attend in 2003. I hadn't even looked at that website in at least a year, so it was a surprising inner directive. My inner guidance grows stronger and clearer all the time. The distinction, between the guidance I receive and my own thoughts, becomes continually sharper. I always obey that inner guidance, when it makes itself apparent to me.

251

So I got up and pulled up Jayem's website. Some words immediately 'highlighted', that is, there was a difference in the quality of 'light' around them. They spoke about Jew and Arab making peace in Jerusalem. All at once I realized that on that original Israeli trip I was the only Jew and Abdy was the only Arab. On some level, the interactions that had arisen between us in Bali were those of an Arab and a Jew. From my Jewish perspective, I felt that an irrational Arab, who had refused to see my good will and service on his behalf, had senselessly attacked me. I entered into a state of blaming and choosing to be the victim, in a sense to validate my innocence. Ah, if only I could as coherently see myself from his viewpoint.

Actually, Abdy is Persian, and Persians are not Arabs, but actually Aryans. So I am really talking about the split between the Jewish and Muslim Middle Eastern perspectives. Yet, at that time I did not understand this distinction.

On a practical level, I tried to imagine his perspective, if he had purposefully orchestrated this separation between us. I had perhaps been calling him too frequently and not at the best times. In the stress of his years as a new father, he likely felt that I wasn't sensitive enough to his needs.

On a cosmic level my days as his student had passed and it was time to stand on my own feet and move toward being my own teacher. Yet one more mentor awaited me before I stepped fully into the reality of taking that voice of my own higher being as my ultimate authority.

In any case, I received the information in looking at Jayem's website that day, that until Jew and Arab make peace, Abdy and I would not reconcile. I instantly understood that on some subtle level, he and I were the hologram carrying the 'Arab/Jew' template of interaction within us, as it was manifesting in the world. There was no way for us to resolve it at this time. We would jointly come to peace as it grew between Jew and Arab in the world.

EQUINOX 2006 IN BALI

During that last March 2006 equinox trip with Abdy, there was for me one potent moment that jumped out from the rest. It was the moment of the equinox itself.

All 90 of us were asked to gather in silence along the ocean at the moment of the equinox at 4:26AM. There we stood in the profound quiet along the water, where still I felt the chaos, death and destruction that had been generated not so far from where we stood.

I am deeply a water loving person. Usually I would have entered into the warmth of the Balinese ocean early on. However, there was something about this particular water that repelled me. I never even made contact with it the entire time of my stay there.

At exactly the moment of the equinox two great gifts descended upon me. Instantly, I realized that my planetary healings had been two dimensional, focusing solely on the surface of the planet. At the moment of the equinox, they switched to beaming not only on the earth's surface, but also above into the atmosphere and beyond and below into the core of the planet and the depths of the seas.

Simultaneously, again at the second of the equinox, a download of an entire piece of music came into my mind all at once. This was what I believe to be a quantum process, that is, it occurred all at once, rather than gradually. The entirety of the music for the Peace Invocation from the Isa Upanishad entered me in less than a fraction of a second at exactly the moment of the Equinox.

Windows of chaos, such as that generated by the tsunami, as well as that happening at the time between Abdy and me, are also windows of opportunity. By the Second Law of Thermodynamics, which I call the Law of Chaos, these times generate a numerical increase in the disorder or entropy of the Universe, which is always required. Since the chaos is so significantly increased, there is more 'numerical room' for other parts of the whole system, such as me, to become more one-pointed. I see this gift of musical creation as a more aligned or ordered process and an example of the kind of potential existing in substantially chaotic times.

I was once at a conference where a video was shown of a particular teaching method for introducing reading to 4-6 year olds in China. It was from my perspective, a quantized reading process, which was employed with the children. A quantized process is one that occurs all at once, rather than in a gradual continuous manner. It also always involves a jump up to a higher state, all at once.

At this school, children flipped through the pages of a book, never opening it. They were then able to successfully answer questions their teacher posed concerning the story. One young boy was able to simply place his hand on the closed book, and through that interaction, was able to relate to his teacher correct answers concerning the material he had just read.

I received the music to the Peace Invocation in just such a quantized fashion. I also received about half of this book in the same manner, as an instantaneous download.

At a period of time when my daughter was hospitalized for 81 days, critically ill, she related to me a remarkable fact. I had never told her about the quantized reading video I had seen. She related to me, near the end of her hospital stay, that a strange ability had arisen in her. She said that she could put her hand on a book and 'read' it without opening the book. She said that she didn't get every word right, but that the gist of the material was transferred to her in this way. Such latent abilities lie in the human Soul of which we can scarcely imagine.

THE VIBRATION OF THE WORD

Personally I believe that, as the bible states, first there was the word and it was good. It was from this vibration that physical reality came into manifestation. With Hindus as well, each Sanskrit syllable is said to vibrate on subtle levels, causing the unmanifest to come into manifest creation. That is to say, words have their own energies and create reality from the fabric of their vibration.

This vibration of words themselves is seen in Professor Masura Emoto's work with water crystals. When he crystallizes water in containers bearing words like 'love', 'gratitude' or 'respect', beautiful intricate crystals result. Such words as 'kill' or 'no good' produce amorphous, asymmetrical and less beautiful crystals.

In essence, all words have their own vibration. So the school in China and my daughter placing her hand on the book and being able to read it, was really a translation of the vibration of the words present, processed and received all at once, rather than linearly, word-by-word.

We are always picking up far more information than we are consciously aware of. Each of us at some point knows who is calling on the phone, can sense another's feelings when entering a room, or has the sense that someone is thinking about you and even what they are thinking. Sometimes this is imagination, yet sometimes it is an actual joining of minds.

When I receive an email that has been sent with strong emotion, I am often overwhelmed by the emotion as soon as I open it, even before I read it. Anger might produce an instant headache or stomachache in me, while love or appreciation might make me feel as if I were buffered by a cocoon of soft nectar.

In this way, I see all thoughts, all wisdom, and all knowledge that has ever existed, as still available to connect with in a direct way. It is in this manner that I have been fortunate enough to receive pieces of music and about 150 pages of this book, all at once, as a quantum download.

It seems to me that if there is a cosmic need to know some piece of information, one can receive it without studying it, in exactly this way, simply as a quantum download of information. Everything is becoming more accessible on this level than it ever has been before. I believe we are moving into an era when these 'psychic abilities' will become the norm.

I also see the thoughts that we are running nearly continually in our heads as actually creating our bodies, our lives and all aspects of our personal world. So I see that the easiest way to change one's reality is to change our 'head thoughts' and activate them with our emotions.

I propose a three-dimensional axis system. Along one axis, let's say the x-axis, is our intention. Along the y-axis is our emotion concerning that intention and along the z-axis is the manifestation that occurs. This is really how our life is created, as a result of our emotions enlivening our intentions.

The stronger the emotion, the more our life will unfold as a resolution of these two vectors. Each of the three, impacts each other. This is completely in agreement with the Law of Attraction, where what we feel is true and already present manifests. In fact it is one explanation of why the Law of Attraction works.

Let me call this principle, Emo-creation or the matrix of manifestation. The power of words activated by emotions seems indeed to result in manifestation in direct proportion to the strength of the intention and the intensity of the emotion. It is important that the language, even the internal language in one's head, be in the present tense. I can almost see how words reshape the space of the energy eggs around us and beyond.

AU REVOIR ABDY

And so my saga with Abdy was for a time suspended in Bali in March of 2006. I did email a few times, but did not hear back from him until 2011. I am so grateful for the catalytic effect he had on my life during the intensity of our three years of regular interactions.

He showed me how to settle into the perfection with which life is unfolding moment-by-moment, even in the most difficult of times. I learned from him the importance of aligning with no intention. I also 'caught from him' the gift of being able to 'step aside' and allow that energy to work through me. I became able to be an empty vessel, a conduit for the Divine flow.

I am eternally grateful to Abdy for the catalytic effect he had on my life. Yet, something had to split us apart, so that I could more fully center on my own knowledge and abilities and start to step out of the role of follower and into the space of my own power and wisdom. This is a journey, which at some point we each make.

Padma

CHAPTER ELEVEN:
A NEW MENTOR

Ansara

Even before Abdy vanished from my life, my third mentor had appeared. I met Padma on July 12, 2005.

I had been walking one day at the Reservoir across from my house, when I encountered a friend from the ashram walking with a woman. Within minutes of meeting her, I had received strong internal guidance that I was to chant for her the Lord's Prayer in the original Aramaic that Jesus had spoken.

By now, that inner prompting had become so clear that I would never think of denying it, no matter how silly I might appear. I asked if she would like to hear it and she enthusiastically said, "Yes".

I chanted for her and immediately, she burst into tears. She had just asked God for a sign, and apparently I was it. We became good friends. Ansara believed herself to be an incarnation of the energetic of Jeshua (Jesus) and Magdalene's child, Sarah. She also believed that their child was an incarnation of Abraham's Sarah.

At this point of my life I know maybe 30-40 friends, who have shared with me that they believe themselves to be incarnations of various ones from the Christ tale. What is amazing to me is that I run into them in very different places and they don't necessarily know each other. If this is but an illusion, I certainly find it a fun one. I have sent many of them around the planet to meet each other. I used to ask my husband why he thought this might be happening to me on an ongoing basis. He never had an answer for me. This is a time I think, when we are being drawn to our personal 'Soul families'. We are simply drawn to those we are perhaps still interacting with through the apparent fabric of time. Time in the end is after all an illusion.

Ansara had been communicating with Padma on-line. When he arrived in the Bay Area, she and I together attended a performance of 'The One', which he was presenting. Padma chanted original compositions from seven sacred traditions: Sanskrit, Tibetan, Native American, Hebrew, Egyptian, Mayan and Latin. With each one the ancient letters of each language were projected 360 degrees, completely surrounding the audience in the circular performing space, as his group simultaneously chanted them. It was a deeply moving and profound experience.

Beyond this, from the moment I first saw him walk out on stage, I knew that I knew Padma well. My sense was that I recognized him from more past lives and traditions than anyone else I had ever met.

After the performance he gave 'Deeksha', an energetic hands-on blessing, to whoever wanted it. After this we hugged and the energetic recognition on both sides was deep. He also confirmed that he felt that I was a close friend from other lives. I felt from the start that Padma, like Elan and Abdy, carried a signature of awakened Christ energy. He transmitted spiritual vibration through his voice more powerfully than any man I had heard up until that time.

Within a month, Ansara called me and said that she and Padma were going to get together for dinner. She invited me to come along. Since I knew that she was interested in him on many levels, I was surprised. "Surely you don't really want me to tag along on your date, do you?" I asked her. To my surprise, she kept insisting that I was in fact welcome and wanted at the gathering. So, we went together over to Padma's.

Shortly after arriving, Ansara was overcome with exhaustion and ended up sleeping much of the visit. So Padma and I had the opportunity to commune on deep levels. Both of us felt pleased by the inspiration of our dialogue.

Strangely, before the visit, I had felt compelled to write up a global list of people, who I knew, through my internal guidance, that Padma was supposed to meet. Sometimes I feel that one of my strongest roles here is to connect up those who are destined to be important influences in each other's lives.

I listed seven people for him to meet in seven countries. Yet, at the last moment, I erased one of them, somehow wary of that contact. Some of them Padma met on my guidance. Some became his friends. Eventually, I believe, he met five of the original seven I listed.

The name I erased was most interesting. Padma eventually traveled to the country in which the seventh one lived. Randomly, they met each other, I think, simply on the street. They instantly became such good friends that Padma came to live with this man and his partner. During that stay the man's partner fell in love with Padma. She then left with Padma, when he departed and traveled with him around the world. Eventually he sired a beautiful daughter with her. They are no longer together.

Sometimes I think I know the unfoldings of life without having the specifics. With hindsight, I can see why I erased that seventh name from the list. Some non-specific foreboding existed in me. I think that I subtly knew that I wanted to avoid any responsibility for the way the universe was destined to play out around Padma. When one's destiny is mapped out, I believe that those key contacts are programmed to occur in one way or another.

CHRIST COUNSEL'S
HOME INTERVENTION

After our dinner, I didn't see Padma for a while. Then one day he called and asked if he might come over. He walked up to the door of my house. As I let him in he declared, "The Christ Council has told me that I am to move in with you for seven days and seven nights and shape you up." I said, "Come in."

Fortunately, my husband was very tolerant of the strange array of characters I brought into our house to live with us. Of all of them, I think Padma was the most difficult for him. There was a way that Padma treated me exactly the same whether my husband or son were present or not. As neither was on an overtly spiritual path, much of what unfolded was not easy for them to understand. The intimacy of spirit between Padma and I was also unusual enough to seem confusing to my family.

Padma had given me deeksha, a form of initiation, a number of times without anything but the most mild of energetic sensations for me. It was much more his music that interested and deeply touched me. However one night he was sitting on my couch and I on the floor next to him. All of a sudden an energetic wave enveloped me. My head came to rest on his knee and in this strange position, I was completely enfolded into the depths of the inner realms. Although I knew, at least vaguely, what was transpiring around me, I simply stayed deep in that state, my body motionless for the next 3-4 hours.

Apparently Padma covered me with a blanket. My husband walked by and was disturbed by the scene. I was so 'out of it' that after a while, I asked for a blanket, not realizing that one was covering me. My son came up and asked, "What have you done to my mom?"

My family was wonderful in allowing me the freedom to explore the spiritual depths with these mentors. The Divine has provided them for me on my journey towards understanding that I hold all power and teachings and all information I ever will need to know within myself. These mentors have been my stepping-stones along the journey from relying on a guru, to coming to know that it is me and no one else who is the real one leading myself on a path from the darkness to the light. 'Gu' is darkness and 'ru' is light. So the guru is the one leading each of us from the darkness into the light. And ultimately, we come to know that for each of us, our ultimate Guru is none other than our own higher Self. And ultimately, that higher Self is, in Truth, the joined higher Self of us all, together as the ONE we truly are.

THE CHOICE OF HAPPINESS

The secret underlying all of this is that the moment of entry into that light, no matter how much it has been catalyzed by another and no matter how great the other is, that very moment only happens by CHOICE, one's own choice. Not necessarily a conscious choice, but more of an allowing for the light to permeate every molecule of one's being. And at another deeper level, not even an allowing, since the light has and always will be there in every cell and molecule of which we are composed, in every table and car and rock.

So it is only a matter of choosing to see what is really there. Choosing to align with the breath of God breathing one, each and every moment. Choosing, and moment-by-moment aligning with --- the choice of happiness, the choice of love, not fear --- the choice that we are truly ONE, simultaneously dreaming the very same dream of creation.

We seem to be different, being the various characters springing from the one consciousness that creates the entirety of the dream. In truth it is just our ONE consciousness that has separated into the many in the dream, simply to play out all the games of life.

Everyone and thing 'out there', seemingly the Not-Me, gives me a chance to forgive that, and through that, to forgive myself. We know who we are by our reflection through other's eyes. So if we really forgive what we are seeing, that becomes the most perfect route to forgive ourselves. One reason this works is that there is no trait that one is capable of seeing in another, that one doesn't have personally oneself. In this way the separation allows us to forgive all our traits.

This for-giving becomes one's service to the Divine itself. One becomes forgiving when one makes the conscious choice always to see the light in each person one meets. No matter what they have done, it is a definitive knowing that there is no one who moment by moment is not doing their best, no matter how it seems. Holding up a mirror of choosing only to see the light in another, lets one further see one's own light and to further align with seeing the light in all.

It is contagious. Hold up someone's light to them and all of a sudden they can see their light. Magically, they are then able to reflect your light back to you, so that you are able to finally focus on your own light as well. It spreads rapidly.

The analysis of the dynamic spread of longitudinal happiness over a 20-year period was investigated in the Framingham Heart Study by Professor Nicholas A. Christakis and Associate Professor James H. Fowler and published in the British Medical Journal in 2008. It reported that happiness in social networks might spread from person to person through close relationships like friends, siblings, spouses, and next-door neighbors.

Researchers followed nearly 5000 individuals and found clusters of happiness and unhappiness that spread up to 3 degrees of separation on average. The relationship was strongest between individuals who were directly connected, but remained significantly greater than zero at social distances up to three degrees of separation. This means that a person's happiness is associated with the happiness of people up to three degrees removed from them in the network. For example, a person is one degree removed from their friend, two degrees removed from their friend's friend, three degrees removed from their friend's friend's friend, and so on.

This study concludes that a person's happiness depends on the happiness of others with whom they are connected. This provides further justification for seeing happiness, like health, as a collective phenomenon. It was also found that unhappiness is not contagious in the same way. The state of one's human relationships are consistently found to be the most important factor that correlates with human happiness.

Studies have shown that joy can be transmitted even to

houses as far as five housing units away from a joyous one to people whom one has never met. A friend who lives within a mile (about 1.6 km) and who becomes happy increases the probability that another person in the neighborhood is happy, by 25% (95% confidence interval 1% to 57%). Happiness might spread, by a diverse set of mechanisms, over longer spans or perhaps may become viral in social networks. Diverse phenomena can cause this spread of happiness in a large social network. See http://jhfowler.ucsd.edu/dynamic_spread_of_happiness.pdf Overall, all the results suggest that happiness might spread through a population like a virus.

So, Padma moved into my house. He walked through the place telling me to throw away many of my clothes, to simplify and change my meditation room, to clean up many messy areas, to leave my ashram seva (sacred service) and to leave my job. I bristled at his suggestions or should I call them demands. Yet, in each case, I started thinking about what each area represented and signified in my life.

I recently spent 2 1/2 months moving my elderly but lively octogenarian mom, who is on three internet dating sites, from her four-bedroom, four-story house of 55 years in Cleveland, Ohio, to a one-bedroom independent living community in Florida. Every room was crammed full of clothes. She still had her prom dress at 87 years old. Ah, these patterns do run in families and are so hard to alter. I didn't have a model for simplicity in my life. I had never thrown or given away my clothes. Most of my wardrobe I never wear. Removing items allows an inflow of new energies. It keeps one closer to the present. A gradual steady process of removing unused excess was birthed during Padma's visit. It has evolved and still continues.

The same patterns were present with the stacks of papers around me. Just as with my clothes, I had to learn very gradually to throw things away, to file more frequently and with slightly less attention to minute details. The clutter of papers has improved as well, but slowly.

Somehow, as with-in, so with-out. My internal mental clutter is reflected in my environment. So I can clear and clean externally, and it will assist with the creation of a calmer mind. The reverse process is equally valid. Meditating, spending quiet time, doing japa (repetition of a sacred name or phrase or mantra) or chanting a name of God can often result in a cleaner, clearer external living space arising.

So, I listened to Padma. Eventually I brought in boxes and piled clothes in them. Comically, this was so difficult for me that it took me another two years to actually give them away.

At this point, I do donate some clothes each year. However, it hardly seems to make a dent in the abundance before my eyes. It is a gradually improving area of my life. I feel a profound joy and new lightness each time I successfully remove some of the items.

I now know that one always needs to remove something in one's life to make room for the entrance of new energies. Abundance is like a funnel. Something must flow out in order to have room for more to flow in. Abundance in one's life can only manifest if the funnel is open at both ends.

This is true of all life processes. Some aspect of one's life must stop, shift, die, leave or disintegrate or be destroyed for the new to grow. So often, what appears to be a painful loss of people, friends, money, a house burning, or the loss of a pet is actually a cosmic gift of room being made for the gifting of something even better. Painful though it may seem.

This is exactly as it is for any living system. Something must be excreted for new, fresher energies to enter the system. This applies to food, friends, faculties, and even groups. The closed group tends eventually to start eating itself. Those organizations allowing new members and also allowing members to leave the organization are often healthiest in their functioning. A group is a living organism exemplifying these processes as well.

LEAVING ASHRAM SEVA (SERVICE)

Padma's input was appreciated, even as I bristled each time he gave me a directive. I was furious when he first told me to leave my ashram seva (sacred service). For most of my work life, even when I was a half-time administrator in charge of 100 faculty, six technicians, a $200,000 budget and teaching half-time while having two small children, I held onto the discipline of ashram seva to see me through.

Many of those years, I would be at the ashram early 2 to 3

times a week. Twice a week I would be assigned to act as a lead chanter on mike for the Guru Gita from 6:30-8AM. I would then travel a half-hour to teach my college Chemistry lectures and laboratories.

One day a week, for perhaps 15 or more years, I would arrive at 4AM to dress a murti, or living statue, of my guru's guru. There was a formalized process of cleaning, applying sacred ash (bhasma), rudraksha malas (sacred seeds composing a necklace of 108 beads round, with one bead askew from the rest) and finally dressing the statue. I did that every Wednesday morning, and then helped lead the daily chant. I always felt the most blissful and calm on Wednesdays, having done this morning ritual.

I don't believe I could have sustained the balance of work life and family life without the ongoing sustenance that daily meditation, chanting and this morning seva supplied.

There was one intense year and a half period when I only slept 3-5 hours a night, save for maybe 10 days. I could never have done this without the nurturing energy of my practices. Needless to say they permitted me to become very disciplined – the kind of discipline that arises spontaneously, without harshness or pushing. They gave birth within my being to a gentle natural discipline that allows me, through the vertical alignment with Divine Grace, to accomplish a shocking amount with ease.

Now, when Padma said, 'Leave your seva!" I was outraged. Surely he didn't understand what support it provided in my life. Yet, for the previous six months before Padma's arrival, I had an amorphous underlying sense that my mornings dressing the murti were numbered. My thought process led me to suspect that someone in charge at the ashram might decide to remove me from the position. Never did I suspect how my departure would unfold.

Padma told me to leave my seva on a Tuesday while he was living in my home. I had no intention of doing so. On Wednesday morning I arrived at the ashram for my 4AM shift. As I walked into the space of the Temple area, which held the statue, I heard inside myself, "This is your last morning here." It was the statue of my Baba's guru itself speaking to me.

Usually two of us dressed the statue together. However, that morning my partner didn't show up and I did all parts of the process alone. As I took off the necklace mala for the cleaning and spreading of the sacred ash, the murti said to me, 'Put that on your neck'. This is not something that would be considered appropriate by those running the Temple. Usually the mala was placed on a silver tray during the dressing process.

I have reached a stage where I am able to distinguish my own inner voice from the voice of Divine guidance within me. I always follow what I am told by my Divine inner voice. There was no question that this was not my voice. I placed the mala around my neck during the dressing ritual. At the end, I replaced the mala on the neck of the statue. In the potent energetic, which for me was the command of the Guru, I heard,

"And now, GO DO MY WORK!

That was my last morning in the Temple doing seva. It was the third day of Padma living in my house.

PADMA SAMBHAVA

Padma rearranged my meditation room, removing two of the three altars, taking down at least half the pictures on the wall, and placing one Tibetan Thanka of Padma Sambhava in a place of new prominence, though not supplanting the primary altar photo of my guru.

At first I was annoyed and outraged by Padma's insouciance and domineering in making these changes. I thought I would simply rearrange it after he was gone. Yet even today it still remains in the simplified arrangement. There is a way that a calmer exterior space surrounding one promotes internal stillness of mind as well. At this point I have fully embraced the more pristine environment for my meditative space.

The historic, Tibetan guru, 8th century Padma Sambhava, the founder of the Nyingma Tibetan Buddhist lineage, had been my initial focus as I entered with seriousness my spiritual path. My first day in Claudio Naranjo's SAT groups was the first day of a month-long retreat. On that day I received the Vajra Guru mantra, which is Padma Sambhava's mantra, from a Tibetan Rinpoche, or reincarnated master, Tarthang Tulku of Berkeley California's Nyingma Institute. I recited it constantly, well really as constantly as I was able, for the next two years.

One day during Padma's stay in my house, it all of a sudden dawned on me that Padma's name was so close to that of the master of that first ancient lineage with which I connected. I gasped internally as I realized that this was not by chance. I knew instantly with certainty that Padma carried the incarnated energetic of the ancient master depicted in that Thanka. I asked him about it, and he confirmed my suspicions.

I knew that Padma was in fact the fruit of my having recited this, the Vajra Guru mantra, with such love for so long.

Om Ah Hum Vajra Guru Padma Siddhi Hum

Padma Sambhava

In my life, one mantra has always led me to another. I followed a Tibetan Buddhist path with Rinpoche Tarthang Tulku for about three years. I constantly walked through my life, looking for white cars or objects as I recited the OM at the crown of my head, red objects for the AH in my throat chakra and green cars or objects as I chanted HUM in my heart.

There came a time, after I had met my Indian guru, when I felt profoundly confused as to which path I was to pursue. Each lecture I attended praised those following one-pointedly a single spiritual path and discipline. Stories were told regarding the foolhardiness of going downstream with one's feet in two separate boats.

One night during this period, I had what felt to be a conscious dream. I have not had many of these in my life. They are dreams that feel entirely real happenings in the dream state. There is a sense that they are true happenings in one's energy body, called the Ka in ancient Egypt, and sometimes referred to as the lightbody. This was such a dream.

Rinpoche Tarthang Tulku rode up in a beautiful open carriage. Somehow my Guru, Baba, was there as well. A subtle battle for my Soul ensued. Baba won me and Rinpoche rode off. I awoke in a sweat.

I had planned a summer of spending a few weeks at my guru's ashram in upper state New York, then taking a course with Rinpoche Tarthang Tulku in Berkeley, all the while engaging in Sufi practices with a Gurdjieff oriented group. I ended up having a private darshan, an audience, with my guru. I went to him and he blessed me by hitting me with a gentle peacock feather wand, as was his way.

I told him that the lectures I attended all spoke about the importance of following only one path, and yet my heart was leading me to follow multiple pathways at the same time. He asked me which paths and I told him.

He then used his hand to gently hit the back of my heart, as I leaned forward over his knees. Then, he looked me directly in the eye and said, "Are you satisfied?"

Somehow that instant was the first moment of complete satisfaction I felt that I ever had in my life. I walked out of the room, and sat in the corridor, crying for a long time from the feeling of full satisfaction I was experiencing.

From that point, I dropped everything else I was doing. I became entirely one-pointed for the next few decades. I cancelled the Tibetan retreat and left the Sufi group. A good friend took care of my place, forwarded my mail and helped with the logistics that allowed me to stay where I was the remainder of the summer.

At first, leaving the Vajra Guru mantra was difficult. However, at some point I realized that my guru typically gave out three different mantras. One of them, GURU OM, contained two of the same words from Padma Sambhava's Vajra Guru mantra. This allowed me to still feel that I was doing the entire Vajra Guru mantra when I did my guru's Guru Om mantra.

Many times over the years, I felt one mantra leading me to another. Originally I had a Transcendental Meditation (TM) mantra. I did it for a number of years. During my ashram chanting, at one point, a few words of one particular chant jumped out at me and persisted in grabbing my attention for many months. I was able to question a swami as to their meaning and pronunciation. To my amazement, I discovered that I had been mispronouncing them and that they were in fact the mantra I had been given in TM. In this manner, I came to realize that each mantra I practiced bore fruit and led me into my next spiritual lessons.

CHAPTER TWELVE:
A FORK IN THE ROAD

FINDING MY PATH–LEAVING MY JOB

For years I agonized over what was my correct path. Finally, one day in meditation, I was given the undeniable answer. I was told that my path was where my foot came down. I have come to know that in fact my most perfect path is exactly where that foot of mine alights. It is in fact that most juicy place which nurtures me in such a way as to maximize the upliftment of not only my Soul, but also the Souls of the lives of everyone with whom I connect. I also know with certainty that this is equally true for your path and everyone's path.

What a relief to know that there is no way to blow what path we each are on, and to know with certainty that each and every one of us are, in fact, no matter how much it doesn't appear to be so, trying our very best. Even your husband or wife. Even your mom or dad. Even your children. Even the murderer and thief.

Padma, still in my house, also told me to leave my job. I told him that because of pension issues and my husband's financial concerns and perspectives, that was not a possibility. I informed him that there was no chance of that happening any time soon. Yet, everything Padma told me became a catalytic seed of action in my life. It took on a force of it's own.

I found the idea of leaving my career at this time ridiculous, impossible, yet appealing, even though I still loved teaching. When I was with students, I felt exhilarated and of service.

However many aspects of my teaching environment had significantly deteriorated, nearly to the point of being intolerable. A President of the college had shifted the administrative structure to one of full-time deans as opposed to half-time faculty, half-time deans who cycled back into full time teaching after six-year shifts. The older structure had fostered excellent communication and a deep understanding of the concerns and issues affecting each of the eight academic areas of the campus. The resulting heavy-handed change to a structure of full time deans, unfamiliar with the Divisions and campus history and often hired from 'outside', resulted in a 94% no-confidence vote against the President. The faculty was angry and miserable. Morale plummeted.

In addition, a student had assaulted me, while I was teaching my Chemistry laboratory. During a quantitative separation of sand, salt and benzoic acid, he had mistakenly thrown away his salt water. It was a two period lab, so that he needed this product to work with the next week.

When he informed me of his problem near the end of the period, I told him that he would have to re-do this portion of the quantitative lab, and that he could come into any of my other sections to get caught up. I turned to remind the other students not to throw out their salt water and the

280

young man grabbed me from behind by my neck and jaw and twisted me around in the air, injuring my shoulder and hip.

I ran out of the room and locked myself in my office – for a long time. Some physical problems relating to this incident have persisted for years.

What shocked me at the time was the complete lack of support I experienced from the administration, my fellow faculty in my department and the workers compensation medical community. The new Dean of Students interviewed the student and never spoke directly to me. He wrote that the student said I was exaggerating and that he had hardly touched me.

A worker's compensation claims administrator told me that I could not have a counseling session. They mandated that I wait an entire semester and attend a six-hour psychiatric exam before they would agree to give me even one counseling session. Finally, the day before the end of the semester they finally agreed to allow me to speak with someone.

In addition, a laboratory technician had been interrupting my laboratory lectures, and the new interim college President took five weeks to decide to support me in maintaining the integrity of my teaching environment.

So, all together, these situations had fertilized the soil of my Soul to a heightened receptivity to Padma's words and suggestions. During the ten days that Padma lived in my house, a radical idea, one I had never before contemplated, started to blossom in me. My husband had wanted me to teach perhaps 4 or 5 more years. Yet, all of a sudden, I saw how I conceivably might seem to work this time and not actually do so.

It took me two years to manifest, but it was successful. I ended up working another two years, but getting paid and getting retirement credit for four years. I worked more than full time for a number of semesters, yet didn't take any extra pay for two years. This allowed me to bank monies owed to me. I also had a number of years of sick leave that I had never used. I just had never thought it possible to do these kind of legitimate arrangements before Padma instructed me to stop teaching.

A NEW LIFE STORY

It is always true that things are unfolding for the best. By the Chemical Law of Chaos, this student acted as a catalyst for chaos in my life. Once again powerful fractures of potential one-pointedness opened for me, as they must in all chaotic times, bringing with them opportunities for a higher state of conscience and being.

Even being attacked was a gift of the Universe with a purpose. Here it allowed me to the possibility of stepping into a dedicated pathway of service to the Divine, far before I thought possible. It also focused me in giving a new level of attention to my body. I ended up getting many Rolfings, cranial sacral sessions and much physical therapy. Even though some physical manifestations of the incident continued, on other levels my physical body improved due to all the treatments I needed. There is NOTHING that occurs that is not ultimately for our highest good.

One example of this manifested, as I waited all semester for the mandated six-hour psychiatric exam, that I was told I must submit to if a counseling session would be authorized. I spoke with a friend within the worker's comp system who informed me what was the best emphasis in exams of this type. I was told to view my life as normal and positive with just this incident sticking out.

This led me to practice telling myself my life story in a new way. How are we to know how much each of us exaggerates the incidents of our life, emphasizing the lows and highs in our minds? Usually it is the lows we keep bringing up on that inner screen, reinforcing their impact. It is also true, in recently reported studies, that each time a memory is accessed, it is changed. It is like getting fingerprints on a photo each time it is viewed, slightly, consistently, gradually changing what is there over the years.

Our life stories are exactly like this. We are no longer connected to the true reality of our life. This is why siblings growing up in the same family may have radically different perspectives on the same family incidents. In this way, we can align with a warped view of our life.

So, in preparing for this psychological evaluation, I chose to practice a rosier version of my life story than that one, which I typically told to myself, and others.

After many weeks of practicing, the night before the scheduled exam I received a call that workers comp had decided to allow me to have counseling sessions without needing to go to the evaluation. After the initial shock subsided, I realized that the new rosier story of my life was JUST AS TRUE as the story I had told myself all my life. It also was a story that made me happier about myself and who I imagined that I was. I never went back to the old story.

I am so grateful for the opportunity the student attack and the no counseling fiasco created. I was able to redesign and believe a new story of my life and it has changed me for the better. How often do we pull up the past, and in particular our past negative judgments of OURSELVES, based on what we think has been proved about us from the incidents of our lives?

A new kinder, gentler past can be embraced, if we realize that things simply happen, and no matter what is in our history, we truly know our own innocence. Even the murderer has been doing the best he could.

Guilt is never of any use on the spiritual path. Forgiveness of others, allowing them to be who and what they truly are and must be, opens the door to forgiving ourselves. We come to learn and allow ourselves to be exactly who we really are. We could not have been different in any circumstance, because we always tried our best, no matter what went awry.

I chose, at this point of preparing my life for external

review, to see myself more kindly.   Now each time I 'remember' some incident of my life, I am literally re-member-ing it.   It has become another choice of happiness in this kinder, gentler evaluation of myself, which has interestingly extended to my evaluation of others as well. Each of us is perfectly innocent. Each of us has tried our best. We all make **innocent** mistakes, no matter how grave they appear to be.   Every one of these seeming errors has actually assisted us in the perfect alignment for the unfoldment of our Soul.   Our perfect path has always been and will always be exactly where our foot comes down.

My Israel pilgrimage friend, Linda, sent me some great comments about the uselessness of stories in our lives. She said:

"ALL stories are limiting....
No enlightened being 'has' a story.
They use stories to reach out to those of us still embedded in stories.
I see stories as storage.
I see storage as egoic ballast.
I see egoic ballast as time bound and time binding, depriving me of Presence.
I'm working to BE EMBODIED, that is, to so profoundly recover each cell and fill it with Light that the cells and the consciousness are translucent once again...."

Some time after this, I, all at once, had a sense of what it might be like to walk into a room with no stories from my past. Instantly, I became aware of the baggage I usually drag around with me, weighing down my shoulders. I carry my parents, my siblings, my children, my husband and all the other incidents of my life. Just for a moment I felt what it might be like to set that all aside. That would open up as well, all the projections I make about my future, based on the judgments I've made about myself from the way I think the past has been.

What I felt like in that moment of setting all this down was freedom and innocence. I had the joyful enthusiasm, blissful relishing, and awe of a toddler. I didn't have to worry about making judgments to decide how to be. There is an innate sense of the world being safe, because one's higher guidance is in control and will figure out all things for me, better than I could ever do myself.

So this is what evolved for me as an operating mode, of detaching from all the stories I carry about anyone, especially myself. This is still a work in process, of course.

Looking for the gift, in even the worst of situations, opens the doors of gratitude. Gratitude then creates the necessary portal to find happiness even in chaos and in spite of physical or emotional pain. Actually it is directly because of the chaos around one at these difficult times, and since numerically the entropy or disorder of the system is thus increasing, that attaining new levels of life, consciousness and happiness becomes a possibility.

Had this student not attacked me, I might still be teaching rather than doing what I do as my service in the world. I have complete freedom at this time to listen to the voice of Spirit, which is stronger, louder and ever more unmistakable. In following that, my happiness and peace of mind and being are ever expanding.

What appeared to be a terrible attack, evolved into a profound and worthwhile life teaching, which ultimately led me to a happier life. I can truly say, unequivocally, that the worst incidents of my life were also eventually those, which gave me the most progress in moving toward the choice of happiness.

MUSICAL ALIGNMENT WITH THE ONE

During the time Padma resided in my house he also catalyzed a tremendous quantum leap in my musical skills.

I had an extensive background in music. I sang from kindergarten through sixth grade with a Jewish Temple choir. I also sang with my middle school and high school performing and touring choirs. I was Josephine in a Gilbert and Sullivan production of *HMS Pinafore* and was in madrigal groups. I continued with Gilbert and Sullivan operettas as well as choirs in college and graduate school.

My first truly transcendental experience was falling into egolessness while singing Bach's *B Minor Mass*. I lost all sense of myself and simply became the music itself and nothing else. Again, this was the feeling of the Holy Instant described in *A Course in Miracles* section VI. on Beyond The Body, which had so aptly described my encounter with Elan, both when he told me he could give me shaktipat with one finger, and when he hugged me, Both his hug as well as Bach's music, led me into a new 'reality' of Union, where separateness disappeared.

Music has been a major portal to the Divine for me all my life. I sang in a San Francisco Opera Production of Wagner's *Die Meistersinger* under Kurt Adler's conducting, with Oakland Symphony Chorus, at a Democratic National Convention helping to sing the national anthem, at an Oakland A's game, with the Oakland Ballet, while they danced *Carmina Burana*, and with various Bach groups in San Francisco and Berkeley, California, as well as with the Rockefeller Chorus in Chicago.

For decades, I played an Indian tamboura and cymbals in the ashram, and was a lead chanter for long text chants, as well as Nama-sankirtana, the shorter, repeating chants. I was also a conductor for 150-300 person concerts at an ashram for about a year. I often led warm-ups of perhaps 20 musicians.

One day, Padma invited his producer, Stara over to my house. This was a catalytic moment for me, where I felt that my musical ability jumped up a quantum level.

I discovered that at least half of the original performance that I heard on the day that I met Padma, had been generated by him and his group spontaneously. Spiritual improvisational music was a new concept to me. I could see one person doing this, but realizing that four people were able to align their energies with the Divine to produce overlays of rhythms, harmonics and melodies that perfectly flowed together was radical for me.

First he and Stara demonstrated the technique to me. Then I was instructed to attune to the ONE that we are and sing/chant melodies from that place. This oneness is a technical and real truth, not a metaphor. Since in fact, we are ONE being, it would be a natural ability to know which notes would complement in each moment and which would be discordant. It would be obvious which patternings would come next. The unfolding rhythms would support each other completely.

In this way I learned to improvise tunes, melodies and phrases, and to spontaneously compose a harmonious and cohesive piece of music together. We did this for five or six hours, with Padma giving me feedback on my degree of success in this process. It completely shifted my perception of what was musically possible.

There came a time, much later, when I was able to practice what I had learned that day with Padma. I was at a Conference, where the performing master musician, Arjuna, played a 15-foot Tibetan longhorn while simultaneously doing harmonic overtone singing. He had the unique ability to play his horn, using circular breath, while chanting the harmonic overtones in the manner of Tuvan throat singers. He teaches what he calls Harmonic Fusion singing. I eventually studied with him.

On that first day we met, I chanted for him the version of The Lord's Prayer in Aramaic, which had come to me after the 2003 Israel Pilgrimage, and the Peace Invocation from The Isa Upanishad, which downloaded into me on the March 2006 Equinox I spent in Bali. He loved the music and invited me to join him in the Saturday Evening concert.

We had never rehearsed a note together. We started the concert for the 30 conference participants who had gathered. He played and sang and then had me sing various pieces of my music, both the channeled ones and some songs I had composed. And then, we jumped off that exhilarating cliff into ONE-ness.

He had me start toning and then came in on the Tibetan longhorn. Instantly, I knew that we had entered the magical juicy realm of Union, because, the random note I had picked to come in on, was in exactly the same key as Arjuna's longhorn. We sounded great as we extemporaneously composed our first piece together.

Then, we dared another piece, which for me, was my chance to apply what Padma had taught me so well. We simply sang a duet. We were both together in that place where harmony exists. Melodies flowed, music formed and it all sounded shockingly good. Afterwards Arjuna told me that he was astounded how long we continued and how extraordinary we sounded. I had learned so much that day with Padma on how to enter a state of divine One-ness with other musicians, who are able to do so, and how to make music from that place. It was magical and something I had never before imagined. It led me to contemplate the nature of our ONE-ness with each other.

What does it mean that we are ONE?

THE HOLOGRAM OF ONENESS

I view this One-ness much like one's dream state. In a dream there are different people, animals, and objects, yet all of this is fabricated from the self-same ONE-ness that is one's own consciousness.

That is, my dream is really entirely, just composed from my consciousness, even though it surely seems real that there are things apart from me while I am in the dream. This is exactly the nature of our true reality in the waking state. Although it appears, through the very act of buying into the idea of separation, that there are many of us here, in fact, we are **actually**, not simply metaphorically, ONE.

Psychic-ness is thus the natural state. Why would you not know different parts of yourself? From the perspective of *A Course in Miracles*, there is but one of us here. We have decided to view ourselves as separate from the Divine and each other and in this our suffering, always based in fear, arises.

This course teaches that only love or fear exists. From one perspective love can be viewed as the state of knowing oneself as a holographic part of the Divine whole, containing all within us. From a higher vantage, love is the eternal, unchanging, continually joined and expanding, merged state where God, as well as each and every one of us is literally identical and undifferentiated. This state of love is identical to perfect peace, perfect joy and perfect happiness, eternally present and never changing.

In Judaism the holiest prayer is the Shema, which is a confirmation of the One-ness of God and us all. It is:

Shema Yisrael
Adonai Elohenu
Adonai Echad

Hear O Israel
Adonai our God
Adonai is ONE

For me this most profound statement of Jewish faith confirms the unity of the Divine as God, as myself and as you, together in our One-ness. At times I can palpably feel this Love with its aspect of complete peace, embracing me, which is identically all of this self same ONE.

The necessary key to entering the One-ness is through the door of forgiveness. The ark is entered two by two. We are rescued into the metaphorical protection of the ark during the flood or devastation we appear to be living in, by forgiving what we see, one person at a time, through forgiveness.

Chapter Thirteen: Forgiveness

FOR-GIVE-NESS THROUGH SEEING ALL TRAITS AS ONE'S OWN

So how does one forgive the unpleasant traits one sees as characteristics of another in front of you?

I use a number of techniques. The **first is:**
Forgiving every trait one identifies as a characteristic that is one's own.

The way to return to love is to see everyone and everything that makes one uncomfortable as a projection one's own self creates, which allows forgiving of what is seen. Successfully forgiving what appears to be out there, automatically results in the forgiving of that self-same trait, or characteristic, in one's self. There is no other path to love and peace.

All we have is our own experience. All that we experience is ours. Therefore any trait I attribute to anyone, i.e. if I see someone as selfish, immature, ungrateful, dangerous, competitive, cruel, inconsiderate, a liar, untrustworthy, envious, stupid, greedy, vicious or lazy, EVERY SINGLE TRAIT that I can disinguish, MUST in fact be something I possess. This is seeing my part in any situation.

So, when I find someone acting reprehensibly in some fashion, I KNOW with certainty, awful that it may be to admit, that I'm reacting to some trait I possess. In fact, every time this happens, I've projected my trait onto the other person in order to give myself the opportunity to forgive them.

When I realize that it is ALWAYS true that each of us is ALWAYS doing our very best in that moment, it is then that I can use that as a gateway to forgive the other. When I am able to do so, I have in fact forgiven this exact trait in myself as well. It happens automatically in forgiving what I've projected onto the other.

In the same way, I have come to know with certainty that the way I can best contribute towards world peace is to make peace with every single person with whom I have any issue at all, one by one. Then, just as when I came with peace in myself to the Western Wall in Jerusalem, creating peace in those around me, I will be able to seed peace in the world. Since we are all quantized fractals of the whole, it cannot be otherwise.

By the Law of Attraction, we are continually creating and drawing to us those individuals who populate our lives. The very fact that a devious or a gracious person exists in one's life, always indicates a deviousness or a graciousness in one's self that needs for-giving or embracing. For-giving allows one to be 'for giving' rather than be 'for taking' – that is, forsaking.

FOR-GIVE-NESS
THROUGH GRATITUDE

The **second technique** to generate forgiveness is **being grateful** for what is present.

When I finally did leave my work arena, which in the end was populated by difficult, unsupportive people, I knew that more than anything I wanted to leave cleanly, holding no grudges and having attained a state of forgiveness. I also know that for me the most powerful door into acceptance is gratitude.

I had a long teaching career. The manner of commemorating the departure of a faculty member at my academic institution is to have a going away party and give them a gift.

On my last full day at work, I had no particular responsibilities. I spent eight hours generating gratitude for each person there, no matter what my relationship was with him or her, and no matter how I felt 'they had hurt me.' Knowing that there is only one of us here, and knowing that I was leaving permanently, I knew that this was my last opportunity to forgive myself through forgiving them.

I spent my last eight hours writing each person a thank you note, specifically indicating what I most appreciated in each one. Sometimes it took considerable searching to find these traits or characteristics. Really they are always there, but I had to overcome my own stubbornness in choosing to see these individual's darkness rather than their light.

Everyone, yes even murderers, Hitler, Stalin, and Ku Klux Klanners, carry light. By choosing to see that light, one has a chance to align with it and when that happens, the light is reflected back, so that it can be seen. Belief in one's own light then arises, no matter what dark corners are imagined within.

So, on that last day, with lovely cards I had specifically selected for each one, I wrote a letter of gratitude to each and every one of my faculty colleagues and to our Division Dean. I left them in their campus mailboxes.

On a subtle, internal, personal and one might think fanciful level, I am keenly aware of my 'past lives' and the past life connections with many of those who show up in my life. For years during this period, I found myself in groups of people who I believed to be incarnations of those I associated with the worst deaths of all my lives.

The group of people at the end of my career, were from the viewpoint of my past lives, those who had been responsible for my crucifixion death in a life I had during Christ era times. My Dean was the magistrate who had decided upon my death for transmitting the teachings we had learned from Jesus. The lab technician was the one who did the deed, and the rest were either there, or helped carry out the sentence or supplied testimony against me.

Therefore, the forgiving in these letters, I believe extended not only to this life, but also to past and future lives with this group. Sometimes emotions about someone are far out of proportion to the present life stimulus. At these times, emotions from past and future lives might come into play. In forgiving in the now, one is also healing the past and future.

Since from some dimensions of consciousness time no longer exists, the whole of everything one ever has been or ever will be can be healed. This is why forgiving sometimes seems so hard. More is being forgiven than is obvious.

Since we together, all of us, are truly one, forgiving affects everyone and everything. Your personal forgiving truly matters and makes it easier for every single person that exists to forgive as well. So the effort, no matter how hard, is an enormous service to the whole that you are, and to the whole that we all are together.

Besides the letters, I decided to give each colleague a specially selected gift, which I distributed at my going away party. I had brought along with me one extra wrapped gift, in case someone did not seem happy with what I'd chosen for them.

The department presented me with a lovely gift. Then I gave each one of them their presents. They seemed quite surprised and pleased. I looked around and to my shock the technician, who had interrupted my class, lied about me and took me to the Dean, that is to say basically crucified me from my perspective, had come to my party. I was shocked. And then I remembered that last extra gift I had wrapped.

All at once I realized, that I had been set up by God. I likely never would have been strong enough to consciously forgive this man. Yet under these circumstances, I saw that the Divine was playing with me and wanted a good full bellied cosmic laugh. So, what was I to do but join in the unfolding of the passion play?

I went over and sincerely offered the gift, a set of nice wooden desk paper holder/sorters, and he loved it. And I loved it. It was so funny that I forgave him in spite of myself. I felt the joyous lightness and peaceful freedom that this profound forgiving seeded in me. My being 'for-giving' of the presents had become true forgiving. My doorway into this state opened through aligning with gratitude. Somehow, in even the most awful of circumstances, it is always possible to find something for which to be grateful in someone or in the situation. I used the letters to align myself with the best for which I could be grateful in each person.

I left my career in great peace that day. As difficult as the ending years at my job had been, I had put in the work to leave it in a clear state with everyone there.

Our comings and goings in life are of the utmost importance. Coming and going with kindness, taking the time to leave someone, focusing on some aspect of their light, frees one up from having to carry the baggage of that person through the rest of life. This is true freedom.

FOR-GIVING BY SEEING THE WORLD AS ILLUSORY

There is a **third technique** that I have used to reach a state of forgiveness with another. It is **seeing the world as illusory** through **realizing that my thoughts are creating it.**

I came to really know this with complete certainty after reading Gary Renard's book, *The Disappearance of the Universe*. I had never read *A Course in Miracles* before that time, so it took me a year to read this synopsis of its principles. I could only read a few pages at a time, since the material took me time to process and I experienced so much light, and perhaps an energetic download, while reading.

When I finished the book, I had a dream. I was in some large and complex house that I knew. I was trying to count how many full and half baths were present there. So, as I was sitting on the corner of a tub in one room, I saw a large snake crawling towards me. As I watched, various segmental portions of the snake became invisible as they merged into the non-manifest energetic realm and then re-emerged. This process continued a while until the entire snake started cycling from visible to invisible and back again. I could almost see heat waves where it existed in its invisible phase.

As I awoke, I felt this to be a representation of our true reality, as an ongoing oscillation between manifest and non-manifest, between the separation of individuality and the true oneness that we are. Strangely, just after having this dream, I received an email, purporting that we are in fact constantly oscillating in and out of 'reality' at an exponentially many cycles per second rate.

DE BROGLIE and
THE DISAPPEARANCE OF THE UNIVERSE

I believe there is an oscillating between our Source identity and our 3-D world. It is a manifestation of Nobel Prize winner Louis De Broglie's wave-particle duality theory of matter, which was based on the work relating to light done by Max Planck and Albert Einstein. De Broglie conceived of his prize-winning thesis while he was a graduate student. It was actually his doctoral thesis.

His thesis committee was unsure of the material and unable to determine if DeBroglie's work was nonsense or brilliant. De Broglie was so fortunate that this committee was willing to admit their inability to evaluate what had been presented. It was his great fortune that they passed on his thesis to Einstein for evaluation, who endorsed his wave-particle duality proposal wholeheartedly. This earned de Broglie his doctorate in 1924 and his Nobel Prize in 1929, a mere 5 years later! This was always one of my favorite scientific achievements to share with the Chemistry classes I taught over the years.

De Broglie's research culminated in his hypothesis stating that any moving particle or object has an associated wave form. De Broglie thus created a new field in physics, wave mechanics, uniting the physics of energy (wave) and matter (particle). Thus, all matter, that which has mass and occupies space (volume), has a wave nature associated with it. This is termed its DeBrogie wavelength.

This theory has more relevance on a very tiny atomic sized level, however because of it, there is a finite probability of finding one's car outside the garage in the morning, even though it was parked inside the night before.

I propose that we are oscillating in and out of our 3-D material world constantly, and likely with varying individual frequencies. I think this relates to an individual's attention span, the arising of thoughts, achieving a connection with the space between thoughts and the amount of sleep an individual needs.

I believe that the 'spaces' into which we oscillate are at various higher dimensional levels. Since we exist in this three dimensional matrix, I don't believe that the oscillations reach the highest realm of undifferentiated Shiva or unity consciousness. I use that term, Shiva, from the Hindu perspective, but I just as easily could use many other terms such as the all-pervasive, omnipotent, omniscient God.

The definition of the Divine for me at this moment is 'the Divine Matrix of all that is, consciously experiencing the Bliss of Itself'. This would also be a possible place to merge after death.

I believe this oscillation however, is at a somewhat lower level or dimension of existence, where there is still a differentiation of individual Soul present in the all-pervasive matrix of the Divine. The incipient beginning of the spanda, or wave of all that is, into our own individuality can be perceived as a separation from the whole.

I experience the Divine Matrix, as Gregg Braden speaks of in his book by that name, in many ways.

When I was a child, lying in bed at night in the dark, the room would often dance with dots of light that reminded me of the pixilated dots of a TV screen. I saw them as many colors and swirling beautifully. Recently, that has become my perceptual field, which is prevalent day or night, no matter where I look. All things, people and objects for me, with just a slight visual shift in the way I am viewing them, are always composed of tiny, luminescent scintillating swirling dots. Before reading *The Disappearance of the Universe*, I thought this was a cool, somewhat psychedelic phenomenon. After reading that book, it all of a sudden, in a quantized way, dawned on me that the dots are actually what IS real, rather than the object filled world of 3-D!

For me the holo-deck of the Star Trek television series is a close approximation to my present view of reality. We enter the holo-deck, which is the Divine Matrix of all co- creative possibilities. Our thoughts, activated by the intensity of our emotions, engage the holo-deck programming into its active mode. We live out what we have created, and then re-oscillate back into the co-creative mode, by generating a new thought again, which is activated in proportion to the intensity of our emotion.

Finally after many co-creative rounds, we end the program. This can be done temporarily by retreating to the sleep state, either still practicing our routines more fluidly in the dream state, or returning to the profound rejuvenation of the deep sleep state, which I see as the re-merging with the Divine Matrix.

Since we are truly ONE, all beings and things exist within every cell of our bodies. The Universe also exists in fractals, so that patterns repeat at every level.

For instance, all that we know is composed of altering regions of no matter and dense matter. So, there is the nucleus or center of the atom, and then a region of nothingness before each shell of electrons appears in its quantized shape. Most of the Universe is nothing, that is non-matter. Each atom contains only about 1/50,000 of anything at all, at least anything that we call matter, that having mass and occupying space. The rest is 'empty space'.

This same pattern repeats in our star systems, with the star at the center and planets at huge distances out from the central sun. Again the pattern is seen with galaxies and the enormous space of seeming nothingness between them. This is the fractal, repeating patterned universe we live in.

So, just as we are oscillating in and out of this reality at a subtle level of which we are not aware, the same fractal pattern is occurring with our sleeping and waking states. In exactly the same way, I believe death is a mirror of this oscillation of co-creation. That is, as we die, I postulate that the individualized Soul consciousness is just taking a rest, as we do each night in sleep, before re-oscillating in to a new co-creative process, that is, a new life.

So, after reading Gary Renard's book, I came to believe that the dots are reality, and this world an illusion that I am choosing through my thoughts to co-create. The dots are what I see of the Divine Matrix out of which everything emerges and of which everything is composed.

For me, there is also an auditory aspect of the Divine Matrix. Just as I can always choose to focus on the dots, I can also choose to focus on the shimmery, fairly high-pitched sound, which underlies everything. When I am in profound energetic states, this sound increases in amplitude.

I have a feeling that at least some cases of tinnitus are just this, a spiritual awareness of the sound of the Divine Matrix. I fall into bliss when I hear this. Perhaps fear of the unusual and unexplainable at times governs the difficulties some have with this condition. Of course I don't know, since the only sounds I can hear are mine and not someone else's. Inner sounds, like inner lights or even smells are difficult to describe accurately to another person. Really, all we have is our own experience and accounts told or written by another.

So for me, Gary Renard's book, *The Disappearance of the Universe*, gifted me with ideas that catalyzed my shift from finding the 3-D physical world most real, to dwelling primarily in energetic realms. This in turn de-emphasized the dramas of my life, and let me live more enjoyably in the ongoing joy and juiciness of the energetic realms. This let me take the difficulties of my life circumstances far less seriously, since I was starting to see everything and everyone as swirls of energy. It let me move forward towards accepting life's flows with more humor, even the worst tragedies, and made living life far easier and more fun.

This **energetic view of reality** became a **fourth door** for me to **forgiving**. I might call it **aligning with the vertical**.

FOR-GIVING THROUGH ALIGNING WITH THE VERTICAL

One way I used this energetic view of reality was in dealing with a situation that arose in my work life. Near the end of my teaching career, after the point where a student had assaulted me in class, there was the technician that told lies about me. He went to the Division Dean and said that I had called him a traitor and other names, none of which had any reality. Who knows, perhaps he really believed these illusions.

The Division Chair chose to side with the technician, and my colleagues and the Chemistry Department Chair seemed to me not sympathetic, neither with the student assault

305

incident, nor with the slander from the technician. I felt overwhelmed, angry, alone and without support.

Somehow at that time, I saw nothing was working and tried an experiment. I truly feel that perhaps the most valuable tool I have for my spiritual journey, or sadhana, is the scientific method. What I see as its usefulness is the willingness to run an experiment. One first makes a hypothesis or guess about something. Data is then gathered. Next the experiment is done again with more data being collected to see if it is reproducible, giving the same results. A final conclusion is delayed until sufficient experiments are done over time, in order to gather enough data to substantiate the conclusion.

I knew that I was not happy with the personalities of the people involved in my work situation, and didn't believe that I could alter the way they viewed me. I saw no way of rationally convincing them to rally to my perspective of the incidents, given who I was and who I believed them to be.

My experiment was to align with the vertical, that is, a higher or divine aspect of each of us. The way I chose to practice this was to view all of them as energy eggs. So whatever was said about me, I viewed as a protrusion of energy from their egg to mine. And, whatever I said or did was an emission from my egg of energy towards theirs. It all became, in a strange way, very funny and beautiful watching all the egg-y energy emissions back and forth. It was my way of escaping the pain of the situation and in retrospect, an alignment with that Divine energy matrix of all that is, that is to say, an alignment with the vertical.

What happened shocked me. Within a week of my initiation of this process, to my surprise, the Chemistry Department Chair all of a sudden became my champion in the situation, supporting me with the Division head. It showed me that things could reverse very quickly by aligning with the vertical. This provided a door into forgiveness of myself and of others in a complex situation.

Often now, the underlying light matrix of everything is starting to be my predominant perception of all the things and people around me. When difficulties arise, I find that by viewing any difficult person as a benevolent bundle of light beaming at me, the situation sometimes resolves in bizarre and unexpected ways.

It works so much better than trying to process any specifics of the situation or person. It ignores egos and stories and directly connects us as similar slices of Source.

FORGIVING MOM

These days I often use this technique of aligning with the vertical through finding the thought or the energetic to shift a situation. I recently used the energy egg to resolve a life-long difficult relationship with my mother.

At some point I came to realize that my mother was getting on in years. I longed to clear our relationship of negativity. I felt that with her, I had nearly never been able to finish a sentence in my life. In my maturing viewpoint over the years, I gradually came to see that I had a part in the cyclic pattern of insults, attacks and outraged outbursts that cycled between us. I held up the relationship to the light for about two years fervently desiring to atone for my part in this process but not knowing how to do this or how to extricate myself from our habitual pattern.

At some point I came to realize that I had fused a mother dent into my energetic egg, so that BY MY EXPECTATIONS OF WHO SHE WAS AND BY MY EXPECTATIONS CONCERNING HER, she was only able to fit into the mother dent in my egg that I provided for her. It was like the lock and key patterning that the body provides for enzymes to function.

Enzymes are proteins, which catalyze, that is, increase or decrease the rates of chemical reactions. In reactions involving enzymes, the molecules at the beginning of the process are called substrates, and they are converted into different molecules, called the products.

The specific action of an enzyme with a single substrate can be explained using a Lock and Key analogy first postulated in 1894 by Emil Fischer. In this analogy, the lock is the enzyme and the key is the substrate. Only the correctly sized key (substrate) fits into the keyhole (active site) of the lock (enzyme).

This was the only shape I had been offering to my mother. So I in essence was creating this difficult relationship by only holding open the energy egg pattern I had always known with her and no other. I was thereby locked into the past and not open to the potential newness of NOW, the only place change can ever occur.

I pondered for a very long time how I might change the shape of my egg with respect to her. I knew from my work with mantras, and my studies of how reality is created in this dimension, that in the beginning was the word. So it must be the words I was using in my mind about her that held my energy egg in this mother-shape. Words like, "My mother never lets me finish a sentence."

I then pondered what words described the way I wanted our relationship to be. I knew that I had to state the 'creation words' in the present tense and to invigorate the words with the strongest intensity of emotion that I could muster to 'launch them'.

What I eventually picked was simple and succinct, but contained everything I wanted our relationship to be. As chance and the perfect manifestation of the divine would have it, a perfect opportunity to try to re-shape my energy-egg arose.

For years my mom had been trying to find an independent living community she liked. So, she went around the country visiting and staying at various facilities. She had just stayed at one for a month and wanted my brother and me to fly down to Florida to help her decide if this was the one.

My brother stayed a day, but I spent a month with my mom—one week living at the facility with her, two weeks traveling back to California with her and a week with her visiting with me.

In addition there had been a family gathering in Ohio for about a week and two more week visits to assist her in figuring out her finances and in packing for the move.

This period was a stressful situation for us both. She was an active 87 yr old, on three internet dating sites. She had lived about 54 years in Cleveland, Ohio in a four-bedroom, four-story house, chocked full of clothes in every room, including even her prom dress. She was moving to a one bedroom independent living community in Florida.

So before each of my four visits with her, I practiced for two weeks, twice a day, my positive affirmations in the present tense with a depth of emotion to activate them. For ten minutes, morning and night, I would walk around repeating: "My mother and I have a nurturing, supportive, fun-filled relationship". "My mother and I have a nurturing, supportive, fun-filled relationship". "My mother and I have a nurturing, supportive, fun-filled relationship". That's all.

On the first visit, we went an amazing 7 days before a blow-up ---a particularly bad one. On the second visit, we lasted about ten days before problems arose. The third visit lasted a month –a week of it sharing a small bedroom.

The effects of my practice were beyond imagining. The breakthrough in the relationship occurred when we were living at the independent community in Florida. My mother was in agony trying to decide whether she should opt to move there. She asked me how to decide. I suggested that she ask her inner guidance, her higher power. We then went to bed.

In the morning she recounted an amazing dream that she had. For my mom, her guidance is my deceased father. He had died about 22 years before, three weeks after the birth of my son.

When she went to sleep, my father appeared in her dream. He told her to move to Florida, that it was time to start a new life there. He told her that she would be happy there after her initial adjustment. He also told her that she was being mean to me and that she should kiss my foot. And then to my shock and disbelief, she did.

I can always feel when the Divine, my higher guidance, comes into play, because what actually occurs is unthinkable. Solutions to problems arise in a manner that I could never have conceived. At times like that, I know with certainty that my calling on my alignment with the vertical has been successful and that the Grace of the Universe is embracing me.

This was such a moment. Our relationship somehow mysteriously and permanently shifted instantly. The truth of our relationship is now truly that my mother and I do have a nurturing, supportive and fun-filled relationship, for which I am eternally grateful. We are no longer locked into the habitual drama of getting offended and then attacking each other. We have a normal flow in our conversations where I am able to finish sentences and thoughts. We listen to each other in a respectful manner, which I would never have thought possible. We enjoy each other and truly have fun together.

I have learned thereby to forgive by aligning with the vertical and seeing my part in the situation. And I thank God for my scientific training and my willingness to run such 'experiments' in my life.

JUST SUPPOSE

One of my favorite Sufi tales involves Nasrudin, who is often portrayed as a simpleton with great wisdom mixed into his naïveté. This story is called "Science", from *The Pleasantries of the Incredible Mulla Nasrudin* by Idries Shah. It reminds me of how I, as a scientist, dared this experiment with my mother.

A scientist and a logician had met Nasrudin and wrangled with him as they walked along a road. Nasrudin was hard pressed. The scientist said: I cannot accept anything as existing unless I carry out a test, or unless I see it with my own eyes.' The logician said: 'I can not attempt anything unless I have worked it out in theory beforehand.'

Suddenly Nasrudin knelt down and started to pour something into a lake beside the road.
'What are you doing?' they asked together.
'You know how yogurt multiplies when you put it into milk? Well, I am adding a little yogurt to this water.'
'But you can't make yogurt that way!'
Nasrudin then said,
'I know, I know...but - just supposing it takes!'

I never would have imagined it would take with my mother. Thank goodness that my scientific background led me to try the experiment.

Chapter Fourteen:
Transmissions-Out Of Bondage

THE ENLIGHTENMENT TEST

Padma has a brilliant mind and writes beautifully. When I first met him, he worked with people through using a model he had developed called the enlightenment test. He determined a number on his enlightenment scale for various aspects of one's spiritual level of attainment.

The Enlightenment scale is based on the Hawkins scale, where your unique frequency is measured on a scale from 1- 1000. For example, 1 is the feeling of shame, and 500 which represents the feeling of love, going up to 700, which is the entry level into enlightenment and beyond.

The fields that he calibrated on the Enlightenment scale, he determined kinesthesiologically (using arm testing), clairvoyantly and psychically. Padma gave 'enlightenment' numbers for physical, emotional, mental, lightbody, and love embodiments.

Rankings were also provided for Brain Glands and chakras, such as the amygdala, (the heart of the brain), the hypothalamus (the seat of compassion), the pituitary (the third eye chakra), the pineal, the crown chakra and the altamajor (the manifestation chakra).

When he described this to me, I said, please do not send my numerical rankings. My ego will get involved with this, so I'd rather not know. The next thing I knew, he sent me my numbers. He also said that I didn't have to look at them. Of course, I could not resist looking. At the time I found them fascinating.

Padma said his goal was to do various clearings on individuals close to being enlightened, so that their numbers would rise to be above 700, the point of enlightenment. I found the Hawking scale, ranking the vibrations of different emotions, to be fascinating.

What impressed me most about this material was that Padma's materials listed three different levels after enlightenment, with a description of each. Much material exists documenting individual's transition into states of enlightenment, however there are few existent readings on the progressions of advancement, which most certainly must exist after the liberated state is achieved. So Padma's delineation of three further levels led me into years of pondering more profound expansions existent beyond the initially liberated soul.

The three levels after enlightenment were described as follows:

The first level of Enlightenment is the end of suffering and distortion. This is the end of ego identification, and personal attachment. One has mastered their ego, and the soul is fully in charge of your thoughts, words, and deeds.

The second level of enlightenment is Universal and personal unconditional love, wedded together as One. Both human and divine are fully lived, expressed, and experienced as One flow of Love. Nothing is left out, and we can enjoy all that life, and our senses, have to offer us on every plane. Here, Sacred Relationship becomes a key pathway.

The third level of enlightenment is the ultimate aim of Life itself. It occurs when we have fully integrated spirit into matter, and are a Co-creator of the divine plan with God. We have the ability to enlighten others, and we embody all of humanity within ourselves. This joining with the Divine and with all seemingly separate beings, as the ONE that we truly are, must expand into being the Quantum field of the Divine itself.

As I have mentioned, from my own perspective, I had long contemplated that lower states of consciousness leading to 'enlightenment' have been well documented yet this was the first map I had come across for those ever evolving states of consciousness, which must lie after enlightenment.

From my perspective, enlightenment is a state in which a permanent connection with one's own inner light has been established. For me, one candle-like flame resides in my heart, one in the region of my third eye and sometimes one over my crown. Sometimes I see my entire body in a flame, especially a violet flame, usually associated with St. Germaine's healing energy. I think of Saint Germaine's violet flame as a merging of the pink divine feminine flame of the heart merged with the blue divine masculine flame and joined by the golden flame of our Mother/Father Creator Her/Himself, all on the sacred alter within each of our hearts. This threefold flame is the original trinity.

I have come to view these inner lights as representative of a permanent connection with one's higher power, or over-lighting Soul. I postulate that these phenomena are the fruit of a steady ongoing connection to one's higher Self, or God.

The next major roadmap, of which I have some awareness, is that which the Hindu's call moksha, or liberation. This is the point that one experiences one's unity with all beings and all things. So not only has one made that vertical alignment, but one sees that it is the identical higher energy matrix of all beings. One lives in the knowledge of the ONE that we all are, the unity of Soul connectedness present in moksha. One might think of this as an ongoing awareness of the Divine horizontal interconnectedness.

It is from this place that true kindness can arise. From this place one knows beyond a doubt that what one does to another is actually and truly being done to one's Self---not metaphorically, but in actuality. The guilt one causes to arise in another instantly becomes one's own guilt. Every act of vengeance is indeed an act on one's Self.

Another map of consciousness is evolving. Physics string theory delineates 11 states or dimensions of consciousness. I have been intrigued by their animated depiction at: http://www.tenthdimension.com/flash2.php

I have only a vague idea of the feeling states of these dimensions. I look forward to more maps of the ever-evolving states existent on the 'high' side of enlightenment. I relished Padma's presentation of three of these higher realms.

THE CHRIST COUNCIL

Padma also wrote a book called *The Christ Blueprint*. It is a map of thirteen qualities of Christ Consciousness. Each quality is held by one of the Apostles. Each of these thirteen is over-lighted or guided by one of what Padma called the Masters of the Christ Council who were actually each Apostle's Higher Self. Therefore, twice thirteen or 26 aspects of the Christ were delineated. Padma had received, as a transmission from the higher realms, a symbol for each of the 26 aspects as well.

For maybe five months I meticulously went through Padma's book, editing it. It was a wonderful journey. His book can be found at http://www.christblueprint.com/ As I entered into a deeper mentorship relationship with Padma, the following communication transpired.

I wrote Padma the following: "A life roundup is happening for me. There is a loosening of wants, or self-directedness or even caring. The one and only intent I cling to is to solely function as God's intention manifesting and if that is to be enlightened, then fabulous and if not, then great. And if I'm off to be God's instrument resonating, fabulous, but if the Divine Intention is for me to take up knitting instead of supporting the evolution of earlier medical diagnostics, then svaha, so be it. Whatever Spirit leads me to do, I am now willing and I am willing NOW."

"Padma, I couldn't feel more graced than having your support and guidance and assistance in the metamorphosis I feel overtaking me. I feel as if I am entering a ministry in Truth as I leave my career and I am God's, 24/7, with no restrictions or limitations."

I feel more under the auspices of or maybe in some way a part of the Christ Council all the time. Interestingly my concept/questions/contemplation of the nature of the Christ Council began during my baptism in the Jordan River when I first became aware of the idea of any of us being able to become 'Christed'.

I believe the Christ Council to be the overlighting energy of the ONE combined mind of Ascended Spirit, which highlighted Jesus and is now available as never before to bring humankind into the state of Christedness. It is this joint Christedness of the One mind we truly are that is the second coming. An unprecedented support by the Council of Christ to embody itself into humanity exists now. This is part of the divine plan set up 2000 years ago, and ready to flower now.

Then, I asked Padma, " How do you define and recognize enlightenment? What would you call the leap I experienced in 2001 where happiness and joy became a possible moment by moment choice?"

Padma wrote back that one of his passions is to work closely with people who are close to an enlightened point and just need the breakthrough energy and support to open themselves up to Self fully. For him, to have one enlightened person is better than 100,000 moderately happy humans.

He said that he felt that Holy Spirit had told him that this is so. "I feel I can assist you in reaching this state in a number of ways", he said. "One is through a breakthrough scale called the Enlightenment Test. The other is through specific transmissions for specific clearings, which you still need to open up further to Holy Spirit.

Your vessel is a vessel for Holy Spirit to flow through, and for that to be made powerfully effective in your singing and energy transmitting, you have to be enlightened.

The Christ Council has big plans for you, which can now be activated as you are finishing your old life obligations, and are free to pursue the next step and octave freely, and without worry, on a worldly level."

Shortly after this communication with Padma, I received a download of information on the Christ Council during the night in my dream state. This is the information I received.

'The Christed state is characterized by a cyclical connectivity to Supernal Mind. Large and detailed bodies of information are downloaded in the NOW and hence in a time frame that seems instantaneous. This occurs on a 'need to know' basis. In fact ALL knowledge, existent and never before accessed, is thereby available without study or external access mode. It is only and always what is necessary and all of what is pertinent.

This occurs from a stabilization of the opening of the crown chakra and its eventual flow to higher chakra fields existent between body and Universe. These, some purport 17 chakras twixt Central Earth and Central Sun, are connected and thereby create an individual's 'ley line' flow to the Universal Mind in all of its manifestations.

The Christed State is only accessible, when an individual has consciously and fully requested it. It is also necessary that receipt of it be consciously and fully acknowledged. This Universal contract with the all-pervasive Divinity is a mutually agreed upon arrangement.'

I felt that during the night, as I consciously surrendered my being to the Christ Council in preparation and for whatever is meant to unfold. In the morning, I awoke from a deep sleep to a knock-knock joke.

Knock, knock!
Who's there?
Christ.
Christ who?
Christ Your Self.

And instantaneously there were six or seven versions of the last line,
with 'Christ' a verb, noun and adjective,
with 'yourself' being one and two words and

with all of the words having capitals or not,
and with various commas.
It was like a continually varying echo of the last line with
multitudinous meanings,
for me
for us
for us all.

Padma and Sundari

ISIS

At this time, Padma had started offering downloads of these energies. One could book sessions with him where he 'virtually transmitted' each archetype's energetic at a specific pre-arranged hour for a fee.

Over the next year, I booked a number of clearing or activation sessions with Padma. He was somewhere in the world, and I would sit for a prearranged hour meditation where he sent a clearing or activation or download. For me the experiences were quite 'real' and impacting.

I was preparing for my first pilgrimage to Egypt, so I thought I would book an Isis activation from Padma. Throughout this recounting, I am referring to the ancient goddess Isis, not the radical group, which did not exist at the time of these adventures. Isis, a goddess figure from ancient Egypt, is the black light, the black Madonna, the womb of the Universe out of which all creation emanates moment by moment. She is one of the 13 'higher self' aspects of the Christ. In Padma's work, she is the over-lighting energy of Mother Mary.

The day after I booked my Isis download with Padma, I awoke, did my morning meditation and afterwards brought in my San Francisco Chronicle from the driveway. I glanced through the paper, turned a page, and my jaw dropped open in shock.

There in front of my eyes was a full-page article on a place called Isis Oasis. This 10-acre site, in Geyserville, California was only a few hours from my house. From the pictures it looked like an amazing Egyptian Temple.

I discovered that Lady Loreon Vigne established Isis Oasis. It's religious branch, the Temple of Isis, is a legally recognized church in California established in June of 1996. Members honor the Goddess Isis, who is also associated with the goddess energy manifesting as Mother Earth. Their goal is to create a spiritual community of like-minded people who live by the Ideals of Maat, the ancient Egyptian goddess of Truth.

Their sanctuary also has overnight rooms, each with Egyptian décor, an Egyptian meeting room, theater, sarcophagus room, temple, pool, spa, sauna, exotic birds and endangered cats such as servals and ocelots.

I called Lady Loreon on the phone and discovered to my joy that it was possible to be ordained in her church as a Priestess of Isis, recognized as clergy by the state of California and the federal government.

Such an ordination would allow me to legally conduct weddings or funerals, do prison or hospital visitations, and do hands-on healings. For years I had wanted to be ordained. I wanted a more spiritual than religious ordination, aligned with principles I could wholeheartedly embrace. I had tried for years to enter the Order of Melchizadek, but the circumstances necessary to accomplish that had not arisen. I had never before heard of the possibility of actually becoming an Isis Priestess.

Immediately it aligned with my heart.

Loreon had me write an essay on the ways that I **was** serving and supporting the planet. She also had me send in the necessary papers and fees. I studied the 42 Ideals of Maat, which are the only principles that one needs to align with in order to be ordained. I was pleased to discover how deeply each of them resonated with my own principles.

Maat was the Egyptian goddess whose primary role in Egyptian mythology was to weigh the hearts of those who had recently died. She represented truth, balance and order. Her feather was the measure that determined whether the Souls of the departed, who were believed to reside in the heart, would reach paradise successfully. If the Soul was not 'lighter than Maat's feather', it could not transition to the higher realms after death.

Below Anubis is weighing a human heart against Maat's feather.

**Anubis, Egyptian God of Death,
weighing a Soul using Maat's Feather**

The 42 Ideals of Maat

by the Temple of Isis in Geyserville, CA:

1. I honor virtue
2. I benefit with gratitude
3. I am peaceful
4. I respect the property of others
5. I affirm that all life is sacred
6. I give offerings that are genuine
7. I live in truth
8. I regard all altars with respect
9. I speak with sincerity
10. I consume only my fair share
11. I offer words of good intent
12. I relate in peace
13. I honor animals with reverence
14. I can be trusted
15. I care for the earth
16. I keep my own council
17. I speak positively of others
18. I remain in balance with my emotions
19. I am trustful in my relationships
20. I hold purity in high esteem
21. I spread joy
22. I do the best I can
23. I communicate with compassion
24. I listen to opposing opinions
25. I create harmony
26. I invoke laughter
27. I am open to love in various forms
28. I am forgiving
29. I am kind
30. I act respectfully of others
31. I am accepting
32. I follow my inner guidance
33. I converse with awareness
34. I do good
35. I give blessings
36. I keep the waters pure

37. I speak with good intent
38. I praise the Goddess and the God
39. I am humble
40. I achieve with integrity
41. I advance through my own abilities
42. I embrace the All

The very day of my Isis download from Padma, was the first time I traveled to Isis Oasis. I was drawn up to Geyserville to the Isis Oasis Temple to join with Isis energy before the transmission, and magically it was the very day, July 23, 2007, that I was ordained as a Priestess of Isis.

Loreon, the High Priestess/retreat site owner /wild cat and bird preserve head, was not there when I arrived. I walked into the empty, open Temple and made my way around to each of the altars at the four sides of the room, with each corner representing one of the four elements. First I went to the fire corner, with a candle to represent the fire. Air had lovely feathers as part of its array. Crystals of many types adorned the earth quadrant.

Finally I approached the water altar, with it's beautiful statue of Isis and its 'unusual carving' and bowl of water below. I reached up to touch the strange portion of the statue and was shocked when it moved. To my surprise, the carved part of the statue was in fact an enormous 4-5 inch moth that had allowed me to pet it. Here below is a photo of that moth. I discovered later that it was a Cecropian moth. Later in the day, I learned that Loreon starts and finishes her life story about founding Isis Oasis, in her book, *The Goddess Bade Me Do It*, with a tale about her encounter with a huge moth – this identical variety. She took my interaction with the moth to be a synchronous sign of the goddess.

**The Moth on the Statue of Isis
on my Ordination Day at Isis Oasis**

I spent the day at Isis Oasis and was pleased to be able to be officially ordained as a Priestess of Isis, recognized as clergy by the State of California, at 7 minutes to seven, about 9 hours before the Isis download from Padma. It seemed to me so magical and perfect.

Constance Demby called in, and in that way became part of the process, as a needed witness to the ordination. She is a masterful musician, and has a last name differing by one letter from mine. It felt pre-arranged by divine forces.

My last hour there, I was handed a key, which had earlier been difficult to find, to the Tomb room. Loreon was on the phone and I was given access alone. I unlocked the door and found stairs leading down into cold, almost pitch-blackness. The faintest candlelight and a flashlight I carried illuminated a large sarcophagus, an ancient Egyptian coffin, and an altar. My flashlight revealed that the ceiling was painted a dark blue with stars and the goddess Nuit. I investigated and found hinges on the box and with difficulty opened it by myself. It was comfortably lined. I wondered how long the air would last inside and how hard it would be to open the lid.

Oh well, I was there and it was my Isis download day. I turned off the flashlight, lifted the lid, removed my shoes, climbed into the sarcophagus, and boldly lowered the lid on myself. I crossed my arms over my chest, somehow wanting to etherically hold an ankh, the ancient Egyptian symbol of long life.

☥

I relaxed. The air stayed good and remarkably fresh, although I had seen no ventilation in the sarcophagus, except for three small holes. I relaxed ever deeper into the blackness.

Somehow I was remembering lying in a sarcophagus in an ancient Egyptian life as part of an initiation ceremony in the pyramid of Giza. I vaguely recalled that to be successful in this initiation one needed to spiral out using a golden mean mathematical spiral into other dimensions or realms. I remembered my elation at succeeding in that test and that there were dire consequences for those who failed.

I loved lying there. I felt a profound sense of deep relaxation permeate my being. I would have chosen to stay there for hours, but probably only remained about 20 minutes. It was late in the day with a long drive ahead. Loreon said I could come back and spend hours there in the sarcophagus. I have returned over the years, but have only spent about an hour at most in the sarcophagus. It is my favorite spot on the grounds.

My experiences that day put me into such an altered state that I got lost three times on the way home. I didn't go to bed until 1:11AM.

For the energetic downloads from Padma, I would sit in meditation at a pre-arranged time and see what arose. I then wrote up what transpired internally for me during that time.

On this particular occasion, I got up at 3:45AM, immediately doing a Hindu Central Channel breathing process, which Padma had taught me. Tears without emotion, as well as yawning, often arose in the process of doing the Central Channel breathing.

Images arose on my internal screen of awareness. Padma picked up and put on the hat of Isis – the red disk and

331

horns. He took it off and put it on me. The red disk sun got darker and darker. It descended down through me into my heart, which became an enormous black hole in the middle of my body. It started swirling, pulling everything into it. It was pulling me into it and from a distance I saw me being pulled in, resisting, with fear and screams – quiet screams somewhat far away from my observer self. I was detached and amused to see my screams. I joined with myself being pulled into the hole of my black sun – the black hole in my chest. Down, down, down into me. I heard, "How far down the Rabbit Hole are you willing to go?" And I immediately responded, "All the way!"

I saw a region of all the stars of the Universe around me. Down, down, down. I am swirling into the Universe's dark matter. I go through the asteroid belt between Jupiter and Mars. It too, is full of miniscule, swirling little black holes, where I realize much of the true dark matter, the unaccounted mass of the Universe, is found. In that region are an infinite number of infinitesimal black holes leading to an infinite number of other Universes.

I fall deeper down into my body, down into my womb, which I find to be full of bumps and gurgles and aliveness. I'm really there in my womb – and there I find another black hole – the one in a bottle I'm sucking. My mouth makes many sucking movements, there in the womb, before my birth. I want a black hole of a nipple to suck, but I'm sucking the hole of a bottle in the womb, waiting to be born. I go deeper into the womb of the Universe and into the blackness between aspects of matter.

Many black holes, swirling, floated by, in my inner visions – an esophagus' dark hole, a stomach - a penis, the penis becoming as large as me, in place of my entire body, the black hole through the shaft of the penis, the dark vaginal hole, contracting – back to the womb.

The black hole pupils of eyes are also black holes of Isis. I think of Egyptian eyes, the eye of Horus, like the eyes of Shiva, which had hung in the entranceway of a huge tent, during a month long silence retreat at an ashram I attended. At the retreat we had all been required to wear the same white outfit. At the time I was sure that it was exactly what I had once worn at a similar gathering in an ancient Egyptian mystery school.

The Shiva eyes and the Isis or Horus eyes lead to infinity within each of us, lead to universes and worlds.

Eye Of Horus   Shiva Eyes

This ended the transmission and the miraculous day I became ordained as a Priestess of Isis.

As time went by, I had other transmissions from Padma, perhaps seven in all.

Moses Transmission

About a month before I was to take my first Egyptian pilgrimage I also decided to book a Moses transmission with Padma before I left. The Journey was called Out of Egypt and followed the route of the exodus from Egypt through the Sinai Peninsula and into Israel at Eilat. Our group was going to the burning bush located at St. Catherine's Monastery in Egypt, and then spending the night atop Mt. Sinai.

For each transmission, which was timed for Padma's convenience wherever he might be on the globe, I first meditated. He was always traveling, so he was in varying time zones. I often awoke in the middle of the night to receive them at the time they were being transmitted. Although this seems like it would be a very subtle phenomena, for me it was rather strong.

So I sat for the Moses transmission at 2AM and this is what ensued.

A cartoon I had seen came to mind showing Moses on Mt. Sinai, the burning bush and innumerable tablets. In it, Moses says, "Wow. Okay. Hmm. Um.......give me the first ten and I'll come back for the rest later."

During my sitting, there came a knowingness that arose in me, that there are not many laws but only one law and that is the ultimate Oneness of everyone and everything.

The name Adam Kadmon came to me. In the religious writings of Kabbalah, the Jewish mystical tradition, it means primal man.

During this download, I see myself in an alley, sitting slumped over my knees, a cap on my head, so no skin or features can be seen. The cap comes off and I am golden-haired beneath. I look up and laugh. I am entirely made of golden light. I appear as a homeless alley-living outcast, but really am entirely a laughing, smiling golden light being.

I refocus in and drop down into my golden light DNA level. I see it clearly. It is a VERY complex multidimensional web-like latticework, not really describable by any ordinary references. It is partially light vibrations and 'semi-vibrations'. It has/creates it's own song in some subtle non-audible/audible non-ordinary and non-describable region.

I see myself, as a golden flying one, encumbered by a hanging, not yet separated chrysalis.

FREEDOM. I am Moses' child – his Golden Child. I am now permitted to enter the land of milk and honey – the promised land – Out of Egypt (the name of my immanent tour to Egypt). I bring my father, Moses, with me. Through me, he is finally able, along with all the generations that will ever be, to enter into Paradise too, through this portal.

Tears flow. I taste the freedom of the Body of Light.
I AM.
Gratitude engulfs me.

335

The Moses cartoon described above, again arises on my inner screen. I see the parting of the Red Sea. Moses is the Holy Zealot. The whole Moses story seems to me, from this space, as being inevitable. Moses was distraught on Mt. Sinai. This seems to me much like letters of Mother Theresa, which came to the public awareness years after her death. She is shown through these to strongly doubt the very existence of God. I am told that the burning bush is Moses himself on fire. How many laws are unfolding within each of us in our DNA. The laws are carved on our own heart. They are being burnt into the fabric of our being.

In this transmission from Padma, I was thus reminded of an actual experience, I had had many years before, where I felt that my guru's name had been carved into my heart in fire.

I thought of my real world experience so many years before during a stay in my guru's ashram. My guru often peeked out from behind a curtain in South Fallsburg at the ashramites ascending to their rooms after the final Shivah Mahimnah chant each evening.

On this particular night, I felt an arrow come from his eyes and pierce my heart. I reached up and clutched my heart. The piercing felt so real. I went upstairs to my eight-roommate bedroom with its four bunk beds and silently cried for hours, with a longing for God the depths of which I had never before experienced.

In the early hours of that morning I cried out, silently, for

God, and I heard God answer, " Go to him." I knew what was meant was real and not figurative. So, still dressed, I left the room, walked down a flight of stairs in the totally still, long ago silent and sleeping ashram.

There was Baba; my guru was waiting for me, totally alone. I walked over to him and pranamed (bowed) placing my head on his feet, tears spilling from my eyes. In perfect unaccented English, which I had never before heard him speak, he said to me, " What is your work and what do you do?" On a mundane level, he knew the answer to these questions. So in the years that followed, I pondered them at a deeper, more spiritual level.

This experience revealed to me that whenever one calls out to God from the depths of one's being, God is there, not in fancy, but in fact. For me at that point in time, my guru was a manifestation of God.

This past experience of mine flashed through me during the Moses transmission. Then my inner process again unfolded. I heard/felt the following:

Moses is Freedom.

The Holiness of the Law is order. The Second Law of Thermodynamics, that the disorder of the Universe must always increase, is reversed. Order is generated from chaos. This is the Reversal. The Moses story is unlikely, improbable. The natural unfoldment of the given law brings order from chaos.

The second coming is the entering the internal land of milk and honey. I feel honey pouring over my head – Amrita, meaning 'nectar', in Sanskrit. In Indian scriptures this internal nectar is described as that which is released from the thousand-petalled lotus of the crown chakra. This internal lotus turns over, releasing its golden fluid, when the kundalini energy, which is initially dormant and coiled at the base of the spine, begins its upward journey to the crown chakra. The rising of this energy from the base of the spine to the top of the head constitutes the entirety of the spiritual path to enlightenment. The kundalini energy is awakened by practices or by contact with a master.

Moses is my heritage, my genes, my family. All goodness and order lies within me. The unfolding is inevitable. The unfolding is life itself. Evolution will happen in me and in all, no matter what we might do. Holy Law is to retrace that journey backwards to the Light Source, which is the retracing of the pathway we traversed to incarnate into this realm. This is the Reversal. This is the reversal of the Second Law of Thermodynamics as well, since internal order rather than disorder is being generated in this process of the return to the light. ΔS (the numerical value of the entropy or disorder) must be less than or equal to zero for this journey to Oneness. Thus ended my Moses Transmission from Padma.

OUT OF EGYPT - THE EXODUS JOURNEY

Within a month of this transmission from Padma, I found myself with a group of 43 pilgrims on an 18-day trip, retracing the exodus journey from Egypt into Israel. This trip was once again, led by Jon Marc Hammar, Jayem, just as my previous Israel trip had been. It was a profound journey.

I believe that one reason these trips were so powerful was the pre-trip preparations, which Jayem required. For months before the trip, the group was asked to daily focus on a joint intention, specific meditations and breath work. Each day for months the group did this individually as a preparation before actually coming together. This seemed to put us into a similar energy vibration, which significantly increased the potency of our group process when we finally met.

For this trip, we were asked to repeat this intention:

Pilgrimage.
Outer places, and inner spaces.
I surrender to a journey deep into my own heart.
I open to be healed into God,
As I invite the Christ Council to surround me, fill me,
Uplift, and transform me.
With my brothers and sisters,
Our pilgrimage begins,
Now.

I was amazed that at the end of this pilgrimage, this intention correctly and precisely had become the flavor of my journey, exactly. Perhaps the repeated exposure had supplied the activation energy input over time, needed to result in the quantum leap to a new state.

THE ELEVEN COMMANDMENTS

One of the most powerful experiences of this pilgrimage for me seemed to be a continuation of my Moses transmission from Padma.

The group spent the night at St Catherine's Monastery at the base of Mt. Sinai. We each were assigned monk-like cells. This is the purported site of the burning bush. Today, much like at the Western Wall in Jerusalem, people put prayers and blessings into the cracks of the stone wall surrounding the burning bush. For me the energy there was thick, peaceful, still and embracing.

**The Burning Bush at St. Catherine's Monastery
Near Mt. Sinai in Egypt**

Looking Down on St. Catherine's Monastery from Mt. Sinai

The next day we started up Mt. Sinai. The terrain is amazingly rugged. It is easily understandable that it took Moses and the fleeing Jews forty years to cross the Sinai Peninsula. I had never seen more formidable geography.

We started up Mt. Sinai on camel early in the morning. As I mounted the camel, the herder assisting us looked at me and said, "Bedouin." It felt exactly right.

Sundari and her Camel on Mt. Sinai

I rode the camel steadily upward for the next 2 ½ hours. It felt the most natural thing in the world to me. At our ranch, my husband and I rode horses. I always felt uncomfortable and insecure doing so. Here however, a lifetime of riding camels in the desert and living in tents floated before my eyes. I felt that I was remembering some wonderful life that had simple, harsh conditions, yet a life that I deeply enjoyed. I especially liked the peculiar rhythmic roll of the camel's gait. Other than traversing some truly precipitous edges and drops, it was a familiar, joyous ride for me.

After the 2 ½ hours, the camels could no longer negotiate the steep, rocky path before us. The next 1 ½ hours were a tiring, difficult uphill climb. The road before me left me shocked that the tour guides had not more fully warned the group about what lay before us on this particular portion of the pilgrimage. I was exhausted when we finally reached the upper ledge of an ancient, now unused church at the top of Mt. Sinai.

It was almost sunset. The group prepared to settle in for the night. We had paid locals to bring up mats and thick, coarse camel hair blankets. The setting sun was beautiful beyond imagining. The stars grew more bountiful and were clearer and more pristine than I ever had seen. As night's stillness enveloped us perched on the top of the world, we settled in for the rather cold night atop Mt. Sinai.

I awoke about 2AM. Everyone was asleep. I felt a stirring in my Soul and Being. The urge to wander off and meditate became a demanding feeling within me. I had no flashlight and there were precipitous drops all around.

There are times when I know with certainty that I have received a calling and this was such a moment. I refuse to doubt when that clear voice is within me. So I wandered off in the dark. Eventually I found a spot to meditate and did so for about the next hour and a half. Sometime during this period Eleven New Commandments downloaded into me in such a way that I did not forget them, although I wasn't able o transcribe them until the next day.

They seemed to me a positively stated version of the original ten with a shift of emphasis. The originals basically say what not to do – 'Thou shalt not...", not what to do, which I consider the 'positive statement of principles. Only after I received them did I consider the effect of the original ten from the perspective of The Secret. That is, the effect of creating with the words we choose to use.

In the Secret, tableaus are acted out depicting the effect of one's word choices. So, if one says, either mentally or out loud, "Please God, remove debt from my life", the effect is to create more debt, SINCE THAT IS THE WORD USED!!! And words create. The word debt causes one to run pictures of debt through one's mind and the pictures elicit feelings, which attach to the picture activating it into manifestation. Similarly, if one says, "Please God, manifest abundance in my life," then abundance is created by the choice of words used.

In the beginning there was the word. So it is the exact word choice that we use, not only audibly, BUT ALSO IN OUR THOUGHTS, that creates the specificity of our reality.

The questions we ask ourselves in our heads are of particular importance. Every item in your home has come into manifestation from your asking yourself a question. Should I buy this computer? Ring? Dishwasher? It is the questions we ask ourselves that lead us along a particular direction in life. What career should I pursue? Should I be a doctor? An Artist? An entrepreneur?

It is the broadest questions, which deal more with goals than means, which serve us best. Such as 'What career will provide abundance and satisfaction in my life?' versus 'Should I be a firefighter?' Broader still might be, 'How can I live in unlimited abundance?' versus "What job should I take?' Instead of 'How can I find a boyfriend?' the internal question might be 'How can I live feeling the abundance of love surrounding me?' The deepest, widest questions allow our inner guidance more possibilities of manifestation in our lives.

Words, with their innate inner vibration, carry the power to create. And so it has been with the original Ten Commandments. They have in fact created and wreaked havoc in our world due to their wording. When one says, 'Thou shalt not kill', it is images of killing that arise in one's mind and hence are created! Similarly, when one says, 'Thou shalt not commit adultery', adultery is exactly what is created in our society. It cannot be otherwise with the particular statement of operating principles that was given from Mt. Sinai.

So, after Padma's Moses transmission, and after going to the burning bush, here is what I received from the download I was gifted on Mt. Sinai.

345

From Mt. Sinai:

The Eleven Commandments

1. **Love your Self. Honor your Self. Worship your Self, for God dwells within you as you.**

2. **See God in each other.**

3. **Serve each other. Make your life a blessing.**

4. **Live in Peace.**

5. **Honor your Mother Earth and Father Sky, whose living elements birthed you.**

6. **Embrace Gratitude.**

7. **Honor Breath.**

8. **Align with your Soul's Passion and the Universe will support you.**

9. **Center in Love's Flame in your heart.**

10. **Visit Silent Stillness regularly.**

11. **Trust. Dwell in the knowledge, All is Perfect – NOW!**

I AM

I found my way back to the still sleeping group and snuggled in under my Bedouin coverings for the remainder of what was to be a short night. As the pre-dawn light started filling the sky, we all awoke in shocked surprise. Around us were hundreds of people who had climbed up the mountain to watch the dawn. It turned out to be a Muslim holiday on which it is particularly auspicious to climb the mountain to see the dawn. The dawn truly was beautiful beyond description.

We spent the next number of hours using a different route to climb down Mt. Sinai back to St. Catherine's monastery. We arrived before breakfast. After a shower and packing up, we were on the road. By mid-day we crossed into Israel at Eilat.

The buses and bus drivers were not allowed to simply drive into Israel from Egypt. There was an extensive 'dead zone' between the two countries. In an eerie scene, we each had to pull all of our luggage from the bus, through a perhaps 50-yard region, with troops with guns on both sides watching us. Eventually we reached the post of Israeli immigration. Finally after being screened, we were allowed to board our new bus with our new Israeli tour guides.

By mid-day we had reached the Jordan River for a five-hour Baptism ceremony. It was powerful beyond measure. How profound had been the fruit of my Moses download!

England

On the way back from this pilgrimage, which followed the Exodus journey through Egypt and Israel, I stopped in England. About half the group was continuing to the Mary Magdalene sites in Southern France. By the time I realized I was interested in doing this, all places were taken. So while this segment of the group was in France, I decided to simultaneously do my own pilgrimage to London, Stonehenge, Avebury, and Glastonbury.

Padma had told me of a wonderful Healing Center on the Tor in Glastonbury, which was run by a friend of his, Elyssis. I spent a night in London, and then took the train and eventually a taxi to Shambalah Healing Center, very close to the Chalice Well in Glastonbury. It was an exquisite spot, to my surprise having extensive Egyptian décor in the common areas.

The garden had a star on the ground, under which it was said an Atlantean energy crystal existed many miles down. Each room had a theme. I was given the Tibetan room, which looked out onto the star. I found the energy of that room to be magical. Each time I entered it, my thoughts ceased-nearly completely, for the entire time I remained in the room. This cessation of the ongoing ripples of my inner landscape was profoundly relaxing.

I enjoyed exploring Glastonbury and it's environs

Elyssis had arranged a private touring car for me. It transported me for a brief, yet potent visit to Avebury, which Abdy had called the earth's heart chakra. From there, the driver took me to a pre-arranged inner tour of Stonehenge. I was able to sit amongst the large boulders, meditate there and feel their solidity.

Stonehenge

On another day, as I was exploring the Tor, I sat on top at the junction of the Mary and Michael planetary ley lines, where the energetic grid lines of the divine feminine, Mary, line meets the divine masculine, Michael, energetic grid line.

The Tor in Glastonbury, England

Just at that moment I heard singing. A group of six women were hoding hands and singing in the Tor. Instantly I knew without a doubt that I was a part of them. Without hesitation, boldly, I stood beside them. I felt so joined with them in every way. We interacted for a moment and I offered to chant for them.

I sang the Lord's Prayer in the original Aramaic and the Peace invocation from the Isa Upanishad in Sanskrit. They honored me with gifts of gratitude – a wonderful book (*The Sacred Quest* by Louise E. Langley) one had just completed writing and which had just been published, a scarf and perfumed Isis oil - all of which surprisingly they had with them at that moment.

I discovered that they, like myself, had just returned from Egypt. Furthermore, many of them had also worked with Abdy, my previous mentor. They had attended energy sessions of his when he was in England. Beyond even those coincidences, most of them also were connected with Edwin Courtenay, my psychic reader. Altogether, the synchronicities along with the large group of friends we had in commom was astounding. I spent the next few days with them in joined activities in Glastonbury. I also visited Glastonbury Abbey, where King Arthur and Queen Gueniviere"s remains are interred. Eventually I returned to London.

HINEYNI – HERE I AM

It was there, alone in a small hotel room, that I reached a state where nothing had any meaning for me other than serving Spirit and the planet. I became willing to surrender every bit of myself to the Divine.

There, alone, I reached my personal epiphanal moment of jumping off the internal 'cliff of the fool' into the abyss of complete trust in the Divine.

I called out to God three times, using that Hebrew word , which Abraham uses three times, to answer God calling him, his son Isaac calling him and finally the angel calling to him to spare the sacrifice of his son Issac. "Hineyni'" he says each time, meaning "Here am I!"

In just such a manner, from the depth of my being, three times I called out, "Hineyni! Hineyni! Hineyni! Here AM I! Whatever, whatever, whatever You need to do to maximize my service to this planet, do it. If you want me never to see my husband again, if you want me never to see my children again, if you want me never to see my house and my clothes and all my things again, I am ready. I will do whatever you want, whenever you want. I will take this case (my large one was stored at Heathrow airport) and I will go wherever you indicate from this moment forward, AS LONG AS YOU MAKE IT CLEAR ENOUGH TO ME TO KNOW THAT IT IS YOU ASKING."

I didn't know then that within one year, every aspect of my life would alter so radically, that the practical possiblity of following Divine Directive moment by moment became an ongoing reality for me and continues to this day. This was not an easy window and involved my life as I knew it crumbling around me in flames. Yet from the ashes, a new life was uncomfortably birthed. From the far side of this transition, I would choose it again. For today God's directives are clear and unmistakable. They take me on unimaginable journeys, lead me to amazing connections and make the day to day fabric of my existense a constant miracle. Even with its considerable trials and tribulations, I would pick this exact life again a thousand times over.

When I purchased an Isis download from Padma, I became a living, functioning Priestess of Isis. After booking Padma's Moses transmission, I lived out Moses' journey and receiving of the tablets. These powerful unfoldings led me to choose to obtain further energetic transmissions.

CHAPTER FIFTEEN: DOWNLOADS AND CLEARINGS

Amygdala

A dramatic download ensued when I booked an Amygdala clearing from Padma. He describes the amygdala as the 'heart of the brain'. This brain region is an almond-shaped structure nestled into the oldest part of the human brain, near its base.

The amygdala detects danger or emotion associated with past experiences from childhood that were stamped within the brain as being dangerous or emotionally significant. If it detects incoming stimuli that match these stamps, then it will alert us to potential danger by pumping increased levels of stress hormones and neurotransmitters through the body and brain.

As this happens, one will typically experience only fragments of the experience, but with the full force of the original emotion, which keep playing out, resulting in repetitive cycles of reaction.

The amygdala, along with the hypothalamus, is also a major brain pleasure center, which generates serotonin production. Serotonin is the hormone of ecstasy. The amygdala is also responsible for the capacity to transcend the known. It is the region in which the dualities of fear or love, attack or peace play out.

Padma says that to open the amygdala to its full potential requires that one travel into the greatest dualities and taboos hidden deep within the subconscious. One has to challenge, and provoke, the underlying fears, anxieties and judgments about oneself, and bring this into a unified recognition, acceptance, and resolution.

So again, I booked a clearing session with Padma, this time of the amygdala. Even before the session time arrived, I felt the gradual descent of a tangible energy noticeably envelop me. A thoughtless state more solidly grounded in peace than I ever have felt, caressed me in stillness and silence.

It was difficult to make dinner. I kept forgetting where I was and what I was doing. Finally, I sat for the clearing keenly aware of the ever-thickening energy. I was virtually thoughtless, and visionless but aware throughout the whole period.

Halfway through the download, there was a jolting and palpable explosion of the lower back area of my brain, a flash outward from the brain stem area in all directions for maybe 6-8 inches. It shocked me and shook me.

Still the thick energy and thoughtless aware state maintained. I was unable to move at all for the next half-hour and did not leave my meditation room for another hour and a half. I was headachy in strange places. That brain stem, rear head-neck area, was sore, tender, hot and aching. I feel very delicate and vulnerable in some undefined way.

354

Heat throbbed down my spine across my whole back down to behind my heart and then after a while, further. I felt feverish. I keep rubbing the amygdala area gently. I think the shape of my lower skull had actually changed. I had noticed it getting bonier over the years and pulled in and now all of a sudden it seemed soft and supple.

At the time, I was surprised to get such a strong distinct reaction to what many would surely judge as the imagined hallucination of someone halfway around the planet sending energy. And to have it be so specific.

Much later from *A Course in Miracles* perspective, I came to realize my own power as the causative principle for all that transpires for me. So one could say that I paid Padma to catalyze my belief that I would have a profound experience of exactly the topic of the clearing. And with my powerful ability to co-create (with exactly the same level of power available to us all), precisely that experience of my amygdala manifested. At the time, it would not have worked without Padma to help me make the space in my awareness to receive these downloads, that are really from my own Self.

PRIDE

As time went by, I decided to book a clearing on what I considered to be a pillar of my egoic structure, pride. I enjoyed what arose in this clearing as I sat in meditation, while Padma transmitted to me from wherever he was in the world.

My internal process during this clearing unfolded in this manner. The word PRIDE appeared like a cartoon, with feet, a face and eyes. I pranamed (bowed), putting my head on its tiny feet, and thanked it for a lifetime of support and for molding my worldview. I told it that I was grateful, but that now it must go.

In essence, I was, from an enneagram perspective, accepting, allowing and honoring the core pillar of my ego. I often think in personality enneagram perspectives, having taught the enneagram with Claudio Naranjo's SAT groups, long before books on the subject existed. We had been required to sign secrecy contracts every three months on the orally presented materials.

During this particular processing with Padma, the little living cartoon of Pride still stood before me. Both of us, the cartoon and I, were a bit distraught. I felt an emotional attachment to it and wanted to cling to it and it to me. I was reluctantly resolute in firmly, but gently, telling it to leave.

It started crying and trying to approach me, sinking emotionally into its heart, in melodramatic four. Then the word blew itself up and growled and tried to scare me, from it's stressed out 8, or venge (vengeance) position. Then it made itself small and helpless trying to win my pity and sympathy through manipulating me. Shucks, it was using every trick of MY book on me!

Finally it went away, leaving me feeling lonely and off center.

A bit of a tight throat cycled in for a moment. Then a really deep energy descended upon me. Deep nothingness grew in me. I thought that was going to be it. I popped out to the rest room for a moment.

I re-sat. I don't remember which came first - the pain, the nausea or the explosions. A groin pull that originated when Abdy pushed me into a woman in the Bali session was reactivated. It became very painful and throbbing, making it hard to sit. Then the nausea in my solar plexus, the third chakra control center, started in waves. Then golden light solar plexus explosions shook me mildly at first and then kept up but on a more subtle level. Lots of golden solar plexus explosions and nausea ensued.

When I was 6 or 7 and molested, I first experienced this flavor of nauseous experience. I think that is when my ego crystallized. My grandfather died, my grandmother moved into my bedroom for the next 6 years, my brother was born and I lost my 'super special only-child' status. Following this period in which I was molested, I must have chosen relatively quickly to hide the events from myself in the realm of repressed memory. They were not recalled until much later in life when my daughter reached about that age.

When in later life I became sexual, romantic activity was for many, many years accompanied by a mildly nauseous feeling.

The golden explosions and nausea of the download continued. I saw, not for the first time, that as a child, I had had to pretend I didn't know what I did know, to survive. I also had to puff myself up to keep from feeling like garbage, which I felt was the way I had been treated. I had to not know what I knew, because at the time he said he'd kill me if I spoke the truth.

The rest of the session was very uncomfortable - a constant golden explosion or outpouring from my solar plexus and nausea.

At the end of the session I 'felt' Padma kiss my forehead and hug me. Telepathically, I asked to be hugged a long time and I did feel that I experienced its reality. I had known all of this before, but I felt very exposed, vulnerable and brave letting it unwind. I also felt somewhat sad and alone.

It was a powerful unwinding of my egoic pillar that occurred and I gained a deeper clarity into the functioning of pride in my beingness.

Aeon Clearing

Next, I booked an Aeon clearing from Padma. Although I didn't relate to Aeons per se, which Padma presented as this realm's energetic entities holding the suffering of the collective unconscious, the clearings had been so powerful and rich with internal imagery and external synchronicities that I decided to experiment with even this.

I am forever grateful for the application of the scientific method to my spiritual life. It has trained me to suspend my judgment that I know how things are and test out various perspectives, giving them my full belief, at least for a while.

So, I decided, "Well, I don't believe in Aeons at the moment, but I'll test out the hypothesis that they exist in some form and run an experiment to see what results ensue. Then after a while of being fully engaged with the system, my experiment, of booking such a session, I'll return to my observational mode and come up with a conclusion. I can then return to the experiment and see if the results are reproducible and whether my conclusion holds." There has been nothing so useful in my life as using this scientific method of suspending my beliefs and what I think I know, and then running experiments on life.

In truth we generate a world around us from the very fabric of our beliefs, thoughts and convictions. We draw to ourselves and in fact create exactly that which supports our views. See demons and evil and they will be there for you in what appears to be reality. Believe you need protection from such and you will. The step that *A Course in Miracles* led me to, was choosing to see the truth of the light, goodness and innocence of everything and everyone around me. From that perspective protection is unnecessary.

Now this takes great practice, perseverance and dedication to foster the seeds of forgiveness within one's being. Dropping blame and victimhood is not an easy task. Yet with choosing to call upon and align with the light of one's inner guidance has led me to ever deepening and a more consistent alignment with these truths. And with the ever increasing conviction of this, combined with an internal vigilance to conflicting thought, my life becomes ever more, peaceful, joyous and happy.

I find that often in groups where I dare to espouse my beliefs about darkness not existing, anxiety and anger may arise in those around me who feel their convictions about evil, demons, and the devil are threatened. Yet darkness is simply the absence of light. Darkness is dispelled as soon as a light is flipped on, just as a shadow has no mass or true substance to it. In the same way I have found that bathing myself in light and joy removes the need for protection from the darkness that seems to exist. This is the choice of happiness.

When I go to make that phone call and realize that I'm expecting my mother to be a difficult person, or my daughter to be caught up in some dramatic difficulty, or the doctor I'm calling to have been as uncaring and rushed as he was before about really hearing my problem, or I discover that I'm assuming that making a particular air reservation will be hard and expensive, I STOP. I adjust my attitude to bless myself with a nurturing, loving mother, a daughter dealing well with her own life waves, a doctor that is competent and caring or a feeling that this reservation will unfold easily. I find with all of these that I need also have a willingness to accept and ALLOW whatever outcome ensues. With this there arises an ever more peaceful life. It is all these little aspects of the darkness that I choose to shine light upon in this manner.

So although I didn't really believe in Aeons, in the manner Padma presented them, I did value and believe in Padma. So, using my scientific method of running an experiment and holding off on judgment, I booked this Aeon clearing to see what would ensue.

Padma spoke of Aeons, mentioned in the Gnostic Gospels, as the Rulers of Earth. They are the prime reason for humanity's suffering and are a deeply ingrained aspect of the collective consciousness. They are sustained by one's very life force, until one is ready to be exorcised from the collective consciousness grid. When one chooses to leave the collective consciousness, one leaves the ancient mind of fear that has governed humanity for millennia.

There is truly only ONE mind dreaming this joint dream of creation. Padma purports that when one is unplugged from the collective consciousness, that is, detached from the Aeon, a basic change in the brain itself occurs allowing an establishment into witness consciousness, leaving the ancient fear mind behind. Through there being only one mind, this unplugging affects the whole, loosening the fear of everyone.

All day I thanked 'Aeon' for this life and all my lives and expressed deep gratitude for its being with me. I declared it was now time for it to go. I was very calm, yet ever so deep within me there was a slight anxiety at telling it to go - just a slight whisper of that awareness.

On my daily walk before the session, the energy was already moderately strong. The beaming of my planetary work was much more expansive than usual. My energy beamed beyond earth, stars and space until it actually touched the Divine All-ness of God and I was immediately shocked at how deeply God was touched by MY energy and by how much God NEEDED my energy! Needed each of our energies to complete Himself!

God thanked me. And I thanked God.
I was deeply moved by that surprising realization.

I bathed, oiled my agna (third eye region), throat, heart, crown and the kundalini area at the base of my spine with oil from St. Marks, the site of the Last Supper in Jerusalem.

I pulled a God/Goddess card from a deck in my meditation room. It was Andhanarishwar, the Divine Androgyne -the merging of Shiva and Shakti, Christ and Magdalene, the Divine Masculine and Divine Feminine.

I thought, 'I am ready no matter what. The energy grew so thick that I had to sit. So deep was it that I was unable to think preparatory thoughts, even though I tried. So I just sank into the depth of the state. There was some slight occasional something, but I was far too deep to remember.

I tried to say goodbye to Aeon, but I couldn't. Somehow, I'd already done my process on my walk; the energy was too deep to redo it. It was not necessary.

Padma appeared on my internal screen at some point and did a curt and formal bow to me. He had a sword and held it above his head swirling downward in patterns like the manner in which the lasers were wielded in Star Wars.

He asked me if I was willing to be rid of the Aeon. I said, "Yes!" He then said, "You realize, you will die." I said, "Yes, I know. It's OK. Do it." This repeated a few times.

I am resolute. It matters not what must go. I am entirely committed to existing solely as God's Christed intention, whatever that might mean. I see less and less far - only barely my next step and really not even that -- only the vector of my next motion's inception. In life, I've stopped thinking about what to do next and am just acting. Not remembering what I'm supposed to do next - just doing it.

For the next half-hour my experience was pretty subtle -a very subtle feeling of a heavy cloak over my back with some energetic rustlings of it. Then at some point it came off the back of my throat and it was a great relief. Then the back of my heart also felt a loosening sensation.

There was some lower sacral, lower spinal, energy movement, yet the cloak stayed attached there.

Suddenly Padma appeared directly in front of me in this vision, with an ax held over my head and to my shock swung it, splitting me down the middle, a bit more than half way, through my skull to below my navel, literally and physically jolting my meditating body.

The two halves of me fell to each side, still attached to the bottom intact part and the legs. Then I realized that I wasn't all gone. A golden Light-being with a larger skull, thereby at first appearing more masculine, was inside the shell that had been me. How perfect that the Divine Androgyne had been pulled before the session.

The more I looked, the more I realized how beautiful, fluid and free this golden being was. I remember seeing slits in my legs, releasing the rest of the golden being that I had become.

I picked up the shell of me in my golden hands and didn't know what to do with it - how to properly dispose of me. I thought of burning me, like a cremation, but it wasn't right, and of water, but that didn't seem right either.

Padma had left. I had no idea, so I asked the Universe what to do with the shell of me. I held me in my hands as high as I could reach as an offering. God appeared and inhaled me into His/Her right nostril. I thought, how perfect. Returning to the place from whence I came.

I turned with fascination to the light, fluidity and freedom of my new form. I marveled at the light extensions that were my feet. I could be earth and let them be tendrils growing deep into the soil, like fast growing plants. I swished up into the air and they were feathery wisps of golden light trailing me. As I became watery, they were like diffuse light flippers propelling me. And as fire, they flickered their light-flames under me. What fun!

I flew. I've always wanted to fly. I was flying along - imagining really flying - and really walking on water.

Padma appeared. I swished right through his golden energy body - feeling there was no resistance. I knew I could be anywhere, do anything in my golden Light-being state.

I merged vaguely in the same region as his 'body' and he laughed soundly, as was his manner. Then I laughed too, and our mutual light body echoed with the sound of us. There was no longer, 'Here I am. Here I'm not.' I could just co-mingle with anything, anywhere. What fun!

I love swishing around in the freedom of my gorgeous, fun Light-body. I felt like the first time swimming worked, where I could just move about freely with such lightness and fluidity.

After swishing around a while, I felt energy under me, like something electrical, turning on, vibrating a little bit- stopping and starting, perhaps rhythmically. I kept thinking it was 'real', but couldn't make sense of it and wasn't sure if it was "external or internal."

I left my meditation room and came downstairs. I lay on my bed. The rhythmic vibration continued. I felt that I was in God's nostril feeling the vibration of God's in-breath and the silent calm of His out-breath. I wondered if I was actually feeling the Universe breathe - or snore!

St. Germaine Transmission

I continued to book these virtual downloads from Padma. I was led to request a Saint Germaine transmission. I had never heard of St. Germaine until Elan, many years before had told me he used St. Germaine as a healing guide and since then, had often called upon this saint's energy to assist me with various healing processes in which I engaged.

In Padma's book The Christ Blueprint, St. Germaine is the overlighting energy for Joseph of Aramathea. The violet flame, which catalyzes spiritual transformation, is associated with St. Germaine.

I booked a 4:30AM transmission from Padma, as he was halfway round the globe at the time. I anointed myself with oil from St. Marks and changed into a deep purple silk robe covering a pale violet silk gown. I wrapped myself in a yak shawl I had purchased in Nepal.

I sat. Over and over, I heard inside me, "I am the Violet Flame". In my fluid violet/purple garments, I felt as such. Yet the internal statement referred to much more than garments. My body lit up as a violet flame.

Violet is technically the highest visible energy color with the shortest wavelength. It is also the hottest colored flame. I became aware of a newly purchased large amethyst crystal rock in the center of my altar, where I had only recently placed it. That was before I had decided to book St. Germaine through Padma.

The symbol for St. Germaine, which Padma received for his Christ Blueprint book, is what is technically in Chemistry, known as chiral. A chiral molecule is one that has an internal plane about which there exists a perfect image, one side of the other, as if the internal plane were a mirror.

Any molecule exhibiting this type of internal reflection is called chiral and once, whimsically, when I was teaching organic chemistry, I listed my name for the semester as Chiral Dembe.

At this moment of the transmission, my identification was as this symbol itself, both in terms of it's chirality as well as looking like a flame to me. The chiral 'Z' 's of the symbol, I see as representing Archangel Zadkiel, the angel of transformation, who seems to me to be innately overseeing and assisting the alchemical transformations that St. Germaine catalyzes.

When I first heard of St. Germaine, Elan was living in my house and he used St. Germaine as a healing guide. I also utilized healing guides but had never before found any as powerful as what I observed with my inner vision while watching Elan do a healing. I, on the internal planes, 'saw' St. Germaine use a vortex patterning to heal, rather than the linear translational energies I had always previously 'observed' with healers. From that time, until the moment Yeshua entered me, and totally changed my modality of healing to shining from my heart rather than using guides, St. Germaine was the only healing guide I used.

For years I had no idea who St. Germaine was and did not know if that one was a woman or man. I think I supposed St. Germaine to be a woman for quite a while, until reading Edwin Courtenay's book, *Reflections*, which contains first person channelings of nine Ascended Masters, each through multiple lifetimes. That book made clear to me that St. Germaine was a man.

I came to hypothesize that Padma seems to be doing long distance Reike, by transmitting the symbols he received for each aspect of the Christ described in his book, *The Christ Blueprint*.

The day or so, before each transmission, I reread the pertinent section of *The Christ Blueprint* relating to the transmission I had booked. Before this download, I reread the five chapters, representing five past lifetimes, pertaining to St. Germaine in Edwin Courtenay's book as well. One of these described his life during the last days of the ancient mythical island of Atlantis. There he was taught a system of 364 symbols, called Inspiration, imparted in short doses, to evolve the people to whom they were given. It was transmitted too late to stop Atlantis' destruction.

There are descriptions in Edwin Courtenay's book of how some Inspirers escaped to Tibet, where 5 symbols were cautiously given out. Some, to whom they were given, did well with them, whereas others twisted the symbols for darker manipulation and control. The Atlantean Inspirers removed themselves from earth, horrified at the man-made disaster resulting in Atlantis' demise. They left 21 symbols, high in the Tibetan mountains, which have become today's Reike. The other symbols have been found over time and are also available on the Akashic level.

As the transmission commenced, I felt the coldness of Tibet. The violet flame surrounded me protectively.

There is an amethyst crystal cavern of my heart that I find myself in. Many years before, I had experienced my heart as a ruby crystal cavern. At another time, I experienced the left half of my skull as a ruby cavern, connected to my heart, and the right half as an amethyst cavern, connected to my womb.

Intuitively for me, the heart is the ruby cavern and the skull the violet amethyst space. In this way, it seems to me, that I have found my red magnetic belly center (kath -leading me to right place, right time, right people) and my heart (oth) in my violet skull and now in this transmission, my violet skull (path) in my heart (oth). The three centers seem to be interconnecting in the transmission. This is a very good thing I think, though I couldn't say just why. My head, heart and belly seemed to join.

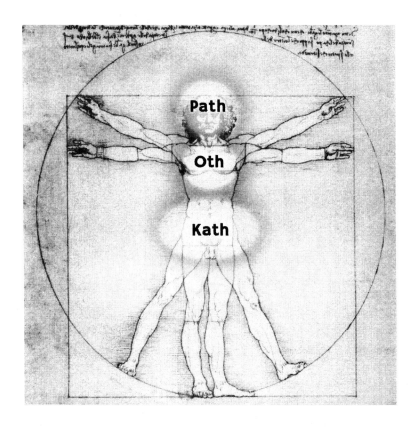

The Three Body Centers or 'Three Brains' of Esoteric Gurdjieff Teachings

In the amethyst chamber of my heart, I look for and find the sacred altar. Christ is there in great golden light. He offers me the Eucharist, I have so longed for, for so many years. I take it. I see the cross symbol of St. Germaine on the Eucharist. Then, I see a dove descending, holding a piece of the Eucharist imprinted with the cross symbol in its mouth.

I look at the Tarot card I had pulled just before this transmission and laughed. The card I picked was the Ace of cups – with a dove holding the Eucharist, with a cross on it dropping it into the chalice, the Holy Grail, which was me. This ended my St. Germaine download.

CORDS of CONNECTION

Padma asked me to join him and two others in joined long-distance transmissions on what he called cords of connection. After the downloads, he planned to compile our joint meditation/visualizations/experiences into a combined book.

Padma formed a theory that the placental cord should not be cut at birth, but only when it became lifeless after a few days. He postulated that the newborn fared better by allowing the cord to finish pulsating and dry out on it's own, rather than being cut. This was because it was still pulsing with life and sending nutrients to the baby. According to Padma, the abrupt, artificial separation, which cord cutting creates, causes terrible trauma leaving a residual and significantly detrimental energetic patterning in the child.

Letting the energy and fluids diminish and leave organically, results in a gentler birth, an easier transition between the womb and the external environment and an easier adaptation to life.

My 'meditation' from Padma's transmission on this process, which he called 'the first separation', felt to me to touch upon scientific 'truths' far more expansive than the original topic, yet holographically and fractally related to it. Here is the information that downloaded onto my internal screen.

I watched as galaxies popped from 'out to in', like an 'outtie' belly button to an 'innie', and back again.

I believe both galaxies and chakras to have an associated vortex energy, expanding out in one direction and going in, in, in at the other, leading to other dimensional portals. On another level this is true as well for fetuses, who have entered from other dimensional portals connecting through the umbilical cord with the physicality they are assuming.

This 'popping in' reminded me of a Tesla chakra meditation I had practiced. I'd received it from a medium of Nicola Tesla's energy. In this session the galaxy phenomena I was 'seeing' was much like chakras, which I experience as vortices, becoming smaller and smaller until they reverse and spread out into a huge vortex into the dimensional space on 'the other side'. For a while I had practiced a channeled Tesla zero-point 12 chakra meditation, in which I visualized each of my chakras becoming smaller and smaller, down to a zero point sizing on the subatomic level....and then smaller still until they 'popped'. I re-felt the inspiration and catalysis that arose from Tesla's meditation while doing this Padma session.

I experienced myself as the cosmic mother who Egyptians called Isis, the all-pervasive Divine Matrix of Black Energy out of which all comes into creation, and which extends out to the edge of the Universe in all directions. The black universal womb of all that was before manifestation is like the field of the cosmic mother before birth of anything from the Divine All-ness of the ONE.

The galaxies are the 'navels attached to umbilical cords' to other dimensions of existence. All galaxies are included. The galaxies are many navels of the ONE, just as the umbilical cords to all the babies eventually extend to the same one pre-birth placental realm of the higher sphere of Unity.

The many navels of all the galaxies are connected to unseen vortices, or tornado-like umbilical cords of dark matter that can't be seen, to the same kind of Oneness realm that all the baby placenta emanate to energetically - Source. The curved hyperspace that I see existing at the edge of our Universe in every direction in my healing work, itself seems a twisted umbilical like cord-tube to I know not where- to other unknown and undefined realms or to Infinity.

The twisted structure of DNA, which itself has a tertiary and quaternary configuration, as actually described in

Chemistry texts, seems again to be an umbilical cord-like structure on it's tertiary level, reminiscent of the corded form I see of our Universe's curved hyperspace edging. So DNA also seems an umbilical cord-like structure as well, leading to some subtle inter-dimensional realm.

For the years following this internal visualization, I have used this other dimensional, curved hyperspace in my daily planetary healing. Cubes, which I experienced at times as merged with Gaia, our planet, came to be removed through my body. Since the entirety of the planet and creation rests in me holographically. to me they represented earth using me as its vehicle to attempt to expel its disorder from various locations.

Long ago, I knew that due to the Second Law of Thermodynamics, which states that chaos must always increase, disorder was building up on this planet, threatening apocalyptic destruction. The only way to alleviate this condition that I could see at the time, was to expand the system, so the disorder had somewhere to go. That's when I became aware of the curved hyperspace on the edge of this 3-D realm.

By adding to the other-dimensional side of that space, thus increasing the system size under consideration in my 'healings', I was able to remove 'the cubes of disorder' from such spots as Yellowstone, Bali, Israel, etc and propel them into where ever it is that the curved hyperspace leads.

The instant the cubes go beyond my view into that curved

space, I feel a rapidity of my breath, a sort of pranic panting, along with a radical shift to feeling more grounded and more 'in my body' and centered instantly, sometimes also with light and color perceptional shifts, although that is much more subtle than the other effects. The ground itself feels more immediate and closer. Over time, it seemed to me that the level of planetary disorder has dissipated, bringing it below the critically dangerous level I had originally seen.

There is another fascinating aspect of our cords of connections that focused for me during this transmission. Cords provide the basic modality of energy sucking or sharing between the egg-like energy beings we call humans.

When the egg-beings, that is, us, throw their silly putty like cords, they stick in various chakral locations. This supplies the mechanism and umbilical routing for all intra-chakral, meaning between chakra, connections. This is like a cord between two placental-like masses, which are the chakras connected between two people's subtle energy bodies. Chakras, actually being vortices to other dimensions, are placental-like in supplying nutrients from other realms. Energetic connections between people thus have an innate placental, umbilical modality.

This is the basis of energetic non-verbal communication. The way we humans connect with each other is to 'throw sticky cords from our chakras to another's chakras.

If I was trying to control the way you see me, I might throw out an energetic cord from my third solar plexus chakra, that of power or control, to your sixth chakra, near the 'third eye, the area between the two physical eyes, which governs how and what one sees. If I felt love, I might cord your fourth chakra near the heart, whereas if I were feeling more like connecting sexually, I would cord your second, lower belly region, sexual chakra.

This is how we feel out the places each of us allow to be connected. When the connection is allowed, the communication of that particular flavor of energy is exchanged between two people.

This would also hold true in psychic healings in which 'healing guides' might be used to 'pull off cords' present, theoretically freeing up one's energy. We might no longer want our parents' cords to our first or lowest, peritoneum level chakra, the survival chakra, but might never have removed them. Similarly, it is our choice whether to allow someone's cording of our solar plexus or third chakra, thus giving them the access to control our energy.

The normal chakra connection cords between others and us must be honored on the energetic level to the same extent that one needs to honor the umbilical cord separation. If the wrong moment and method is used to severe these energetic connections, the same result transpires as severing the cord. There is a leaking and pulsing out of the life force of the Ka, the Egyptian term for the light body or auric field, and a dropping into lower vibration emotions.

This is why the manner in which we come and go is particularly important to our light bodies. We are constantly, every time we interact with anyone, reliving our umbilical separation through the chakral cords. This is a good reason to practice self-healing, rather than receiving healing from someone else. It is also a reason that healing work on another may not hold. We are likely to re-establish that which someone else removes, yet if we personally decide on an energetic change for ourselves, it is likely to hold.

Truly it is always our own choice, whether conscious or not, as to whether we feel drained by another and whether we take in too much or block the flow of energy into our system. Illness and disease can be caused by these circumstances we choose for ourselves. We can always choose again. Knowing this, allows us to re-open or unblock these flows as well.

It is also for this reason that all our comings and goings in life need to be done with kindness and gentleness and why both parties are equally hurt by leaving any relationship or interaction in a violent, abrupt, or hurtful manner. In this case a prematurely cut 'interaction cord' damages us, as well as the other being, and we leak vital light body energy when this happens, until the cord 'dries up'. It is why a painful breakup can hurt for so long. Our cords are leaking our vital energy fluids unless we seal them, usually through forgiveness, mainly of ourselves as well as our partner. Many romantic break-ups occur in this manner. It is for this reason, that the manner of coming and going between people, is of great importance and needs to be done with care and caring.

These ripping away of cords, or leaving them present past their usefulness and not taking responsibility for the energetics of cord connections, is also what is responsible for the ongoing grudge. It is why the pain of that can still be felt, through the leakage or blockage of a cord that has never been attended to. This is also what allows one to heal oneself by removing a cord or sealing its leakage of vital force energy.

This type of energetic pain can thus arise in all kinds of settings, large and small, from leaving a marriage to leaving a party. One might experience all kinds of emotions, when the true causality may be linked to the energetic level.

In this transmission, my consciousness again returned to galaxies' centers leading to other dimensions. We are all still in Isis' womb with umbilical cords of black holes, black light, dark matter leading into the fifth and other dimensions. Our galaxies are like placentas (now viewed from the perspective of the higher dimensional realm) with an electromagnetic umbilical cord supplying nutrients to those other dimensions as well, through the modality of gravity, magnetics, location and mass, cording us to the fifth dimension and beyond.

It is not only God supplying us with nutrition of all kinds through the umbilical system, but we are also supplying God, that which is necessary in the higher realms.

So what nutrients are supplied to the pregnant mother from the baby? Surely that magical glow of pregnancy is something – maybe connected to the father as well. Since there are shared strands of DNA involved, subtle induced electromagnetic feedback loops between the higher dimensional regions of DNA triggered by junk DNA sequencing during pregnancy can supply new, never before experienced resonance harmonics that the fetus and later the child activates.

The common strand of DNA sends out, using induced currents, magnetic signals to the parent strand and visa versa. This is the unbreakable, never severable special connection between DNA blood relatives which stands out over all time in its potency. Marriages can be severed. However the tie to one's children or parents is a bond, which in our 3-D world has no parallel for its power and strength.

The flow of these ideas through me during this transmission was very different from the others. I felt that I was touching Supernal mind, universal truths. They felt to be portions of concepts not yet known, but about to be birthed in the world.

CHAPTER SIXTEEN: LEAVING PADMA'S SPHERE

SANSKRIT

Padma and I emailed frequently between transmissions. There was a common thread of having studied and aligned with the philosophy of Indian Kashmir Shaivism. Padma knew Sanskrit and I had perhaps a 400-500 word Sanskrit vocabulary, although no grammar. I had spent three months in my guru's ashram in India, where I was assigned the seva (sacred service) of changing their chant book from one form of Sanskrit transliteration to another. As part of this work, I was directed to study with a Sanskrit scholar for an hour each day. So it was great fun for me to attempt to email Padma, using some Sanskrit, fairly often. I think we both enjoyed that considerably, although it is quite possible that my attempts at Sanskrit poetry were comical. I used some of the ashram chants as my base.

At one point I wrote this poem for Padma and his Suki Hrudaya (sweet heart). I said, "May your unfolding together bring ever-increasing joy, satisfaction and contentment to your lives".

Namastute suki Padmaji,
para teja nivedayet,
setave ajnana jnana,
tasy Namastute Padma,

Sadananda,
saubhagya dayakam sada,
duhkha bhayam vighnam harakam,
mohanam priye,
hrudi madhyastham,
namastute.a matam!

Sarva saubhaagya vivardhanam

Shveta-ambaram shveta-vilepa-pushpam
muktaa-vibhoosham muditam dvi-netram
vaama-anka-peetha-sthita-divya-Magdalena
manda-smitam saandra-krupaa-nidhaanam

This was my valiant attempt at trying to say:

Salutations, sweet Padma,
Dedicated to illuminating with radiant energies,
Bridging the gap from ignorance to knowledge,
I honor and greet you, Padma.

Ever blissful,
Always bringing good fortune,
Remover of miseries, fears and obstacles
Captivating the beloved
Situated in the center of the heart,
Salutations eternally.

May all your good fortune increase.

Contemplate the one clad in white garments,
Wearing basma (white paste) and white flowers,
Who is adorned with pearls and has two eyes.
On the left side of your lap sits the divine Magdalena,
Who is a treasure house of abundant grace.

At least, this is what I thought I wrote.

SHATTERED TRUST

So, the communications with and transmissions from Padma continued smoothly until December, 2007. At that time Padma had asked three women, including myself, to join him in writing a book. We had all sat for the transmission on Cords of Connection, and he was going to combine what information each of us received into the chapters of the book. When the first combined materials came back, all the women were credited as to their parts, except me. My contributions were written as if Padma had composed them.

I emailed Padma that it was not OK with me to use my material unreferenced. He felt that since the material I wrote resulted from a transmission he initiated, that whatever I wrote from it was his as much as mine. I felt that what I wrote was my artistic product.

This situation shattered the trust between us. He stopped

working on that book. Really what was happening on a more cosmic scale was that my time of having Padma as my mentor was nearing its end. My time of needing any mentors or teachers was also nearing its end. I was being pushed into the Self-reliance of listening to my internal guidance, rather than any external source, for direction and guidance. And, much like with Elan and Abdy before, I was being forced to sever the connection with Padma, even though I could not see that as this meeting of wills unfolded. And just as before, the process was very painful for me. It took me a long time to start to figure out what had occurred, as the intensity of life unfolded rapidly.

Before this incident, I had booked my passage for a pilgrimage through Egypt, which Padma was leading in March 2008. The trip was described as follows:

'This experimental journey is about opening our chakras, each one represented by different temples along the Nile valley. In these temples, while experiencing a transmission of light, Egyptian mantras and some tantric practices, each part of our body, mind and soul will open and activate.

These sacred sanctuaries are originally places of initiation and purification. The rituals that we will celebrate there will ground our heaven into our earth, our body of light into our physical body.

The temples will also themselves receive the benefits of those healings.

Egypt is the heart of the western and eastern spiritual traditions. In its fabulous sacred sites, we find some of the most powerful energies in the world, designed to stir the Master within each of us. Many are being called back to Egypt this year to receive parts of themselves that have long been forgotten, but are now ready to be reclaimed, and remembered.'

Padma

The Tantra of Light Tour

Padma's alchemical journey of personal growth, planetary activation and spiritual transformation was called the Tantra of Light Tour. The group visited the sacred ancient Egyptian chakra temples of the River Nile from the Sudanese border to the Great Pyramid in Cairo. Padma said that each chakra, represented by different temples along the Nile, would be activated and opened through light transmission, Egyptian mantra, and Tantric practices.

In ancient Egypt the temples were used for initiates to

receive and practice energy transmissions, holy breath, tantra yoga, sacred sound and meditation. Light, sound and tantra together have not been done in these places simultaneously for a long time – yet it is what these temples were designed for.

The temples were a progressive set of chakral initiations in the tradition of the ancient Horus mystery schools. If one passed the test of each temple, one progressed to the next. In some, death resulted from a failed initiation, such as flubbing the secret underwater passages, alive with crocodiles, at the Kom Ombo temple. The final initiation in the King's Chamber of the Great Pyramid could also result in death if the spiritual body, exiting along a golden mean spiral path, was not found alive and well in the closed sarcophagus in which one was entombed for the test.

I had already purchased my flight to Egypt before Padma and I had our differing viewpoints on what I had written, so I could see no way out of going. I was wary of the state of the relationship between us. He offered me a partial refund, but I would have lost more than half the money I had already spent. In the end, I chose to go, having no idea of the extent of the unpleasantries to which I was about to subject myself. I did also book myself on a British Egyptian Pilgrimage with a friend of Padma's, Elyssis or Isis, who has a healing center on the Tor in Glastonbury. Her trip began two days after Padma's finished.

Little did I know that these journeys were to be the window into one of most difficult periods of my life.

I booked a two-day pre-trip extension to Abu Simbel on the crocodile infested Lake Nassar, along the Egyptian Sudanese border. The French travel agent who set up the entire journey ran this portion of the trip.

It was very powerful and wonderful for me. I chanted the Lord's Prayer, in the original Aramaic that Jesus spoke, for a small group at this location, close to the border with Sudan. I believe that when done in the original Aramaic, this blessing opens vortices of light, which leave residual seeds of light at any site at which I chant it in this manner. One of my strongest internal directives for taking this trip was to plant these seeds as close to the Sudanese border as I could. It was satisfying to do so this early in the journey.

The Monument of Abu Simbel

The Monument of Abu Simbel, dating from about 1200 BC, is located 280 km from Aswan on the West bank of the Nile in what was once called Nubia. Ramses the Second, also known as Ramses the Great commissioned the site during the 5th year of his long reign. It was not completed until his 35th year as pharaoh.

It is the largest and most beautiful of the many monuments Ramses the Great erected throughout Egypt to proclaim his power. The massive façade, cut into the mountainside, features four statues of Ramses himself, each 20 meters high. Smaller statues of the royal family stand between the four largest statues. These include Ramses' mother, his wife Nefertari, and their sons and daughters.

Within the temple, there are eight large statues depicting Ramses, as the god Osiris, supporting the hefty ceiling. After passing through halls containing rooms for various rituals, visitors arrive at the most famous part of Abu Simbel's inner temple, a sanctuary room with a small altar and four statues of Ramses as different gods.

The temple was designed so precisely for two days each year, in October and February, the morning sun beams its glorious rays directly into the temple and into the small sanctuary room, illuminating the four statues. To the south of the main temple is a smaller temple dedicated to Ramses' most beloved of his many wives, Nefertari, and to the goddess Hathor. The Ramses II and Nefertari Temples, were dedicated to the great God Amon and the

Sun God, RA. There was a wonderful sound and light show our group attended at the temples. To my surprise it was presented in German.

The nearly perfect Solstice alignment of sunlight shining into the inner temple of Abu Simbel at dawn

At dawn, since we were present so close to the February day, which is the birthday date of Ramses II, we were able to view the sunlight rising almost in alignment with the sacred axis of the great temple, illuminating the sanctuary's deities. This portion of the trip was wonderful and spectacular for me. Padma did not join us until day 3 of the trip in Aswan.

From the moment our group arrived in Aswan, the pleasant energetic of the trip shifted for me. I was moved from my room three times. The woman assisting Padma decided to claim the room next to his, which I had at first been assigned. It was a great metaphor for what was about to transpire in our relationship.

I was not happy with the last, very shabby lower room, which I was eventually given. I lay down for a few minutes to rest from all the moves. As I arose, I tried to leave the room, only to discover that the doorknob was inoperative. I was locked in!! Ah well. I went to call the hotel desk and discovered that the phone also did not work. I pounded on the door, yelled and tried what I could for a half-hour and finally realized that there was nothing I could do. I lay down and took a nap, until eventually a roommate showed up, about an hour later, just minutes before the beginning of our group process that evening. This incident foreboded the flavor my pilgrimage would assume.

I hadn't thought that Padma's annoyance with me would pervade the entirety of the trip, but it did. Also, to my shock I quickly discovered that nearly everyone on this pilgrimage ONLY spoke French. Padma was not even conversant in French.

There were only about six solely English speakers in the entire group. They sat together with Padma for nearly every meal of the trip. I was never permitted to join their table. I could speak some rudimentary French, which I hadn't used for about 20 years, and it got a workout. However, I lost all the subtleties of conversations and as I became tired over the course of the trip and the day, I was not able to follow the French at all.

Although we went to powerful sites and engaged in profound ceremonies, there was a constant barrage of criticism from Padma in my direction. I experienced him as constantly finding fault with me and what I was doing. I found solace by sinking into the comforting thought of counting down the days that I still had to tolerate the unpleasant situation in which I found myself.

The group visited some incredible sites.

There was the Philae Temple, also named the Egyptian pearl, dedicated to Isis, universal mother and goddess of magic, reigning over life, death and resurrection. I experienced ancient reminisces from the energy of this goddess temple of a matriarchal period, when women's energies and leadership in religion were key.

At the end of this period, which I associated with this temple, about 12,000 years ago, women priestesses as a whole shut down their 5th chakras located at the throat. Women stopped feeling safe enough to voice their truth. It was the point of the destruction of the Isis and other goddess temples, whereby power became relegated to the men, to the patriarchy.

The key to stepping into the Divine Feminine energies in this present age and thus reclaiming our power to stand strongly beside our men, as full partners, is to reopen the 5th chakra through learning to truly speak our Truth. This is not such an obvious or easy process after such a lack of practice, but more and more the new energies are entering to support this destined evolution.

Next came an early dawn ritual in the sanctuary of Kom Ombo, dedicated to God Sobek, the crocodile god of fertility, water and flooding.

Karnak Temple, the biggest one of ancient Egypt, was designed with great grandeur of height and expansiveness. Most statues there and columns looked like they were built for giants, as are the statues of Abu Simbel as well.

There are myths that the Egyptian gods and goddesses were really the survivors of ancient Atlantis, who were much taller than present day humans. With their never before seen skills and scientific and technological expertise, they were revered and worshipped as holy. Some believe that artifacts and remnants relating to skills possessed by the Atlantean survivors are still existent within the as yet undiscovered chambers in the pyramids, as well as under the Sphinx in what is called the Halls of Amenti.

At the top of many columns in Egyptian temples, one can see the distinct, elongated, extended ears of the Hathors. Some view the Hathors as beneficent extraterrestrials holding the vibrations of love, mirth and melodious sounds. They were said to be particularly tall beings, as suggested by the enormity of some Egyptian structures, such as Karnak.

One highlight of our group's experience was a profound ceremony engaged in at a remote portion of the Karnak Temple, in which there was a larger than life statue of Sekmet, the lion goddess.

Padma's group continued on to the crypt of Denderah, and

then to the temples and tombs of Luxor. It was in this region of Egypt that I experienced my favorite day of any of my three pilgrimages there. My experience involved an intimate communing with the four elements of Egypt.

The day began at dawn, engaged with the element of air, in a hot-air balloon ride over the Valley of the Kings. After our early morning flight, the group was going on to a tour of the Valley of the Kings. Five of us had been to that site the year before and were uninterested in returning so soon. Instead we chose to walk miles in order to see the Valley of the Queens and the Valley of the Artisans, who designed and decorated the walls of the Pyramids.

I felt an deep connection with the earth element of Egypt in this walk. A Frenchman of our little band, Pascal, shared with me the ability to do harmonic overtone singing, similar to that done by the Tuvans. I had studied this technique with my friend, Arjuna of Joshua Tree, who does Harmonic Fusion resonance overtones, while playing a 15-foot long Tibetan long-horn. Pascal and I toned these Tuvan resonances together over many of the tombs.

Pascal and his wife then made a decision to take a taxi back to the hotel. The three of us who remained were told by locals, that if we started simply walking across the desert in a particular direction we would come upon a famous site, Hatchepsut's Temple. It was near noon and we had no water. There was no path. Boldly we three musketeers started walking off into the unmarked desert in the indicated direction. It was really hot and we felt the fire of Egypt burning through us. As time passed and just a bit after we were becoming quite concerned as to whether we had been fools to engage in this undertaking, Hatchepsut's temple peeped into view on the horizon.

After eventually reaching the temple, buying water and touring the site, we three bold adventurers obtained a taxi to the Nile River. Our hotel lay on a ways down the river. We then chose to rent a felucca, a traditional wooden sailing boat, to get to our hotel on the far bank of the river. This allowed us to appreciate the life giving power of the water element in Egypt, especially in contrast to the scorching heat of the desert that preceded it. So ended my magical day of communing with and being deeply grateful for the elements of Egypt, its air, land, fiery heat and life-giving water.

After Luxor, our group went on to a ritual in Abydos, a sanctuary of Osiris. We then continued on to the Saqqarah Pyramids near Cairo, which are the most ancient pyramids found in all of Egypt, and finally to Egypt's most famous pyramid, the Great Pyramid of Giza, a powerful spiritual wonder of the world.

Sundari at the Great Pyramid of Giza and the Sphinx

All throughout this pilgrimage, I experienced Padma as more than icy in his interactions with me. From my perspective there was a barrage of what felt to me insults, attacks and confrontations. I was forbidden to sing for anyone at any time.

When I momentarily stopped doing a healing on a group member, to retrieve my suitcase, while the group was waiting for our luggage at an airport, Padma loudly rebuked me. The delineation of my perceived offenses felt constant. He must have been considerably hurt by our differing views on the writing process to persist in these attempts to separate me from him and the group. I kept counting the days left in the trip, imagining the freedom and joy to be experienced at the end of my time in this fiery caldron of emotion.

EGYPTIAN PAST LIFE

Internally I knew that beyond the mundanities of the present life interactions, I was also processing the depth of emotion from a difficult past life in Egypt.

I had known for a long time of my Egyptian past life interactions with my husband. However, the details of that life came alive with precision as I was actually at the Egyptian sites. I also came to realize how key Padma had been in this story, along with other participants on his pilgrimage. The emotions, which arose in me on this pilgrimage with Padma were those of that life long ago, a life in which I had suffered 'the worst death of all my lives'. Those emotions were added to and fueled by the present circumstances in which I found myself on the trip.

What arose on my inner screen was that in ancient Egypt, Padma had been a great Pharaoh and I had been his wife. Over time the Pharaoh, unbeknownst to me, had come to favor my younger sister. The Pharaoh found a young man, who he thought I would find appealing, and placed him in the circumstances of my palace life. I did in fact fall in love with this young man and he became my cherished lover.

The Pharaoh secretly spied on the course of my interactions with my beloved. After a while, the Pharaoh arranged for my love interest to be placed innocently engaging in activities with another woman, where I could observe them. My consort, the Pharaoh, correctly surmised that jealousy would consume me and it did. In the humiliation of my hubris, I vengefully arranged for my love interest to be killed. And he was.

Informants to the Pharaoh discovered my evil deed and I was tried and condemned to death for my actions. The punishment was death by being buried in the sand and eaten by ants. A scorpion stinging me, by having crawled into my ear, led to my final demise. It was a grateful release into the hereafter that the Egyptian Goddess Selket, the Scorpion Goddess, bestowed upon me.

There was a meditation upon the Scorpion Goddess Selket that the pilgrimage group engaged in during Padma's pilgrimage. She appeared to me on my inner screen and informed me of her role in my history and I thanked her for freeing me from the inner and outer agony I was living out in that life.

In the tale that arose for me during this journey, Padma, as Pharaoh, then married my sister, which had been his goal in trapping me through my own tendencies all along. I shared this story with the woman on the trip, who I realized was an incarnation of that sister. It was exactly my interactions with this woman that had led Padma to his energetic rebuke of me at the airport. So, for me the trip was a re-enactment of the tale involving Padma, my husband and I that had occurred at the very sites we were visiting.

I had been aware of the Egyptian past life with my husband for many years before I met Padma. Yet it was only on this trip that the details emerged. I believe that what I experienced as my husband's most difficult traits, a lack of trust and a hard time just having fun, were traits that I created in him by my cruel actions towards him in this past life. My present life thus afforded me an opportunity to make amends to him by living out our life together. This time around we had the life we both desired, and were never able to live out in Egyptian times.

I realized what I was healing in this lifetime. Better yet, I knew with certainty, that given the choice again, and knowing what I was clearing, I would certainly still select to live out my life with my husband, even with all it's trials and tribulations. It was a great blessing that I was able to share these revelations with my husband when I returned.

My trip with Padma ended and with it my perception of him as my mentor.

Arriving

hOMe

CHAPTER SEVENTEEN: ELYSIS' EGYPT

AT THE PYRAMIDS WITH ELYSIS

For two days after Padma's group left, I stayed on near the Great Pyramids alone, until the gathering of my British group. I had booked a Sacred Geometry trip with them that solely involved time at the pyramids.

I had this group through Padma. The woman running the gathering was a friend of Padma's, Elysis, who runs a healing center on the Tor in Glastonbury.

I had stayed at her inn, Shambhala Healing Center, on the way home from my first Egyptian pilgrimage the previous year. The Glastonbury lodge was a gorgeous place, where each of the seven rooms had a particular theme.

I stayed in the Tibetan room, situated near to the place she purported Atlantean power crystals to be buried a mile down into the earth. To my amazement, each time I entered that room, my thoughts simply ceased for nearly the entire time I stayed there. It was a profoundly soothing and restful retreat site.

Elysis had arranged a private tour of Stonehenge and Avebury for me, where I was able to spend time in the area of the ancient stone monoliths. She first made me aware of her planned pilgrimage to Egypt at that time. I never imagined that I would actually take this trip with her a year later. Had Padma and I been on better terms, I think I would not have decided on this second trip, nearly back to back with his.

Hers was a 12-day Sacred Geometry pilgrimage at the Pyramid of Giza. My hotel room was situated such that I could lie on my bed and stare in awe through the balcony window at the looming Pyramid of Giza directly across the street. For the next 12 days, my room was bathed in the enormity of the energy front the pyramids created. It was profound. I was able to enter the pyramid grounds and explore not only the three large pyramids, but also the many adjoining artifacts and tombs.

Synchronistically, weeks before leaving on this pilgrimage, I had become friendly with a man who believed that he was an incarnation of one of the architects of the Pyramid of Giza. He brought over his drawings of the sacred geometry of the pyramids and of their secret, as yet undiscovered, chambers. Since then Ernie Pecci has completed his book, *The Sacred Geometry of the Great Pyramid, From the Board of its Architects.*

When I wandered on the Giza plateau one day, an Egyptian man approached me and inquired as to whether I would like to see an obscure, usually not visited tomb on the site, which had been that of one of the pyramid's architects. I explored it, with its most unusual figure crawling through a low entrance. I was sure it was the tomb of my friend.

Our group spent considerable time with an older Egyptian man, Hakim, the holder of the 10,000-year-old Khem tradition. Abd'El Hakim Awyan (1926-2008) was an Egyptologist, archaeologist, and indigenous wisdom keeper. He, his wife and some of their 11 grown children lived across the street from the Sphinx, which could be viewed from the balcony of his house.

We asked him questions about the pyramids, their purpose and Egyptian history, as he smoked his sheesha pipe, sitting on the floor in his nearly furniture-less house. His family could arrange many Egyptian adventures, some of which bent local rules. We communed and sang and musically jammed together. His story can be found in Stephen S. Mehler's book, *The Land of Osiris*. Here are Hakim, as he is known, and I together outside his home.

Abd'El Hakim Awyan and Sundari

'WOO WOO'

Right from the start of this pilgrimage, I felt Elysis' program was 'woo woo', that is, far out there, even from my perspective. The group's intention on this Sacred Geometry gathering was to open a Stargate on the Giza Plateau. I knew none of the participants before this trip. I was shocked when, at our first group gathering, Elysis requested those present who were purportedly from various Star systems to stand up.

"Sirians, please stand up", Elysis said. A group did so. "Pleiadians! Alcyons! " I'd never even heard of that star. "Arcturians!" Group after group stood up as my jaw nearly dropped open.

Finally, she said, "Hathors, please stand." Much to my shock, as if some unseen hand had grabbed the rear waistband of my pants and pulled me up, I found myself standing. I had always felt a great affinity for the Hathors, who were supposed to be beings from another Universe who came through a portal on Venus, arriving in ancient Egypt to teach the Egyptians about compassion, love, sound and humor. The Hathors were about 15-16 feet tall. Their images can be seen atop many Egyptian columns. On my first Egyptian tour, I would wager that perhaps 20% of the photos I took were of Hathors. I would seek out their images in each temple.

The Hathors differ from the individual Egyptian goddess Hathor, the goddess of fertility, love, beauty, music, motherhood and joy.

A Hathor at the top of an Egyptian Column

At one of our evening gatherings, Elysis alleged that she had been able to download an audio recording of the Hathors. She started playing it during one of our group meetings, and again my scientific heart was shocked. All that all I heard was COMPLETE SILENCE.

As we were listening, there was a distinct feeling of being impacted on some subtle level. Person after person broke out into laughter, some of them nearly rolling on the floor. I was one of the last to be affected and on some level I had decided to somewhat resist the affect, so as to test its reality. Eventually, I could not contain my laughter and ended up nearly doubled over by the force of it. It was a deep inner state of mirth that I can't say I had ever before experienced. Truly it was a bizarre and strong reaction for me to the playing of the silent recording.

In our second night session, Elysis pronounced, "We have Russian karma to clear. All who are part of this Russian karma, please stand up."

Just like the night before, a force grabbed my butt and pulled it up, forcing me to stand, when I had no intension of doing so. Seven of us ended up rising.

Elysis said, "One of you was Ivan the Terrible." A huge, dark, swarthy man, who most certainly looked to me just the way I'd imagine Ivan the Terrible to be, said, "That's me!" He actually had a mean, aggressive personality, which emerged later as the trip progressed. Another of you is Ivan's wife. "Oh, my God, shrieked one of the women standing, apparently in surprise. "That's me."

It progressed. One person was identified as Stalin's secretary and one as Rasputin's student. Finally Elysis pronounced that the two of us left standing were Romanovs. Again I felt a shock run through me.

Since I had been about 11 years old, when I first read the story of Anastasia, I had been fascinated by the end of the tsarist era. I had no concept of past lives at that time. I simply had a vivid internal picture of exactly how each Romanov had been killed, where they were sitting or standing and what had transpired at the end.

After the February 1917 Russian Revolution, Tzar Nicholas II and his family were placed under house arrest in the Alexander Palace. On July 16, 1918, Bolshevik authorities shot Nicholas II, his immediate family, and four servants in the cellar of the Ipatiev House in Yekaterinburg, Russia.

The family was told that they would be photographed to prove to the people that they were still alive. The family members were arranged appropriately and left alone for several minutes. Soon the very people that were protecting them entered and shot them. There was mystery surrounding the missing youngest children, Anastasia and Alexei, until their bodies were eventually found in a nearby forest and positively identified in 2008.

Whether or not I was a Romanov in a past-life, I believed it to be true on this trip. Our beliefs, charged by our emotions, are what results in manifestation in our 3-D reality.

I see a 3-D axis (x, y, z) vector system where on one of these axes lies our intentions, and on another axis, the strength or amplitude of our emotions with respect to this intention. I perceive the resolving third axis vector as being the way our lives actually manifest. This manifestation has formed directly from how intently we feel about the focus of our thoughts. That is how strongly we feel, either negatively or positively, about any situation in our life, creates exactly that. Those pictures and words running through our minds at any time, if we feel strongly enough about them, will manifest.

Sometimes however, there will be just as strongly felt opposite intentions, which can cancel them out. Also, fear activates the manifestation of exactly those things that we fear. Negative or positive emotions equally activate a word or image. So this is another viewpoint of the phenomena described in the movie and book called *The Secret* by Rhonda Byrne.

For me on this trip, real or not, I came to believe that I had been a Romanov, specifically Anastasia, in a past life. Since I believed this strongly, it started to create situations around me.

The day following this revelation, my Finnish friend Linda, the other Romanov of our group, and I decided to go explore the Giza plateau on our own. We found the tomb of the physician for the Egyptian Pharaoh Khufu (Cheops in Greek). It is believed that the Great Pyramid was constructed for this pharaoh.

As soon as we entered this underground chamber, we found ourselves surrounded by a Russian tour group and it's leader. They spoke only Russian. We looked at each other, eyes twinkling. What amazing synchronicity. I always believe that these co-incidences are aspects of the Divine making Itself known to us, so that we can come to see the magic and support of the Universe, the miracles surrounding the daily fabric of our lives. They are always there if we but choose the vision with which to see them.

My Russian experience continued beyond my time with the group. After all the British members of the group flew home, I had two more days to spend in Egypt alone before my flight home since I had found such a buy on the flight two days later. It was Easter weekend, 2008. I wanted to spend my last two days in downtown Cairo, rather than the more tourist-oriented region around the pyramids.

Before my pilgrimage with Padma, I experienced considerable fear as a Western woman, arriving in Egypt alone at 2AM in the morning during Ramadan. That worked out OK. I also gained confidence during the two days alone between Padma's and Elysis' trips. By the end of these two pilgrimages, I had been a month in Egypt and was very comfortable there. Everyone thought I was Egyptian. I felt ready to dare the bustle of Cairo on my own.

I had not pre-arranged lodging and it turned out to be very difficult to find a room. An Egyptian tour guide who had helped to set up Elysis' group assisted me in eventually finding a hotel. It was a bit more expensive than I usually spend, but not excessive. As all the normal tourist hotels were booked, this one was unusual, although right on the Nile River.

A while after the British group departed, a cab drove me the hour into downtown Cairo and the chaos of Easter weekend. As I arrived at the hotel, my cab driver started pointing out the sites around the hotel. "You are right across from the Russian Embassy", he exclaimed, " and across the street from the Russian School. The hotel houses many Russians."

I laughed from a deep place in myself. Then I gathered myself together. I felt in that moment that my identity as a Romanov was confirmed. True or not, as I walked into the hotel lobby and up to the desk in my fairly elegant Egyptian attire, with my turban, I had the bearing of royalty.

As I approached the hotel desk, they looked at me strangely. They talked amongst themselves in Egyptian, which I do not understand. They kept looking at me and took a very long time to issue my key. Finally I was given a key.

I pressed the elevator button, emerged on my floor and opened the door to my room, only to utter a gasp as I saw what room I had been assigned. Before me lay the penthouse suite which extended the entire length of the top floor of the hotel facing the Nile River.

I entered into a foyer, which opened to my living room with sliding glass doors. These doors took me out to my 40-foot balcony, extending the entire length of this Nile side of the hotel. I had luxurious lounging furniture to lie upon to view the city and the river. The balcony looked directly down upon the guardhouse of the Russian Embassy. From the end of the balcony I could watch the happenings at the Russian School below. The view was beautiful beyond belief and at night I nearly completely refused to sleep due to the exquisite, intoxicating, mesmerizing beauty of the lights of Cairo at night.

All the mosques in Egypt have neon green lights glowing

from them at night, so that they can be easily spotted. At one mosque I visited I asked why the lights were green. I was told, because that is the color of life.

My suite also had two large, decadently wonderful bathrooms and the biggest king-sized bed I'd ever seen. I could lie on the bed and look through a second set of sliding glass doors at the Nile far below. I knew that I had been on some subtle, or maybe not so subtle level, recognized and honored for the Romanov I knew myself to be at that time. And even if it wasn't so, what fun to create that vibration in the 'reality' surrounding me. This suite was fully worthy of any Romanov and was surrounded by Russian compatriots.

My last night there, I had to get up at 5 AM for my flight to London, yet was unable to go to bed till 2 AM, because it was so breathtakingly beautiful.

Even when I eventually returned home, the connection continued. My husband and I had just recently lost our car mechanic of the last 15 years. When I did return home, he told me that he had found a new one. We went together to his business, and I noticed on his card a very unusual last name. It began with an O and ended with a yi. "What kind of name is this?", I asked him. "It's Russian," he replied, "and I am related to the Russian royal family." I couldn't help laughing as to how my Egyptian Russian connections had followed me home.

So had one other ominous prediction that a member of Elysis' group made to me in passing. I spoke with a woman named Joy about my husband. Casually, she leaned over to me and said, "You know, he will die soon." Shocked, I told myself inside that Elan's prediction six years before hadn't come true. I knew better now, I thought, than to believe such things.

A COPTIC EASTER

After the group and Elysis had gone I was alone, wanting to explore Cairo, and brave enough to do so.

I boldly attended an Arabic Easter mass in Cairo's Coptic area. Coptic Christianity existed in Egypt before the birth of Islam in about 600AD. The churches in the Coptic region are ancient and beautiful.

Since the time I had been baptized in the Jordan River, reveled in the Lord's Prayer in Aramaic and had my personal communion with Jeshua, I came to partake of communion on Easter and Christmas. It's not that I've left my Jewish origins, Buddhist connections, Hindu ties and Sufi threads. They all are alive, well and deep in my being. I engage in all their practices with the heart of a zealot. They are all the fly's eye views of the totality of the Divine for me.

I sat along benches at the Coptic Easter service, 2008, with a string of Arab women. The service was in Arabic. I was the only Westerner I could identify at this service. I understood nothing, but found the service to be lovely.

As rows of women around me rose to take communion, I boldly chose to join them. As I received the sacrament a shocking event occurred. The priest gave me the wafer and wine and then looked at me strangely. He then reached over and took my headscarf off my head. I was shocked and terrified, for ever so many reasons. Was I about to be taken into custody as a Westerner, as a Jew, as a non-believer, as a heathen? Maybe I had dressed incorrectly. Maybe non-Arabs couldn't partake. My mind raced, however I maintained my outer calm and simply walked back with the women and sat back in my place.

I saw no one who could explain to me what had transpired. So I simply sat there, somewhat in terror, somewhat perplexed and continued to listen to the service, now from my fear heightened state. Time passed. I was still alive and safe. Gradually my pulse slowed and I again sat listening to the waves of the Christian prayers in Arabic.

After some time, the women around me tried to get my attention. I saw they were pointing to the priest and they gestured for me to go up again. I did as I was told and walked toward the priest at the front of the room.

As I again reached the front of the church, the priest handed me back my now damp headscarf. I came to realize that a drop of wine had landed on the cloth. Since after being blessed it is the blood of Christ; they could not let me simply leave with it as a spot on my garment, so they cleaned it.

In more recent years, I have attended Magdalene Gnostic masses at which a sister Isis Priestess, who is also a Magdalene priestess, officiates. Some of the bread dribbled onto the floor. I felt compelled to pick up every crumb and to learn about its proper disposal. The Easter Mass in Cairo's Coptic quarter seared that into my Soul, the preciousness of the blood and wine.

Later during the Easter weekend, I attended one of the weekly free performances of the whirling dervishes, which take place on Wednesdays and Saturdays. They are performed at Wikala Al Ghuri, a gorgeous merchant's palace from about 1200, which is located nearby the Khan Al Khalili Bazaar. This is across from Al-Azhar Al-Hussein Mosque, where Mohammed's grandson's head is interred. The Mosque houses some very sacred items like what is believed to be the oldest complete manuscript of the Quran.

The Whirling Dervishes of Cairo

I always dressed appropriately for the culture in Egypt. When not at the tourist saturated pyramid region, and at the times I wandered alone, I wore long pants or long skirts. My arms and neck were covered. I also kept my hair covered in a turban at most times and places. Any native approaching me nearly always spoke to me first in Arabic. I was nearly universally mistaken for an Egyptian.

I wandered alone very comfortably at night through the Khan Al-Khallili Bazaar after the Sufi Dancing. It was my last night in Cairo.

Afterwards, I returned to the hotel and stayed up most of the night, lying decadently out on the balcony. The lights of the Nile and Cairo at night lay at my feet.

Alternately, I felt myself the Romanov, or the Egyptian Pharaoh's wife and Priestess of lives long ago. Yet, in the timeless dimension of consciousness, I experienced my being dipping simultaneously into present, past and future realities. My consciousness and the wisdom I gleaned from all those lives I've lived at this place blending into my present – the only place we ever actually exist.

The morning I left Egypt, I had no idea of the enormity of what lay before me. Changes were stalking me that were about to shake every corner of my existence. Somehow I had stepped into the full power of my being.

I didn't realize it until much later, but I had left spiritual mentors and teachers behind. I am ever grateful for each of their influences in my life, in fact the imprint of our joined energies is vibrantly alive within my being. I weep at the grace I experienced from my guru and the awakening of the kundalini energy within me. The guidance on my journey has been invaluable.

By one-pointedly following one path, I received its fruits. I became a Finder, not a Seeker. Elan, Abdy and Padma each gave me invaluable lessons. Somehow, however, their influences have brought me to the place of being my own guru. I seek the answers now from my internal guidance and trust that I am being directed and led most appropriately.

Truly, I know less than I have ever known. I never have any idea of what I should be doing or with whom. Each night however, and sometimes each moment, I call internally on the Divine. That inner Spiritual guide, who rings truer than anyone 'outside' ever could be. Somewhere, somehow, I have come to hear the difference within, between the still, small voice of the Divine and 'my voice' of my ego-self. I have learned somehow to align and know the feel of that still, small voice's guidance. I am so grateful.

MY HUSBAND, DON

I returned home to my husband. I shared with him my revelations and adventures from the trip. I told him what I learned of our 'past-life' together in Egypt. I shared with him how I believe myself to have been catalytic in creating in him those traits of his with which I found most difficult to live.

My heart expanded in sharing with him that I knew, without doubt, that even with all our trials and tribulations, difficulties and hassles, that I would, without a doubt, choose this life with him again, knowing what we were learning from each other and knowing what we were karmically clearing by staying together. We had dated for six years and in the upcoming August it would be 25 years we had been married,

Three weeks after my return, suddenly, in a six-hour period, he died.

My husband, Don Brunner, died on Wednesday, April 23, 2008 from a sudden, massive, hemorrhagic stroke. He worked outdoors that day. We had breakfast near our first house at our favorite breakfast spot. He had a doctor's appointment that morning, right next to the hospital in which he would expire before the next day's light. We even went over to the hospital's gift shop and he wanted to buy me a jacket I liked. It was a very normal day.

Don worked outside doing this and that around the house. I made dinner and we ate. As he cleaned up the dinner dishes, as was our normal way, I checked on my spiritual email network, about 500 around the globe at that time. Almost daily someone, with whom I'd been on pilgrimage, would send me something of spiritual interest, and when I was so moved, I'd share it with the others, all of whom I knew.

That night I was watching a link someone in my network had sent: (http://www.microclesia.com/?p=320) It was an uplifting video of Harvard brain researcher, Jill Bolte Taylor, describing her own hemorrhagic stroke. It had been sent to me and I synchronistically watched it, just as my husband's symptoms developed.

Don and I taught Chemistry together at Diablo Valley College, a California Community college. He was from a Forty-Niner gold mining family. His great grandmother, Daniel Boone's niece, California Real, was the first baby to be born in the mining camps of California. Other of his ancestors took a boat from New York to Nicaragua, which they traversed on foot, before the Panama Canal was constructed. After arriving in San Francisco, they walked to Angels Camp, carrying with them everything they owned. Yet other 19th century ancestors of his lived at Sutter's Fort and adopted some of the surviving children of the Donner party.

As a young child, Don had actually lived in Bodie, California, the lawless, wild gold mining town, now a ghost town. After his dad was in a mining accident, when he was four, he grew up with his grandparents, without electricity, running water or a telephone. He never spoke on a phone until he was 20 years old. He rode a horse to school, went on cattle drives and played with groups of wandering Indian children.

Don was a man of the land, single-handedly managing our three ranches, 100 sheep and a horse, irrigating 20 acres six months a year, often awaking at 2 AM to change pipes, pruning 20 fruit trees and tending to the sacredness of the earth. It was his worship and his religion. It was a profound time of transition for the family, of endings and beginnings, of sorrow and joy, of leaving that which was and stepping into the uncertainty and the newness of NOW.

Three weeks after Don died, my uncle with whom I lived with until I was 15 years old, passed and then four close family friends. David, our son, graduated from college in Digital Animation one week after his dad's death and turned 21 a month later. Our daughter, Sabrina, took over running our sheep ranches with her boyfriend, and giving pottery/ceramics classes with an artists colony near the ranch. She bought a goat, born the day Don died, and brought it home between the two dogs on the back seat of the truck, when she drove in for the memorial service. She trained it not to pee in the car, but to jump out and go with the dogs. She also procured a guard llama to chase coyotes from the 100 sheep we had at the time. With the llama around, we no longer had a third of the flock decimated, as had been the case the previous year. In fact, no sheep were lost as long as the llama was present.

I had met Don as a member of my hiring committee on my first day of contact with the school at which we taught, and the day of his memorial was actually exactly my last official day of work at that job. It was an incredibly intense period.

It was also an amazing time, where doors opened and I lived between the worlds. I spent three days with my husband's body after he died. I passed many hours after his death that night lying beside his body at the hospital. A few days later, I chanted and looked deeply into his eyes off and on for an hour in the hospital morgue.

I also spent one day at the mortuary from 11 AM to 6 PM. I cleaned and oiled my husband's body. He looked so peaceful. Even a clergywoman at the hospital kept telling me, "He looks so happy!" But it was much more. I felt the reality of his energy there for days and every time I stared deep into his eyes, I instantly became ecstatic from the Spirit union, which took place between us in that space between the worlds.

However, by the time of his cremation about 10 days later, I no longer experienced his energy as 'being there'. In Hinduism, it is said that the Spirit separates completely from the body after 13 days.

I personally performed the cremation, with four goddess women, who dared to join me. Don grew roses, which once a year, only at the first blooming, have blossoms 9-12 inches across. The day of his cremation (also the 34th anniversary of the day I met my guru, Baba) seven roses were in their state of being enormous blossoms and I placed these on his body. I chanted the Jewish Kaddish, the Lord's Prayer in Aramaic, the Peace Invocation in Sanskrit from the Isa Upanishad (Om Purnamidah) and one friend chanted the Buddhist Amitabhah.

One of the women present, I had met at an ashram in India. By chance her father had been my husband's best military buddy when he served. I had also conducted her husband's memorial service when he died.

I placed oil from the altar at the last supper site (St. Marks in Jerusalem) and bhasma, Indian ash, on my husband's body. I turned on the cremation myself, toned in a cacophony of languages and finished by pranaming (bowing) flat on the floor.

The cremation workman, who usually does this alone, was in tears and hugged me. The women, none of whom knew each other, and I chanted the Guru Gita, while the cremation process ensued. It was almost as if we were some ancient goddess cell, rejoined in order to ground a new vision of death into the planet. For me, all this was obvious to do, although I never read, heard or thought of such things before, nor did I know how comfortable I'd be around death. There was an ancient knowingness. I came to feel that in one past-life, I had been part of the transition team leading souls to the light after death, likely in Egypt.

On the 13th day, which was Cinco de Mayo and also the new moon, I picked up Don's remains. Before I brought them home I went to the Lafayette Reservoir. It was a cool, windy Monday with almost no one around. I carried the remains out to the end of a pier and put down a mat on which to sit. I planned to meditate and to recite special mantras obtained from the ashram, which were to be done on the 13th day, and the new moon day for a year following the death.

As I started meditating, the largest goose I ever saw approached walking down the pier towards me. I said, "Shoo, shoo!," waving my arms, but it wouldn't shoo, shoo. It sauntered up and sat down exactly next to Don's remains on the other side, just as close to him as I was. It's neck curved back as if sleeping while I meditated, but as soon as I started chanting, it became alert and attentive, staying in the same place. It remained nearly the entire hour until a boater lost control in the wind and bumped into the pier. I told the boater that I was doing something private and he replied, "Can't you see I'm out of control."

I looked over and the goose was gone. I resumed chanting and moments later the same goose swam up to me from my left (the other side from Don's cremains) and looked at me intently, hissing three times in a communicative fashion. It stayed until the end of my process and then left.

That evening a group of 23 people associated with the ashram graciously came over to my house to chant the Guru Gita for Don, along with a set of three special mantras for those who have recently died. I was so moved by their kindness.

Don died during Passover, the Jewish festival of Freedom (Liberation). My father died on 4th of July, the celebration of Freedom. My guru's swami name means the bliss of Freedom. Don's cremation was exactly the anniversary of the day I met Baba. This helped me know the perfection of how things had to unfold.

There are ways that I feel I have been gifted to be with my husband during the post-death process, in a real and wonderful way, that I never could have been in life. I came to know, without doubt, his identity as myself, and that I had split into he and me to learn and play out the games, sagas and adventures we did with each other. This dispelled the discomfort, which arose just after he died, when a lens instantly focused and I became acutely aware of all the little ways that I could have been kinder. Our Soul contract with each other revealed itself clearly after his death and I knew with certainty, that given the choice, I would pick exactly this life that I had, even with ALL it's trials and tribulations.

Within four months of my husband's death, our daughter, who had been holding her father's hand when he died, became critically ill. She was hospitalized for nearly three months. Doctors came in regularly telling me that it was likely she would not make it. I consciously knew that I had a choice of buying into my fear or simply holding her in wholeness, light and love. In order to do this I had to internally make peace with it if she chose to die or if she chose to become incapacitated.

I understood that her life was in essence her business, no matter what choices her Soul was making. My only option was to decide how to respond to this. I was able to find peace, even in this tumult around me, by allowing her to be who she was, having the experiences she was having. By seeing myself having a good life no matter what my daughter's choices were, I was able to be there for her, more usefully, without excessive anxiety.

I spent 81 days, 10-16 hours a day, in the hospital with my 23 year old daughter, being told that she likely might not make it. I settled into watching her heart shine, my heart shine, and holding her in wholeness by seeing myself at a lecture she would be giving in the future about this time in her life. And, she made it through.

CHAPTER EIGHTEEN:
The Guide Within

THE END OF NEEDING MENTORS

Thus ended my life, as I had known it. My husband's death removed him as a teacher in my life. I left my lifelong career at this point as well.

My intense interactions with Elan, Abdy and Padma had transitioned me from a long, one pointed guru path. Elan had helped catalyze my first experience of ongoing, extended bliss, completely independent of circumstance. When I met Abdy, I could finally have the conversations at the juxtaposition of metaphysics and science, which I had longed for all my life. He led me into believing myself to be a conduit for the transmission of Christ Maitreya energy. My interactions with him flowered in me the belief in the perfection of life at every moment, even the difficult ones, even my husband's death and my daughter's illness.

Sound is manifesting at a profound and deep core of my Beingness. My life has always flowed along channels of science and music. My essential heart-self rides the silence into pure sound, spilling out eventually as the molecular matter of the universe. Music is one of the stongest ley lines of God's intention expressing through me, yet not the one I aligned with professionally. Padma gifted me with a new depth of connection to a dimension of sound creation emanating from the ONE.

I am eternally grateful for the magic and miracle of having these mentors catalyze and enliven the fabric of my life. I worked and played 3 years with each of them. And then with each, joltingly, like lightening striking, our time was done.

I was at a meditation program soon after my last trip with Padma, but before my husband passed. We were asked to visualize a teacher, mentor, guide or someone we deeply respected standing in front of us, sending energy to us. I was surprised and delighted to find that the person appearing in my visualization was myself, over-lighted by the Christ Council, seven Archangels, the Ascended Masters, the Elohim and Seraphim, that is over-lighted by my connection to my inner Divinity, to that one we might call 'Higher Self' or 'Holy Spirit'.

For me all of these now feel the same. The alignment I speak of is to that Inner Wisdom which is ever greater than our individuality and which guides, directs and supports each of our lives. It is the ONE that we truly are together, not limited by our apparent body containers. It is the place of 'I and my Father are One'.

Seeing that it was me standing before myself, as my own guide, validated for me the success of the process of reclaiming my power and hence my personal responsibility for every aspect of my life. Hopefully any remnants of blaming or victim-hood will fade entirely. As Teddy Roosevelt once said, "The buck stops here."

HERE I AM

I had been on a guru path for decades. I had sought out spiritual teachers and mentors most of my life. However, I am no longer a Seeker, but rather a Finder. I have no further interest in guru's or mentors and guides like Elan, Abdy or Padma. Therefore no more mentors appear.

My only interest is to serve in every moment what that Divine force guides me to do. My path is aligning to hear that voice ever more clearly, moment by moment, and finding the Inner Will to align with That. For me the age of external gurus and teachers is passed.

I only want to bathe constantly in the bliss of existence. I envision this to include Divine Service, Divine communion and play with whoever appears before me on the path, and the exploration of sacred relationship anchored in Truth with everyone. I have much to learn on these topics, but relish the amazing wonders of people and circumstances that sprout around me.

As my life burned about me, I had the choice to fall into misery or enjoy with awe the opportunities and marvels that lay within the difficulties. The only place I found to turn was again that Hebrew word 'Hineyni' --- Here I AM!

As I adjusted to life without my partner, to solely managing what had been our finances and properties, to leaving my career, being there for my children and launching myself into new realms of writing, singing, and energy work, I knew my function in life had become to be in the space of Hineyni – Here I AM. I no longer needed mentors and teachers because somehow I learned that I was the ultimate one who could always be here for me.

Along my guru path I had heard about the quality of a guru described in Sanskrit as 'niralambaya', needing no eternal support, like a strong tree, independent in one's existence. It sounded appealing at the time and I fervently prayed for this quality. It is not looking to others for one's opinions or for guidance. It is being supremely free and effulgent, always sparkling and shining from within. At the time, I had no idea what I was asking for, yet looking back, I was blessed to have these amazing guides leading me ever closer to the niralambaya for which I prayed.

In that state of being niralambaya, it becomes ever more unclear as to what is happening, what to do or what to say in any situation. Yet the inner teacher and guide becomes reliably present to continually lead the way with no planning or even understanding needed on 'my' part. I need do nothing. The best I can simply do is to show up and listen. Hineyni! HERE I AM!

THE PERFECT LOVER

I had been delving into a particular self-exploratory process for 1 1/2 yrs. Just at the moment I finished writing it, I had an epiphany. It was as if my whole life my inner voice and perspective has been more of a witness/parent/judge and all of a sudden it switched to being a lover. With that change of focus, extraordinary happiness arose as I wrote the following:

I am the perfect lover I have always sought. I am the one I have always waited for. And I am available!!! It is me that I have longed for, through all ages, all times. I am the only one in all creation who is the exact, perfect match for all that I am – now and always. I am the only one I can be with in perfect sacred relationship. It is me who can be here for myself 24 hours a day, eternally, now and always, in this life and in all lives. I am so grateful to have finally found myself.

It is such a shock to know - to really know – that this is true – in a deep profound way – not just a play of words or ideas. I am the perfect lover – the one who knows every nuance of my Soul and how to make love to that. The one, who appreciates all the hidden and overt strengths and abilities; the one, who can acknowledge the Power beyond all power within; the one who can always, 24/7, say, I am here for you – I care – I love you infinitely and always – I AM and We Are. I feel like a new bride with her beloved – ever so much gentler, ever so much more caressing –

appreciative of the exotic, special, unique blossom that I am. How could I have been here all along and not truly noticed myself? How fortunate, blessed and graced to finally open my eyes and discover that I am here – at my very own feet.

I don't have to search me out in the four corners of the globe. I am here. And I can actually trust completely that I will always be here – now and forever. I will never abandon myself. I could never imagine anyone else taking my place – ever. I am the one I have always sought.

Dear newly beloved – be my bride – be my husband. Let our marriage and unity exist eternally, from this moment forth – now and forever. So be it. Svaha.

And it was, and it is, and it always will be.
Amun, Amun, Amen.

With that switch to discovering and cherishing
the ONE within,
now, forever and always,
moment-by-moment,
that which becomes available is
The Choice Of Happiness.

Glossary

Abhishek – the ceremonial or ritual bathing of a statue, or murti, of a guru thought to contain the living energy of that teacher.

Absolute Zero – the lowest possible temperature, 0 Kelvin, which is -273.15° Celcius or -459.67° Fahrenheit, where nothing could be colder and where no heat energy remains in a substance.

Adam Kadmon – primal man, the first who contained all future human souls within himself.

Aeon - as used by Padma, energies of the earthly realm, who are the prime reason for humanity's suffering and are a deeply ingrained aspect of the collective consciousness.

Agna – the third eye, or sixth chakra, region in the space between and just above the eyes.

Akashic Records – the etheric record of all knowledge, available on a subtle level to all as needed. Some say these records lie stored in the Halls of Amenti below the Sphinx.

Alpha Particle – a positively charged particle, indistinguishable from a helium atom's nucleus, containing two protons and two neutrons.

Amrita – nectar, especially the internal honey-like taste that can be experienced when the coiled kundalini energy rises into the crown chakra of the head tipping over the thousand-petalled lotus releasing this sweet tasting fluid.

Amygdala – one of the oldest parts of the human brain, just above the topmost vertebrae, with a clear role in processing emotion and memory.

Ankh – an Egyptian symbol of long life.

Anubis – the ancient Egyptian jackal-headed god associated with death and the afterlife. He uses Maat's feather to weigh the recently departed's heart to see if entry to higher after-death realms is warranted.

Arati – a Hindu form of worship involving waving a tray containing a burning candle, representing the light of the Soul or Inner Self, in circles in front of the form of a deity.

Archangel – an angel of high rank.

Archangel Zadkiel - the angel overseeing the process of transformation.

Ascended Masters – those high beings who are no longer embodied on this plane. They have achieved complete mastery and enlightenment, and hence are in a joined state of One-ness with each other and with us all. They are equivalent to the 'Christ Council'.

Ashram – the residence of a guru and his/her followers.

Atlantis – purportedly, an ancient and advanced civilization, contemporary with the final era of Lemuria, located in the Caribbean Gulf region. The scientists of Atlantis ended up destroying it with misuse of their technology, sinking the island civilization. Survivors made their way to Egypt, where they came to be regarded as gods and goddesses due to their advanced knowledge.

Atom – the smallest piece of a pure substance that still retains the properties of that substance.

Aura – the subtle luminous energy around a person or object.

Bambino – a word for baby in Spanish.

Bell's Theorem – a 1964 proof by JS Bell that demonstrates that quantum mechanics is not consistent with locality, that is, that if quantum mechanics is assumed correct, then events can affect something far away, non-local.

Bhagavan – Lord, God, the Supreme Being with specific reference to the aspect having a personality, hence the personification of the Divine.

Bhasma – in Hindu practices sacred ash from a fire ritual worship applied to the body for purification and to connect with the Divine.

Bindi – a small spot of red kumkum placed in the middle of the forehead just between the eyes to represent the 6th energy center (chakra) also known as the third eye, representing inner vision and the flame of the intellect.

Boon – a benefit or favor granted in response to a request.

Brujo – a Mexican or Spanish name for a shaman or sorcerer.

Chakra – one of the major energy centers of the body.

Chemical Bond - a pair of electrons shared between the nuclei or center of two atoms, holding them together.

Chi – a term for the subtle body energy in the Buddhist or Taoist systems.

Chiral – in chemistry, a molecule that has an internal plane about which there exists a perfect image, one side of the other, as if the internal plane were a mirror.

Christ Council - those who are no longer on this plane, no longer embodied and who have achieved complete mastery and enlightenment. They are hence in a joined state of One-ness with each other and with us all. They are equivalent to the 'Ascended Masters'.

Coptic – the Copts are the native Christians of Egypt dating from 600AD before the birth of Islam. There is a Coptic Christian area of Cairo.

Cosmic Rays – very high energy, small wavelength, light radiation from outer space that can cause biological damage.

Cryogenics – the study of substances at very low temperatures.

Darshan – a group gathering to see or meet a guru (spiritual teacher).

Dantien – a Taoist term for one of the energy or chi centers of the body.

Deeksha – a spiritual initiation, or blessing, bringing an expansion of consciousness.

Dervish – a member of a Muslim sect that twirls or whirls for long periods of time to attain states of spiritual ecstasy.

Electromagnetic Radiation – a name for any energy moving at the speed of light, 186,000 miles/hr or 3×10^8 m/sec. It has both electric and magnetic field components, which oscillate in phase perpendicular to each other and perpendicular to the direction of energy.

Electron – a tiny negatively charged sub-atomic particle much smaller than a proton or neutron located in the outer portion of an atom. The study of where it is located is called quantum mechanics.

Elohim – this is a plural or singular term for gods or god in Hebrew. It sometimes also refers to the seraphim, the divine or angelic musicians at the right hand of God.

Enneagram – a nine-pointed geometric patterning, originally introduced to the west by Gurdjieff, relating to universal interlaced relationships of 9,7.3 and 1, used to explain musical scales, and functionings in the natural world. Since the seventies, as introduced first by Oscar Ichazo and then Claudio Naranjo, it has represented a map of ego structures and their dynamics.

Entropy – a scientific quantity for measuring disorder or chaos.

Enzymes – are proteins, which catalyze, that is speed up, biological processes in the body.

Eye of Horus – one of two Egyptian mystery schools, the right and left eyes. Horus was a falcon-headed god of ancient Egypt, the son of Isis and Osiris.

Feng Shui – the Chinese study of the orientation of tombs or houses and flow of energy through them.

Ferromagnetic – the magnetic fields of individual atoms align creating a larger field capable of being attracted to a magnet. Iron, cobalt and nickel are the only ferromagnetic elements.

Flight 93 - the terrorist commandeered flight, which crashed in a field in Pennsylvania on 9/11.

Fractal - a geometric patterning, such that each part has the same character as the whole.

Frequency – the 'wiggle' of energetic waves or a measure of how many cycles per second at which the wave is vibrating.

Full Lotus – a meditation or sitting posture in which both feet are twisted to rest on each thigh.

Gamma Rays – the region of light having tiny wavelengths less than the diameter of an atom and very high energy, dangerous to biological systems.

Gravity - the natural law by which physical bodies are attracted to each other by a force proportional to their masses.

Guru – a spiritual teacher who can take one from the darkness (gu) to the light (ru).

Guru Bhava – a spiritual practice of feeling that one's own energy is identical to that of one's guru; an imitating the guru to feel one's own energy as identical to that of the guru.

Guru Gita – a major Hindu chant extolling the glories and inner meanings of a true guru or spiritual teacher.

Hacienda – in Spanish, the main house on an estate.

Hathors – tall extraterrestrials from another universe, who entered this realm through Venus, carrying the vibrations of love, mirth and melodious sounds. Their visage can be seen at the tops of many Egyptian temple columns. Also, Hathor is a specific Egyptian goddess of fertility, love, beauty, music, motherhood and joy.

Havdalah – the closing ritual that ends the Jewish Sabbath.

Harmonium – an Indian musical instrument played like a piano with one hand, while the other pumps a bellows creating the sound.

Hindi – one of the many languages of modern India.

Holographic – a system, where each and every individual part completely contains the whole.

Horus – the falcon-headed Egyptian god, who was the son of Isis and Osiris.

Hypothalamus - is an area of the brain that produces hormones that control body temperature, hunger, moods, sex drive, sleep, thirst and the release of hormones from many glands.

Hypothesis – a reasoned guess as to what the result of a scientific experiment will be.

Ida – along with the pingala, an energy channel or nadi, twisting around the spine and represented as part of the medical symbol of the caduceus.

Impedance – the measure of the opposition to an electrical current that a circuit presents when a voltage is applied.

Isis - the ancient Egyptian goddess, who was worshipped as the ideal mother and wife, as well as the patroness of nature and magic. From a more expansive perspective, the essential female energy, or dark universal womb, out of which all creation emerges.

Ka – the ancient Egyptian name for the energy body or lightbody surrounding but larger than the physical body.

Kabbalah - Jewish mystical traditions and teachings.

Kaliyuga – the darkest and most unenlightened of the four major long eras or epoch time periods in Hindu philosophy.

Karma - the idea in many eastern religions that our past actions, both 'good' and 'bad', will govern that which transpires in our future lives.

Kath (sounds like *koth*) – in the Sufi tradition, the energy center located in the belly, at the body's gravitational center.

Kibbutz - a collective community in Israel that was traditionally based on agriculture.

Kinesthesiology – applied kinesthesiology is a technique in alternative medicine to help diagnose and determine treatment by using relative strength or weakness of muscles.

Kinetic Energy - energy due to movement.

Kriya – means action. It is an involuntary movement or breath pattern that occurs spontaneously, often during meditation, often arising from the release of inner blockages to the flow of energy in the body.

Kundalini - the dormant spiritual energy coiled at the base of the spine, which can be awakened by spiritual practices, or by a spiritual teacher or guru. It is the movement of this energy to the crown chakra or top of the head, which constitutes the journey to enlightenment or spiritual awakening.

Le Chatelier's Principle – a chemical principle describing how a system in equilibrium, which is perturbed, will shift in such a way as to reduce the applied stress.

Lemuria – an ancient, advanced and more feminine civilization, older than but overlapping time periods with Atlantis. Various land masses around the Pacific Ring of Fire were at one time part of Lemuria, before continental drift pulled it apart. It existed about 26,000 years ago.

Ley Lines – a planetary energy grid, much like acupuncture meridians, around the globe, along which or at junctions of which can be found most 'sacred' planetary sites.

Maat – the ancient Egyptian goddess of Truth, who weighs hearts of those departed to see if they are 'light as a feather', which thereby allowed entry into the higher post-death realms.

Maitreya – this is the overlighting energy of the bridging personality to the Divine, who has been expected for generations by all of the major religions. Christians know him as the Christ, and expect his imminent return. Jews await him as the Messiah; Hindus look for the coming of Krishna; Buddhists expect him as Maitreya Buddha; and Muslims anticipate the Imam Mahdi or Messiah.

Major Arcana – a suit of 22 cards in the Tarot deck.

Mala – in Hindu practice a necklace or bracelet, usually composed of rudraksha seeds, 108 for the necklace, used to count repetitions of sacred words or mantras. This repetition process throughout the day is called japa.

Mantra – a sacred word repeated during the course of meditation or as one goes about one's day.

Melchizadek –king of the righteous, a priest of God. A figure honored in Judaism, Catholicism, the eastern Orthodox, Armenian, Mormon, Lutheran and Ismail churches.

Merkabah – the transmigratory vehicle of the Soul, figuratively the cart or chariot, allowing the ascent to heaven.

Microwave Radiation – the region of light having wavelengths ranging from one meter to one millimeter, used to cook food.

Minor Arcana – one of the two major divisions of a Tarot deck containing the four suits.

Moksha – liberation or a highly evolved spiritual state.

Molecule – the smallest piece of a compound, a pure substance containing two or more atoms, that still has the properties of that substance.

Mridang – a classical double-sided drum of South India.

Murti - a statue of a holy being or guru, thought to contain the living energy of that teacher.

Nadis – one of the 72,000 major energy channels in the body. The three major nadis are the ida, the pingala and the sushumna. The major spinal channel with the ida and pingala twisting around it, is represented in the medical profession by the symbol of the caduceus.

Nama-sankirtana – a Hindu practice of repeating call and response musical chanting.

Niralambaya – from the Sanskrit meaning needing no external support, like a strong tree, independent in one's existence.

Nuclear Reaction – a reaction of the innermost core of an atom, the nucleus, in which the substance itself changes identity, giving off a tremendous amount of energy.

Nucleus – the core or center of an atom containing positively charged protons and neutral neutrons.

Nuit – the Egyptian sky goddess covered with stars and the mother of Isis.

Om Namah Shivaya – a traditional Hindu mantra or sacred words in India meaning 'I bow (or honor) the inner Self in all'.

Ocelot – a South American wild cat, also known as the dwarf leopard.

Oth – in the Sufi tradition, the heart energy center of the body located at the heart.

Path (sounds like *poth*) – in the Sufi tradition, the body energy center, located in the center of the head.

Perpendicular – at a 90-degree angle to each other.

Pingala - along with the ida, an energy channel or nadi, twisting around the spine, and represented in the medical symbol of the caduceus.

Potential Energy - energy due to position.

Prana – the subtle energy of the breath or life force itself.

Pranam - to bow, usually with the head to the ground or lying completely flat, face down on the ground.

Proton – a sub-atomic positively charged particle found in the nucleus or core of an atom and determining its chemical identity.

Puja – in Hinduism worship through a ritual practice or an altar established for rituals.

Punyatithi - the anniversary of the death of a great being.

Quantitative – a scientific process relying on numerical results.

Quantum Mechanics – the study of the shapes and positions electrons occupy in atoms, derived from the four quantum numbers, which are the solutions to Schrödinger's wave equation.

Quantum process – a process occurring all at once, in one big step, not as a gradual unfolding.

Rabbi – a Jewish scholar, teacher or religious leader.

Raga - one of the ancient traditional melodic patterns or modes in Indian music.

Ramadan - is the ninth and most sacred month of the Islamic calendar; Muslims worldwide observe this with a month of fasting.

Reike – a hands-on healing system employing the use of symbols.

Resonance Hybrid – in chemistry, an intermediate truly existing molecular structure blending two or more not actually existing contributing structures.

Resonance Structure – in chemistry, non-existing contributing molecular structures, which are used to help explain the molecular properties of a substance.

Rosh Hashonna – the Jewish New Year.

Rotational Energy – energy due to molecules somersaulting or rotating.

Sadhana – the spiritual path; the term actually means to heat or warm.

Samadhi – the unity state or enlightenment.

Samskaras – impurities, which can be dislodged as kriyas, or involuntary movement releases possibly occurring as the spiritual energy ascends the spine during the course of the spiritual journey to enlightenment.

Sangha – a spiritual community.

Sanskrit - the language of ancient India.

Sarcophagus – a box-like coffin for a corpse. In ancient Egypt they surrounded and protected a royal mummy after death.

Sari – a woman's dress in India consisting of many yards of wrapped material.

Satsang - a gathering with a guru or with devotees, to listen to, assimilate or talk about the Truth.

Second Law of Thermodynamics – a well-established scientific principle stating that the chaos or disorder of the universe, known as the entropy, must always increase.

Sekmet - the ancient Egyptian lion-headed Goddess.

Selket – the ancient Egyptian Scorpion Goddess.

Seraphim - the seraphim, are the divine or angelic musicians at the right hand of god, sometimes also known as Elohim.

Serval – a medium-sized African wild cat with spotted markings.

Seva – sacred service, or work performed, often in an ashram or community.

Sevites – those who do sacred service, or seva, especially in an ashram or guru's community.

Shabbat – the name for the Jewish Sabbath lasting from sundown Friday until sundown Saturday.

Shakti – in Hinduism, the spiritual energy, which is viewed as having a feminine nature.

Shaman – a practitioner who enters into altered states of consciousness, typically during a ritual, to access the spirit world for divination and healing.

Sheesha – an Egyptian water pipe in which different flavors of tobacco are smoked.

Sheik – the spiritual leader of an Arab village.

Shema – the core prayer of Judaism, stating the One-ness of God.

Shivah Mahimnah Stotram - a Sanskrit textual chant devoted to the adoration of Shiva, the Hindu god of destruction or transformation.

Siddha – in Hinduism, an enlightened one, who usually has special powers.

Siddhi - in India, a spiritual power, or psychic ability.

So'ham – in India, a mantra, or sacred repeated word, meaning 'I am That.'

Spanda - a Sanskrit term for the subtle creative pulse of the universe as it manifests into the dynamism of living form.

Spectrum – a grouping of various adjoining wavelengths of light, especially in the visible range of light, such as the red, orange, yellow, green, blue, indigo and violet of a rainbow or the colors into which a prism breaks white light.

String Theory – is a still evolving research in particle physics that attempts to reconcile quantum mechanics and general relativity.

Substrate – the substance that an enzyme works on in a biological system.

Sufi – one practicing esoteric or mystical teachings of Islam or one practicing Neo-Sufism.

Superfluid – a state of matter formed in helium at very low temperatures, in which the liquid displays no friction and can crawl up walls of a container.

Supernal Mind - to create something greater than the human mind can create. The joined wisdom-mind of all.

Sushumna – the central energetic spinal channel in Hinduism around which the ida and pingala wrap.

Swami – a celibate priest in the Hindu religion.

Tai Chi – a Chinese martial art practiced for defense and health, using the body's natural energy or chi.

Tamboura – a stringed drone musical instrument of India, whose lower portion is a gourd.

Tandra – a meditative state most resembling a dream.

Tantra – a set of doctrines, practices, or teachings. The tantric practitioner uses prana, the energetic universal flow, to attain either spiritual or more body associated goals.

Tantric Yoga – a holistic study of the universal macrocosm, from the point of view of the individual, or microcosm, uniting the Divine Masculine and Feminine polarities.

Tao – in Buddhism, the flow or the way, the primordial essence, or natural order of the Universe.

Taoism – a philosophy and religious tradition that emphasizes living in harmony with the flow or universal energy.

Tarot - a pack of playing cards used from the mid-15th century in various parts of Europe for fortune telling.

Tetragrammaton – the four Hebrew letters, Yod, He, Vov, He, representing the unspeakable name of God.

Traspaso – a spiritual practice of staring into the eyes of someone, often involving a transmission of energy.

Vedic – referring to the Vedas, a major Indian scriptural text, or to the period of time in which the Vedas were composed, 1500-500 B.C.

Vibrational Energy – the energy of a molecule due to the motion of its individual atoms with respect to each other.

Vortices (Vortex) – funnel shaped, spinning whirlpools that can form in fluids or gases.

Wavelength – the distance before a wave's shape repeats.

Wave-particle duality – the theory proposed by de Broglie that all matter can either be represented as a particle or as a wavelength.

Yoga – a generic term for the physical, spiritual and mental disciplines originating in ancient India. Yoga means union.

Yom Kippur – the Day of Atonement, the holiest celebration of Judaism.

Yuga – one of the four major epochs of time in Hinduism.

Zhiker – Sufi chanting or devotional prayer.

IN GRATITUDE

Profound thanks go to my daughter, **Sabrina Brunner**, who edited this book, suggested the glossary, and has encouraged and supported the birthing of this volume for so long, my son **David Brunner**, who designed the cover and helped with art, formatting, photography and technical assistance at every juncture, **Elan**, **Abdy** and **Padma**, who so deeply impacted my life, **Baba**, **Uma-Guru**, **Claudio Naranjo** and the SAT (Seeker's After Truth) school, **Jayem (John Marc Hammer)**, every mentor in my life, the spiritual, the secular, and truly each and every person I have ever encountered, **Gary Renard**, who helped me to see the value of my work, **Lee Carroll (Kryon)**, **Dr.Todd Ovokaitys**, **Joe Wolfe**, who offered so much support in the birthing of this work, **David Hoffmeister**, who has helped me bring 'the darkness to the Light', **Dov Fishman** and his encouragement, **Judy Skutch Whitson**, **Ernest Pecci** for his advise and support, **Linda Chappo**, who brought me to a publishing conference, **Chris Forsyth**, who first told me that "You should write a book on that", **Jane Peery**, for her formatting assistance, the '*A Course in Miracles*' community in which I have settled into the non-duality, knowing that I, the Divine and every fellow journeyer along the way are truly ONE together. I am especially grateful to all of YOU, who dare to pick up this volume and join with me in our Journey to the Self.

ABOUT THE AUTHOR

Sundari Dembe 's life has been an intimate mixing of metaphysics, science and music into a seamless solution of Self. She has had a lifetime career as a Chemistry Professor in the California Community Colleges holding degrees in Chemistry and Chemical Physics from the University of Michigan and the University of Chicago. She taught enneagram, meditation and esoteric practices in varied local and international settings, including Claudio Naranjo's SAT Sufi mystery school groups. She has practiced Taoist, Vipassana, Nygma, and Zen Buddhism, Sufism, decades in Hindu practices, Judaism, was ordained as a Priestess and has deep ties with mystical Christianity. She is strongly aligned with *A Course in Miracles* (ACIM).

She has spent a lifetime singing in choirs, Gilbert and Sullivan productions, madrigal groups, lead chanting and being a conductor in an Indian ashram, performing with SF Opera, Oakland Symphony, Oakland Ballet and at an Oakland A's game. She now writes spiritual music, giving solo acapela concerts, leads Vibratory Sound/Light Sessions and sings globally with a 1000 person Lemurian Toning DNA Activation Choir.

She was widowed after a nearly 25 yr marriage and has two children. She runs working ranches. She functions as a Planetary Caretaker, and has traveled to 41 countries, often with groups of Lightworkers.

She has been a psychic and healer and was gifted by Spirit with 150 pages of this book in a microsecond.